THE FIRST
ALCHEMISTS

"In this remarkable and necessary work on early alchemy, Churton outlines a program of research and experimentation into this rich but mostly unexplored area of Greco-Egyptian alchemical philosophies and practices. The depth and range of the material are breathtaking, and it is very satisfying to see the topic of glass addressed so thoroughly. I strongly recommend studying and working with *The First Alchemists* and going deeper, letting Tobias Churton light the way."

BRIAN COTNOIR, AUTHOR OF *ON ALCHEMY, ALCHEMY,*
AND *PRACTICAL ALCHEMY*

"The subject of alchemy has always been shrouded in dense fog. Here at last is a book that probes deeply and lucidly into this age-old pursuit, taking us right back to its roots in the Middle East, examining seminal sources and investigating key avatars of alchemy—of both ancient and more recent times—and what precisely they were trying to achieve. Alchemy has both a practical and a spiritual side. Tobias Churton, writing with his customary eloquence, shines a clear light on both aspects."

CHRISTOPHER MCINTOSH, AUTHOR OF *OCCULT RUSSIA*
AND *BEYOND THE NORTH WIND*

THE FIRST ALCHEMISTS

The Spiritual & Practical Origins of the Noble & Holy Art

TOBIAS CHURTON

Inner Traditions
Rochester, Vermont

Inner Traditions
One Park Street
Rochester, Vermont 05767
www.InnerTraditions.com

Text stock is SFI certified

Cataloging-in-Publication Data for this title is available from the Library of Congress

ISBN 978-1-64411-683-8 (print)
ISBN 978-1-64411-684-5 (ebook)

Printed and bound in the United States by Lake Book Manufacturing, LLC
The text stock is SFI certified. The Sustainable Forestry Initiative® program
promotes sustainable forest management.

10 9 8 7 6 5 4 3 2 1

Text design and layout by Priscilla Harris Baker
This book was typeset in Garamond Premier Pro with Columbia Serial, Futura,
Quiche Flare, and Nocturne Serif used as display typefaces

To send correspondence to the author of this book, mail a first-class letter to the
author c/o Inner Traditions • Bear & Company, One Park Street, Rochester, VT
05767, and we will forward the communication.

For Joanna and Merovée

Contents

FOREWORD
by Frank van Lamoen   xi

Introduction   1

ONE
Ancient Recipes for Gold—
and Other Things   9
Discoveries at Thebes   11
A Theban Magical Library?   14
The Leiden Papyrus   17
Papyrus V   20
Papyrus W   22
Papyrus X   24
The Stockholm Papyrus   32
Pseudo-Democritus   36

TWO
The Origins of Alchemy in Roman Egypt   44
Akkadian Origin of Chēmeu?   55
Heat and Glass   56

THREE

The Pioneers of Graeco-Egyptian-Jewish Alchemy 62

Cleopatra 64

Jewish Chemistry 74

Mary the "Prophetess" 81

FOUR

Zosimos I

Clearing the Decks 89

Was Zosimos an Egyptian Priest? 92

FIVE

Zosimos II

Alchemical Yoga 101

Practical Dreaming 103

SIX

Zosimos III

From Omega *to the* Final Quittance 118

On Destiny, Fate, Worldly Thought, and Noetic Understanding 126

The First Book of Zosimos the Theban's Final Account 137

SEVEN

What Did the First Alchemists Do? 143

Making Talismans? 152

EIGHT

How Did They Do It? 162

Sulfur Water; Divine Water 164

Apparatus 166

Putting the First Alchemists to the Test 171

NINE

Where Did They Do It? 178

A Hermetic "Lodge"? 182

A Guild for Theosebeia? 189

Laboratories? 192

TEN

The Myth of Transmutation 198

Philosophical Background 199

The Stone 206

The Tome of Images 212

Myth and Reality 223

ELEVEN

Forbidden Knowledge 228

TWELVE

A Strange Relation

Alchemy and Gnosis 239

Mercury and Christ 252

THIRTEEN

Legacy 257

Arabic Alchemy 261

The Inheritance 264

"Good Health!" 275

Notes 277

Bibliography 291

Index 297

Foreword

WHEN THE GERMAN CHEMIST and historian of chemistry Hermann Kopp (1817–1892) discussed alchemy in his Geschichte der Chemie (History of Chemistry), he dismissed it as the "Geschichte eines Irrtums," the history of an error. Such ruthless judgments are rare in the exact sciences, even though historians of astronomy, for instance, would also have a point to make. Kopp of course referred to *transmutation,* the alchemical idea that base metals could be changed into precious metals. In Kopp's time, chemistry was firmly established as a science, whereas by then alchemy was taken seriously only in esoteric circles, to be reborn in Carl Jung's psychoanalysis later. It seems that the history of alchemy, too, constantly transmutes. Different periods in history yield different types of alchemy, or rather: alchemy in changing theoretical frameworks. Medieval alchemy bears a strong Aristotelian mark, and a lot of Renaissance and later alchemy carries a Neoplatonic stamp. These changing interpretative frameworks make it very difficult to explore the origins of alchemy. They generate anachronisms that cloud our view of the subject. In this brave book, Tobias Churton points us the way to those origins.

A first step on the path of finding the origins of alchemy is the understanding that theoretical frameworks must be abandoned. Alchemy is not a theory, nor is it an applied science. It is a practice, an art. The alchemist of Roman Egypt has nothing in common with a mathematician; he is in the same league as a potter or a blacksmith. He knows from experience how something must be made and which procedures must be followed. These procedures were captured in secret recipes, sometimes accompanied by a pithy saying, which, for instance, refers to sympathetic coherence in nature: "Nature delights in nature, nature conquers nature, nature masters nature." Self-knowledge and a purified mind are absolute essentials to carry out these procedures successfully. There is a theurgical dimension to alchemical practice: to engage *in* the practice requires a religious attitude that is strengthened *through* practice.

"It is owing to their wonder that men both now begin and at first began to philosophize," Aristotle said in his *Metaphysics*. The metallurgical chemists of Roman Egypt had little use for Aristotle, but they no doubt regarded with wonder those secrets of creation that deal with *change*: evaporating, smelting, burning, and especially the changing of color, a phenomenon philosophers were unable to explain. Transmutation for Greek alchemists was not about making gold. It was instead about making glass out of sand, which made matter transparent. Tobias Churton devotes fascinating pages to it in this book. It takes imagination to look at the world with wonder. We have become wandering rationalists who gaze into the fire only when we want to feel all warm and cozy.

The absolute hero of this book is the alchemist Zosimos of Panopolis, known to students of Hermetic philosophy because of his clear references to works attributed to Hermes Trismegistos. Tobias Churton's portrait of Zosimos is an unequaled tour de force: where other authors usually limit themselves to a single aspect of his work, Churton offers insight into the *whole* Zosimos, without, however, losing his attention to detail. An ironic detail is perhaps Churton's view on Zosimos's commercial instincts. All Hermetic and gnostic insights notwithstanding, the alchemist was also aware he had to find buyers for his products. In his book, Tobias Churton devotes intriguing passages to the changing economic circumstances that caused alchemists to leave the protection of the temple and start working in groups.

The First Alchemists is a brilliant and complex book about a complex world little known to us because there is such limited information. It invites further analyses and encourages new syntheses.

Solve et coagula! There is work to be done.

FRANK VAN LAMOEN,
RESEARCHER, ASSISTANT CURATOR,
STEDELIJK MUSEUM, AMSTERDAM

Introduction

I REMEMBER EGYPTOLOGIST PROFESSOR Kenneth Kitchen descending from Liverpool University to England's West Midlands and kindly giving a Saturday talk to about fifty students in Birmingham's Museum and Art Gallery in 1977. I was sixteen or seventeen at the time, and the visit was doubtless organized by our religious studies teacher, Hilary Docker. (Where are you now, dear Hilary?) It was a kind of foretaste of university lecture experience, and I recall the professor getting on to our level very quickly and effectively. Though it's forty-five years ago now, one thing he said buried itself in the archaeology of my mind only to come back to me sharply while researching this book.

Professor Kitchen was talking about the nature and value of evidence available to scholars of the ancient and late antique world, whether of Egypt or elsewhere. In a potent analogy he asked us to imagine piles of manuscripts, papyri, and objects being cast onto a fire in a large fireplace. What wasn't consumed by fire or hadn't fled up the chimney might leave scattered, charred, disassociated residues on the carpet in front of the fire. And *that,* the professor said, is the residue scholars call "evidence." His analogy gives us a vivid, if dispiriting, idea of the actual material available for generating our histories. The professor warned against the natural tendency of scholars and others to build explicatory

1

pictures and speculative scenarios on what can only ever be fragmentary portions of past, largely unknown, realities. This "warning from history" should be in our minds, as it was in mine, when approaching this investigation into the origins and practice of what Arabic-speaking scholars came to call "alchemy" some 1,300 years ago—then already some 700 years after the composition of our first undisputed evidence for the practice in Roman Egypt.

In so many respects, we don't know *enough*. And it is perhaps for that very reason that the subject of alchemy has invited so much obscurity, contradiction, mystification, elaboration, enthusiasm, opposition, fantasy, and plain incomprehension over the centuries.

While I have now progressed forty years amid some aspect or other of what passes academic muster as Western esotericism, I must confess to a long, abiding confusion as to what we should understand by *alchemy*. The one question that has bothered me when giving interviews goes something like this: "Can you explain what alchemy is?" If I knew as much, or little, as many an encyclopedia, it should be an easy enough question to answer, for you will find in numerous compendia the subject defined as the ancient belief and attempt to transmute base metals, such as lead, into gold, with the common caveat that while the practice is doomed to failure by dint of superstition, some of its practices contributed to the beginnings of what we know as early modern scientific chemistry. Such would have been the easy answer, but anyone familiar with esoteric traditions will have been convinced that intelligent people have believed there's more to it than that—so much more, in fact, that any attempt at clear definition is soon shrouded in mists of philosophical obscurity and contradiction. The traditional reason often given by alchemical apologists for such contradiction is that the practice contains a secret or secrets of such transcendent value that it would be impious or dangerous to reveal them to the uninitiated. Therefore, we're told, alchemy is worked in deliberately contradictory code (on the surface) and that only the purest and most devoted can ever expect to grasp the essence of the matter and perform the Great Work with success, such that the secret may be transmitted to the next initiate. This kind of obscurantism, or even arguably disinformation, repeated over many centuries, makes the subject generally distasteful to science, and further interest in alchemy, as opposed to chemistry, is often dismissed as retrograde and vain in the "real world."

Of course, most everyone has heard of *Harry Potter and the Philosopher's Stone,* and J. K. Rowling's literary interpretation of alchemy as a form of magic with a mysterious and wonder-working apex is pretty much what I thought of as alchemy in my romantic, teenage years. At that age, I imagined an alchemist as a kind of Merlin character in an old laboratory full of aludels, alembics, retorts, and crucibles, working by night with furnace glowing red and gold, amid bubbling emerald ferments of distillates as he delved into the mystery of change in nature, of how *one thing can become another,* and how in that quest, the alchemist, too, might become profoundly changed, gifted with life-enhancing powers of a secret, magical, even spiritually salvific kind. The accreted symbolism of the "Stone" is luminous and unforgettable.

At least one aspect of this somewhat Gothic picture is valid. Alchemy was practiced in a particular kind of place with particular instruments and involved combinations of recognizable materials. Chemistry may not have been its end, but it was at least its means, despite what science would come to see as a lack of theoretical consistency and mistaken and now outmoded theory allegedly underpinning it.

After long entertaining a romantic image of magical alchemy came knowledge of Renaissance and post-Renaissance Paracelsian "spiritual" and medical alchemy, a reformist alchemy leading to the theosophical system constructed by the gnostic Jacob Böhme (1575–1624) in which alchemical terms described Christian spiritual transformations of a micro- and macrocosmic kind. In the eighteenth century, neo-Rosicrucianism combined a theosophical reworking of alchemy with renewed interest in laboratory practice, even as chemistry as a distinct science was leaving its troubled "gold-making" reputation behind. Alchemy became like an old acquaintance whose presence now caused embarrassment to a socially ascending seeker of reputation, eager to shake off past associates. When science turns up its nose, it reveals unseen nostrils.

Despite Isaac Newton's now recognized attempt to integrate alchemical investigation with demonstrable science and theory, alchemy from the mid-seventeenth century found itself embroiled in a long drift toward the occult, from which unscientific (because obscurely esoteric) territory the celebrated psychologist Carl Jung (1875–1961) attempted to redeem it by applying alchemical imagery and processes to his psychological theories. Jung believed alchemy was most of all to do with the *mysteries of the psyche:* the "gold," or perfected stone, was individuation, that realization of the individual in touch with the healing and ascending dynamics of the unconscious. Through a scientific gnosis the psyche could be transformed, or be matured, from a *massa confusa* to a harmonized, spiritually aware wholeness, with attendant release of creative potential in balanced character development, in preparation for the great journey beyond this predominantly organic existence. "I do not need to believe," Jung famously told John Freeman in 1959, "I *know*."

I often wish I hadn't read Jung's involved work *Psychology and Alchemy* (1943) at the time I did, for I may have too uncritically absorbed Jung's tendency to take alchemical "principles" from many different periods and apply them whenever something analogous appeared. This associative tendency makes for interesting philosophical and spiritually stimulating commentary while renewing significant value to alchemy's respectability, but it very easily obscures the particularity of the works of different alchemists in very different periods and obscures distinctions between alchemy as practical laboratory effort and inward alchemical symbolism. There is no doubt at all that the interweaving through time of alchemical texts with religious and Hermetic symbolism has produced a possibility of creating, effectively, an alchemical religion or religious philosophy, whereas, as we shall see, what some early practitioners aimed at was a more religious—that is *purified*—chemical art.

Well, it is hardly surprising that confusion has inhibited understanding of alchemy. The term has perhaps simply come to mean "too much." When confronted by something akin to a Gordian knot, I feel an urge not to annihilate the puzzle by putting my sword through it as Alexander the Great did but rather to retire and try to figure out how the knotty phenomenon actually came about. And that is my explanation for undertaking this investigation into the first alchemists. The job needed doing.

Having decided to undertake a comprehensive investigation into the origins of alchemy, I soon found additional incentives to bolster my ardent desire to bring clarity to widespread confusion—for confusion is endemic to the past history of the subject—and many past commentators have been less than honest about their own confusion and understandable, if seldom admitted, ignorance.

The first thing that struck me was that what has long been the first port of call for scholarly study of Graeco-Egyptian alchemy—the two volumes of *Collection des Anciens Alchimistes Grecs* (Collection of Ancient Greek Alchemists) by Berthelot and Ruelle—was published in French as long ago as 1888 and has never been published in English! This, the largest collection of late antique and Byzantine alchemical sources, I first had to translate from the French. Plowing through that onerous task (finding that even Berthelot and Ruelle were often mystified by the content of what it was they had translated from the Greek), I began to consult the considerable amount of scholarly books and academic papers that have appeared in remarkably increasing numbers since the 1990s, and since 2000 particularly. It is encouraging to see a relatively new wave of serious, painstaking scholarship in this field. I can't help wondering if I myself have contributed a little to stimulating this phenomenal impetus as my first endeavor to popularize the field dates from the 1980s, though I suspect synchronicity helps better explain increasing interest in alchemy.

Be that as it may, I believe it is vitally important to convey clearly to the intelligent lay reader the best of contemporary scholarship on the subject, while laying out a modest tray of my own thoughts and occasional insights into this often recondite, but nonetheless deeply fascinating, story.

The investigation opens with a tale (true, I hope) of adventurers, merchants, and sometime reprobates, without whose appetites we should lack even the flimsy evidence we have on early alchemy. The so-called Leiden and Stockholm Papyri are not our earliest *sources* of alchemical recipes and practices, but they are our oldest physical articles relating to the art, dating from third-century Thebes or Memphis, apparently a fruitful period of alchemical practice, despite, or perhaps because of, the fraught politics of a declining Roman and temporarily imperial Palmyrean Egypt in that period.

Our oldest *texts* date from about the first century CE, about the time Jesus is believed to have walked in Egypt, Judaea, Galilee, and Syro-Phoenicia. They were attributed mistakenly to Greek philosopher Democritus (ca. 460–370 BCE), who allegedly relied on the knowledge of a fifth-century BCE Persian sage called Ostanes. Tradition related "pseudo-Democritus" to third-century BCE Egyptian Bolos of Mendes, perhaps himself inspired by predecessor Democritus. The truth may have been very different.

Fragmentary is our knowledge (if we may call it that) of our first early "alchemists" (they would not have recognized the term). We examine the evidence for alchemical pioneer, the Jewish lady Mariam or Mary, sometimes called the Prophetess, along with Graeco-Egyptian alchemists who are now little more than dislocated names: Cleopatra and Pebichius, to name but two whose reputations reached subsequent practitioners before 300 CE.

It is from about that date that we may locate an Egyptian called Zosimos, a compelling intellect and craftsman who emerged from his hometown of Panopolis (Akhmim) to make a name for himself as a tutor of the craft in Alexandria, and perhaps elsewhere. Zosimos's surviving works had reached Constantinople by the time of the emperor Heraclius in the seventh century.

Zosimos is the single figure upon whom we greatly rely for his knowledge of the "noble and holy art" (as he called it)—and he is even more significant—combining the art as he did, with an eclectic, coherent, endlessly fascinating amalgam of Egyptian temple tradition, Judaism, Christianity, and perhaps above all, Hermetically inspired gnosis. As far as the manuscript record goes, Zosimos introduced a panoply of mystique and symbolic elevation about what might, until that time, have been described (in our terms) as advanced metallurgical chemistry.

Because Zosimos himself deserves considerably more attention than he has received, I have endeavored to show the depth and subtlety of his cosmic art and creative intelligence.

Having established some clear pointers and geographical markers, we proceed to some nitty-gritty questions, questions like: Where was alchemy practiced? How was it practiced? What were the theories and philosophies behind the practice? What kind of apparatus and chemical materials were employed? We investigate Zosimos's view that his art was derived from daimons or angels: the rebel angels, or Watchers, who, according to the Book of Enoch, descended from heaven for lust of human women in antediluvian times and conveyed forbidden knowledge to a soon perverted humanity. Here lies the origin of our trope of the mad scientist. In terms we might grasp today, imagine nuclear fission as a science stolen from above, to be abused on earth for the enjoyment of alien "demons," with the caveat that purified people could use it properly, because it was ultimately derived from the Highest and therefore could enlighten and transform the pure-hearted initiate.

At this point we investigate how it occurred that alchemy came to fixate primarily on the philosopher's stone, or the Elixir of Life. We examine the myth of transmutation (turning lead into gold) and discover whether the first alchemists believed that to be their task.

Late antique alchemy alerts us to remarkable parallels between alchemical theosophy and Gnosticism. Could it be that gnostic theories of the hidden *pneuma* (spirit) in Man derive from alchemical practice—or vice versa? This is a hot subject, and we've not heard the last of it, I suspect.

Alchemy has a curious place in the exegesis of the Bible in the patristic (church fathers) period. We discover that the famous and fundamental Nicene Trinitarian axiom itself (that the Son is of "one substance" with the Father—built around the Greek word *homoousios,* "same substance") may likely have a Hermetic source, with alchemical implications, conveyed through Emperor Constantine's acquaintance with Hermetic ideas.

We conclude with a brief account of the legacy of late antique Graeco-Egyptian alchemy—a legacy vitally active in the world's scientific and spiritual discourses today, coming as it did from a world where what we call science and spiritual knowledge constituted a unified field of practical and speculative science.

We may then ask whether we have benefited from science discarding its spirituality and religion discarding, or opposing, its science.

ONE

Ancient Recipes for Gold
—and Other Things

OUR STORY BEGINS WITH A GREEK from the Macedonian city of Serres, some 50 miles northeast of Thessaloniki. According to the Greek community registers in Alexandria, Egypt, Ioannis Anastasiou—commonly known as Giovanni or Jean d'Anastasi or "Anastasy"—was born in 1765 and interred in a handsome tomb at Alexandria's Greek Orthodox cemetery in 1860.*

Egyptologist Warren R. Dawson (who mistakenly recorded "Anastasi's" nationality as Armenian) believed Anastasiou's father was a Damascene merchant who profited from supplying Napoleon's army during its occupation of Egypt in 1798, involving his son Ioannis in the business. French evacuation of Egypt in 1800 ruined the father and, according to Dawson, probably led to his death soon after. Left to pick up the pieces,[3] son Ioannis did so with alacrity, paying off his father's debts by 1825 while building a reputation in the grain trade, consolidated by influence in high circles, including privileged access to

---

*Warren R. Dawson, first compiler of *Who Was Who in Egyptology,* gave Anastasiou's birthdate as 1780,[1] while researcher Vassilis Chrysikopoulos suspects the true date is likely somewhere between the two, a lifetime of ninety-five years being fairly extraordinary for the period.[2]

modern Egypt's founder, Albanian Ottoman Muhammad Ali Pasha al-Mas'ud ibn Agha (1769–1849), Egypt's ruler from 1805. The pasha's shared origins, having been born at Kavala, only 56 miles east of Serres, may have helped oil mutual relations. The pasha was not alone in recognizing Anastasiou's talents and usefulness. The kingdoms of Norway and Sweden appointed Anastasiou their consul general in Egypt in 1828.

According to Chrysikopoulos, Anastasiou had dealings with antiquities collector Bernadino Drovetti (1776–1852), France's consul general in Egypt. Despite providing Turin, Paris, and Berlin with major collections of Egyptian antiquities, Drovetti is infamous today for ruthless handling, through his agents, of what he saw as rival competitors in digging or paying for antiquities. Excavations launched at Luxor in 1818 drew complaints from excavator and collector's agent Giovanni Battista Belzoni over harassment from Drovetti's unscrupulous agents. Drovetti was also hostile toward Englishman Henry Salt and the now famous Jean-François Champollion—decipherer of hieroglyphics from the Rosetta Stone—whose excavation rights came through Anastasiou. Chrysikopoulos describes Anastasiou as "a humane entrepreneur," whereas Drovetti proved crude in his handling of antiquities, behavior embarrassing to more responsible, less bellicose, Egyptologists. Prussian Egyptologist Karl Richard Lepsius (1810–1884), who acquired a collection from Drovetti in 1836 that formed the basis of Berlin's Egyptian Museum, owed his excavation concession and his contact with the ruling pasha to Anastasiou.

Chrysikopoulos informs us that Anastasiou helped free hundreds of Greek rebels against Ottoman rule from slavery after the pasha's son Ibrahim's attack on the Peloponnese (1824–1828).[4] From among the liberated Greeks, Anastasiou adopted Marie, a young girl who later married Vincent Benedetti, French consul to Egypt (1840–1845). This gives us a good idea of Anastasiou's status in Egypt.

One of numerous Greeks who ventured to make good in Alexandria and Cairo, Anastasiou first emerged in Egyptian records circa 1812. Ruler Muhammad Ali favored Alexandria's Greek merchants, whose numbers included Etienne Zizinia, Tossizza Bros and Co., and Stournari. Such indeed was that favor that until 1829 these merchants sold cotton to Europe on the pasha's own account.[5] By then, Alexandria's prominent figure Ioannis Anastasiou had enjoyed seventeen successful years exchanging, buying, and excavating antiquities, among other profitable goods.

Chrysikopoulos consulted Ermoupolis archives on the island of Syros, southeast of Athens in the Aegean, to get an idea of how Anastasiou's commercial networks operated. The archives reveal a respected Giovanni of Anastasi, tough in negotiation but generous, too. Involving his agents in personal aspects of his life, a letter of November 9, 1835, from Anastasiou in Alexandria to agent Argyrios D. Tarpoktsis in Syros inquired about barley and bean prices before requesting mediation for a marriage of his niece's daughter. Tarpoktsis duly found the minor a bridegroom in a doctor from Lamia, for which Anastasiou instructed his agent to pay a very considerable dowry. He also asked Tarpoktsis to find a husband for family member Penelope d'Anastasi, who Anastasiou trusted to live in the agent's house in the meantime. A dowry of 6,000 drachmas was provided so she could marry a local merchant. This was the way business operated: a bond of trust with one's countryfolk, sealed with personal obligation. Tarpoktsis continued to flourish on Syros, becoming mayor in 1846 and major donor for constructing the church of St. Nicholas in 1851.

An important trade hub, Syros's port welcomed ships from Alexandria destined for Constantinople and the Black Sea, Trieste, Malta, Marseille, and Livorno, Italy.

Discoveries at Thebes

In 1827, Livorno's port witnessed the unloading of a collection of Anastasiou's antiquities, including papyrus manuscripts. Originally intended by Anastasiou for sale to Sweden, the Dutch government bought the collection in 1828 for the Rijksmuseum van Oudheden in Leiden. The museum thus obtained 147 papyri among 5,600 objects, to which Anastasiou added as a gift a Byzantine helmet and two additional papyri.[6] Amid this collection could be found what is now called the Leiden Papyrus (designated P.Leid.), chiefly concerned with "alchemical" recipes.

Four years later, Sweden's royal house benefited from Anastasiou's collections. On August 27, 1832, Sweden's Royal Academy of Letters, History and Antiquities wrote a letter to thank Anastasiou for his gift of an alchemical codex. This is now known as the Stockholm Papyrus, or P.Holm. (*Papyrus Graecus Holmiensis*).[7] This critical text now resides at the Kungliga Bibliotek in Stockholm.

Another cargo of Anastasiou's antiquities arrived at Livorno in 1838, a large proportion of which was purchased by the British Museum the following year. It included some 1,326 objects, with forty-four papyri among them. A number of the papyri from the Papyri Graecae Magicae (PGM V) were translated into English by Charles Wycliffe Godwin (1817–1878) and published by the Cambridge Antiquarian Society in 1853. Godwin's commentary provided the first scholarly publication concerned with the Greek Magical Papyri (PGM).*

A final sale of Anastasiou's antiquities occupied a public auction in Paris in 1857, its 1,129 items subsequently dispersed into several continental collections. Paris's Bibliothèque Nationale obtained a papyrus manuscript now known as the Great Magical Papyrus, wherein appeared the names Osiris, Sabaoth, Iao, Jesus, and other

---

*Godwin's translation provided the text for Aleister Crowley's famous Bornless Ritual, or Preliminary Invocation, which he used to invoke Adonai (the Lord or Holy Guardian Angel). The original reads: "I summon you Headless One, who created earth and heaven, who created night and day. . . . I am the Favour of the Aion; my name is a heart encircled by a serpent" (PGM V, 96–172). Crowley mistrusted the translation of Headless One, believing it a misunderstanding for Bornless One, hence Crowley's adapted Bornless Ritual.

Fig. 1.1. The god Set in the Greek Magical Papyri (note the god's Egyptian hare head, first identified by the author)

"aeons" of a gnostic character. The sales catalog indicated their provenance as Thebes, on Anastasiou's word. The 1828 sale catalogue had attributed provenance of papyri to Memphis, Philae, and Elephantine, as well as Thebes, while the 1838 catalog referred to Thebes and Memphis.

Hans Dieter Betz's study of the Mithras Liturgy Papyrus—an early fourth-century CE segment of the Great Magical Papyrus—offers further insight into the provenance of these and other papyri of Anastasiou's.[8] One of Anastasiou's acquaintances, Cairo merchant's son Giovanni Athanasi (known as Yanni), who hailed from the island of Lemnos, spent eighteen years in Thebes searching for antiquities, serving from 1817 as agent to Lichfield-born artist, collector, Egyptologist, and British consul general to Egypt (from 1816) Henry Salt (1780–1827). D'Athanasi's *Brief Account of the Researches and Discoveries in Upper Egypt, made under the direction of Henry Salt, Esq.* and his *Catalogue of the Very Magnificent and Extraordinary Collection of Egyptian Antiquities*—recording Sotheby's auction of d'Athanasi's own

Fig. 1.2. Henry Salt

antiquities collection—inform us that Anastasiou obtained his papyri scrolls from sealed terra-cotta urns from within, or close by, ancient tombs. Such would certainly explain the excellent condition of many of the surviving papyri.

The hundreds of papyri sent from Alexandria over the thirty years from 1827 to 1857 deal chiefly, and in some cases remarkably—such as the Mithras Liturgy—with Egyptian magical rituals, including theurgic ascents of the soul to higher, spiritual realms with gnostic elements, and most importantly for our purposes, the papyri included alchemical recipes for the dyeing of precious stones, metalware, statues, and wool, with the intent of raising the commercial, aesthetic, and religious value of the objects by subjecting base materials to chemical processes. They were written in Demotic (late Egyptian script, written right to left), in old Coptic, and in Greek.

A Theban Magical Library?

An internal consistency is discernible in the worldview of the papyri: an atmosphere of practical science, willed magic, and protective religion pervades the separated texts, as well as common handwriting and thematic interrelatedness. Such consistencies have encouraged specu-

Fig. 1.3. The Theban Necropolis (photo: Steve F. E. Cameron)

lation that the texts may have originally been drawn from a "Theban Magical Library" situated in a temple of the Thebaid region (the area around Thebes, from Abydos to Aswan). Scholar Korshi Dosoo has looked closely at the possibility of the papyri coming from a single source.[9] Dosoo notes that P.Leid. I 396 is accurately attributed by Anastasiou to Memphis, which suggests the merchant was not cavalier about provenance; the 1828 catalog indicates his agents kept notes of where they bought their goods or in what area they were allegedly found.

In Dosoo's list of possible candidates for a Theban Magical Library drawn from the three sales and the gift to Sweden, the majority are Greek and Demotic magical texts. The Stockholm Papyri are included, along with some papyri from the Leiden Papyri (notably X

and W). Dosoo notes that twenty-one pages of PGM XIII are written in the same hand as the Stockholm Papyrus and P.Leid. I 397,
while recognizing the unlikelihood of papyri coming from one archive
just because related to a single area. We know, for example, the names
of several separate practitioners of alchemy operating in the Thebaid
around 300 CE. They probably had their own collections, though
these may have been copied or obtained from a common source, such
as a temple library (Egypt suffered great instability in 270 CE when
the Palmyrean Empire invaded Egypt). Nevertheless, Dosoo considers
that because the papyri came from one collector, they were likely part
of a cache rather than similar documents coming from different places.
Besides, their shared interest in "revelational divination and alchemy"
is distinctive amid other papyri of the period.10 Furthermore,
PGM Va, P.Holm., PGM XIII, and P.Leid. I 397 display the same
handwriting, which also appears in an annotation on the inside
cover of PGM IV—and they all employ a cipher alphabet unique to
the papyri.

PGM XII contains a brief alchemical section (II 193–204). This
and the Stockholm Papyrus are the only known magical papyri containing alchemical material. Dosoo cites a letter of March 18, 1828, from
Anastasiou wherein he informs his agents that the Demotic Magical
Papyri and Greek Magical Papyrus XII were obtained "from the hand
of the Arabs (who according to their fraudulent custom have probably
detached it from the main papyrus in order to get a greater price from
it by the double sale)." There was no mention of excavation. Yanni
d'Athanasi's book on *his* Theban exploits for Henry Salt makes the
same observation of Arabs dividing collections and selling them to different buyers with attractive provenances.[11]

Dosoo admits that while the onetime existence of a unique Theban
Magical Library cannot be assumed, nevertheless, "on balance, it seems
certain that the Theban Library represents a real archive—the relationships between its papyri seem too certain to easily dismiss."[12] There has
been relatively recent support for the premise that PGM IV was indeed

a fragment of larger papyrus.* However, Dosoo suggests that scholars should be cautious in ascribing Thebes as the sole origin of the library on the basis of Anastasiou's indicated provenance alone given that there are anomalies in documentation. Anastasiou was by all accounts decent, but he was not perfect, and the demands of provenance in his period were rudimentary compared with today.

Whether or not there was once a composite Theban Magical Library, Anastasiou's papyri today still tend to be treated by scholars as separate sources; thus, we have the Greek Magical Papyri, the Demotic Magical Papyri, the Leiden Papyrus, and the Stockholm Papyrus. The latter two constitute, for the time being, the oldest surviving evidence of alchemy being worked in late antique Egypt, and to these we may now turn, not forgetting in the process that their eminently *practical* contents also made sense in a world where magical divination, gnostic cosmology, and daimonic-polytheist and monotheist entreaties for assistance in the business of daily life were normal. They are part of an integrated, even eclectic view of spiritual and bodily life in the cosmos, and beyond it.

The Leiden Papyrus

The contents of this Greek-language papyrus were first published in Latin by Leiden Museum Director and Egyptologist Conrad Leemans

---

*A colloquium held in August 2016 at Montserrat to discuss an edition devoted to Egyptian magical formularies as part of the Chicago University project, the Transmission of Magical Knowledge in Antiquity, was informed of a discovery by Eleni Chronopolou of Pompeu Fabra University (Barcelona) that PGM II and VI belonged to an original, larger roll. The first column of PGM II followed the single column of PGM VI. For Dosoo this proves the link between Anastasiou's second and third sales: two fragments from one papyrus were thus sold separately, whereas it had been thought the sole link between PGM II and VI was Anastasiou's ownership. A complication arises: the sale catalog for PGM VI indicates Memphis as its source. The two parts could hardly come from separate places; in which case there was either misinformation or an error. The sales catalogs have other anomalies. PGM VI was sold in two parts, identified as numbers 3 and 5. Why, Dosoo asks, would the apparently blank margin of number 5 be described in the catalog as "fragment of a Greek manuscript"?

(1809–1893) in 1885. His publication, *Papyri graeci musei antiquarii,* carried over the museum library's labeling of Greek papyri from A to Z. Parts A through U, dealing with Egyptian law, attracted little interest. Three years later, when outstanding French chemist and politician Marcellin Berthelot published *his* technically informed study with C. E. Ruelle's French translation of practically all texts of "Ancient Greek Alchemists," Berthelot confined attention to Leiden Papyri labeled V, W, and X, especially the latter two. For Berthelot, these confirmed much of what he'd gleaned from studying other, mostly later, Greek-language alchemical texts: "My hope has not been misled; I believe, indeed, I can establish that the study of these papyruses makes a step forward in the matter, showing precisely how the alchemical hopes and doctrines on the transmutation of

Fig. 1.4. The Leiden Papyrus

precious metals were born out of the practices of the Egyptian goldsmiths to imitate and falsify them."[13] This view has not appealed to numerous scholars following him (especially when, like Berthelot, scientifically trained), such as remarkable chemist and translator E. R. Caley (1900–1984), who retained a suspicion that the straightforward practical recipes of the Leiden and Stockholm Papyri were not really proto-alchemical or mindful of the by then traditional definition of alchemy as being concerned exclusively with transmutation of base into noble metals. Caley saw the papyri recipes as belonging to a long history of metallurgical and chemical recipes extending back to ancient Mesopotamia. The difficulty, as we shall see in due course, settles over precisely what different people in different times have understood by "transmutation."

Papyrus V

Papyrus V, nearly 12 feet (3.6 m) long and 9.5 inches (24 cm) high, is written in Greek and Demotic, with the Demotic running to twenty-two columns. The Greek occupies seventeen columns. Despite the start and end of Papyrus V being lost, we nonetheless acquire knowledge of thirty-seven secret names for plants given to them by sacred scribes, such as "lion's semen," "semen of Hermes," "semen of Ammon," "snake's blood," and "rat's tail." Berthelot sees the beginnings here of what would become characteristically strange alchemical nomenclature. Similar names appear in first-century Roman army surgeon Pedanius Dioscorides's long and influential *de materia medica,* though referring to different things (in the papyrus, "seed of Hercules," for example, is rocket; in Dioscorides, saffron), with the exception of anagillis (pimpernel) being called "blood of the eye" in both the papyrus and Dioscorides (extracts from ten articles by Dioscorides close Papyrus X). Berthelot wondered if popular botanical names of his own time such as ox's eye, lion's tooth, or dog's tongue went back to such writings, though the papyrus names were often drawn from less savory sources: semen, bile, feces, head, heart, bone, tail and hair, along with Greek names of Egyptian gods, including Hephaestos, Hermes, Helios, Vesta, and Chronos.

Berthelot was keen to see the papyrus contents as analogous to doctrines of the Gnostic Marcus (as related in Irenaeus's *Against the Heretics,* ca. 180 CE), since Marcus used magical formulas, aphrodisiacs, incantations, and daimonic means to procure dream states.[14] It was Berthelot's belief that "the history of magic and Gnosticism is closely linked to that of the origins of alchemy: the current texts provide new evidence in this regard in support of what we already knew."[15]

Berthelot notes how similar code words would be used by alchemists for metals. The "old alchemical lexicon" records "seed of Venus" for copper flower (oxide, carbonate, etc.); "snake bile" could mean "divine water," or mercury; "ejaculation of the serpent" could also mean mercury; Osiris was taken for lead (or sulfur); "black cow's milk" for mercury derived from sulfur; "midge blood" for alabastron water; "Vulcan mud" (or lees), for barley, along with many more of the kind.[16]

As for alchemy in Papyrus V, Berthelot narrows the term to metals and minerals, such as a process to refine gold (*iosis chrusou*), as well as a preparation for the coloring of gold (also given in Papyrus X), as well as a mystical ink recipe made of green vitriol, gum, oak apple, a blend of seven perfumes and seven flowers, and "misy," apparently consisting of mixed ores of oxidized pyrite and copper and iron sulfates. Berthelot reckoned it was for writing magic formulae on niter (potassium nitrate, or saltpeter).

The passage on refining gold is similar to what Berthelot, as a chemist, knew as "royal cement," for separating gold and silver (Macquer, *Dictionary of Chemistry*, 1778). I here translate Berthelot and Ruelle's translation of the passage in Papyrus V.[*]

> Take pungent vinegar, thicken, take 8 drachmas [measures] of common salt, 2 drachmas of lamellar alum (schist), 4 drachmas of litharge [mineral form of lead oxide], grind with vinegar for 3 days, separate by decantation and use. Then add to the vinegar 1 drachma of couperose, a half obole of . . . three chalcite oboles, one obole and a half of sory, one seedpod of common salt, two seedpods of Cappadocian salt. Make a flake [or blade] with two quarters (obole?). Submit it to the action of fire . . . until the blade breaks, then take the pieces and look at them as refined gold.
>
> Having taken four gold flakes, make one blade, heat it with water and with another dry (couperose), beat (one part) . . . with the dry matter, another with the mixed matter; pour out the rust and throw in . . .'[17]

We see in fact two separate recipes, both including copper sulfate, more or less oxidized (rust), under the names of chalcanthon, or couperose,

---

[*]All quotes from Berthelot and Ruelle's *Collection des Anciens Alchimistes Grecs,* Berthelot and Duval's *La Chimie au Moyen Age,* and Bidez and Cumont's *Les mages hellénisés Zoroastre Ostanee et Hystaspe d'apres la tradition grecque* are my translation.

and sory. The second recipe appears to be a mutilated fragment of a larger formula. The first is close to one recorded by first-century naturalist Pliny (*Natural History* 32.25) for making a remedy with gold, by commuting to roasted objects an active specific property Pliny calls *virus:* a literal translation of the Greek *ἰός,* "rust or venom," from which derives *ἴωσις* (iosis), a term we shall see again in the context of refining.

In column 8, 1.24, and column 6, 1.26, we find reference to a significant magical ring with a stone depicting a snake biting its own tail. This has been regarded as the fundamental symbol of alchemy, the ouroboros, showing nature as a single, consistent system characterized by repeated cycles of birth and rebirth, derived from the mystical "One." The ring in question provides glory, power, and wealth.

We also hear of magicians whose names are unique to the papyrus: Zminis the Tentyrite, Hemerius, Agathocles, and Urbicus. The names of Pebechius, Ostanes, Democritus, and Moses, however, we know from Pliny the Elder and other alchemical texts.

Papyrus W

Papyrus W is just over 10½ inches (0.27 m) high and 12½ inches (0.32 m) wide, containing twenty-five pages of text of 52 to 31 lines. Like the previous papyrus it is full of orthographic errors and solecisms, suggesting copyist errors. In it we find the names of the seven perfumes mentioned in the mystical ink recipe in Papyrus V: styrax (attributed to Saturn), malabathrum (Jupiter), costus (Mars), frankincense (the sun), nard (Venus), cassia (Mercury), myrrh (the moon); while the seven flowers turn out to be nard, marjoram, lily, lotus, buttercup, narcissus, and white violet.

Because Papyrus W contains magical invocations with Jewish and gnostic elements, Berthelot considered it linked to gnostic doctrines associated by Irenaeus with Marcus and followers of Carpocrates, but this was speculative. Irenaeus (*Against Heresies* 1.17) accused Marcus's followers of producing many apocryphal works. According to Berthelot, the papyrus quotes, without naming authors, numerous Jewish apocryphal and pseudo-Mosaic books concerning astrology, the Law, and a "Book of the Archangels." Highly syncretistic, it contains Jewish biblical names, Greek names, and references to Thoth and the dog star of old Egypt. It opens with reference to a sacred book called "Monas" (the "eighth of Saint Moses"), and Monas was a name Marcosians (following Valentinus, according to Irenaeus) gave to the great "unknown God" (*Against Heretics* 1.15): pinnacle of the Gnostic Ogdoad, or eight heavenly powers.

The papyrus also refers to a familiar character from the Hermetica and from the Graeco-Egyptian alchemical corpus: Agathodaimon, seen here not as a Hermetic patriarch but as divine serpent: "Heaven is your head, ether your body, earth your feet, and water is around you; you are the Ocean that begets all good and nourishes the inhabited earth."

There is an instruction to paint a sacred "stele" with the following invocation:

> I call upon you, the mightiest of gods, who created all things; you, born of yourself, who see all things, and cannot be seen. You gave the sun glory and power. When you appeared, the world existed and the light appeared. Everything is subject to you, but none of the gods can see your form, because you transform into all . . . I invoke you under the name that you possess in the language of birds, in that of hieroglyphics, in that of the Jews, in that of the Egyptians, in that of the cynocephals . . . in the Sparrowhawk, in the hieratic language.

Following an invocation of Hermes, the above languages appear again before a Gnostic account of creation. These mystical languages reappear a little further on, after an invocation to Hermes at the head of an account of creation. Berthelot calls it a "travesty" of the Genesis account of the seven-day creation, considering it comparable to the Gnostic Pistis Sophia and kindred texts related to what scholar Jean Doresse referred to in the 1950s as the "Egyptian Gnostics."

The God with the nine forms greets you in hieratic language . . . I precede you, Lord. Saying this, he applauds three times. God laughs [seven times]: cha, cha, cha, cha, cha, cha, cha, and God having laughed, were born the seven gods who understand the world; for it is they who appeared first. When he burst out laughing, the light appeared and lightened all things. . . . For God was born upon thy world and upon the fire. Bessun, berithen, berio. He burst out laughing for the second time: all was water. The earth, having heard the sound, cried out, bowed down, and the water was divided into three. The God appeared, the one who is in charge of the abyss; without him the water can neither grow nor decrease.[18]

In the third burst of laughter of God appears Hermes; in the fifth, Destiny, holding a balance and representing Justice. Its name means the boat of the celestial revolution—"another reminiscence of the old Egyptian mythology," according to Berthelot. Then comes the quarrel of Hermes and Destiny, claiming each for himself Justice. In the seventh laugh, the soul is born, then the serpent Pythian, who foresees everything.

Papyrus X

Papyrus X is the core document of the Leiden Papyrus that most interests scholars of alchemy and historians of chemical science. Consisting of ten leaves of about 12 inches by 13 inches (30 cm by 34 cm), folded in width direction, they make twenty pages. Sixteen contain text of between 28 and 47 lines. No less than 111 recipes follow, with no mythological or philosophical elements. There is a hint that copyists of the recipes may have been consciously involved in counterfeiting or deceiving the eyes of receivers of their works. In recipe no. 8, for example, we read that "this will be asem [see below] of the first quality, which will deceive even the artisans."[19] Practitioners could obviously discriminate between origin and contrivance, even if their understanding of chemical difference was, by our standards, crude, and based on different conceptions that conditioned perception (as ours do in their way). Basic approaches to testing silver and gold for purity are found in the papyrus. As these generally involve melting to see if impurities stand out, eutectic mixtures* would likely have deceived them. As far as the experienced practitioner was concerned, appearance was reality, even if they knew the reality was only an appearance; to us perhaps a curious mentality, akin to suspension of disbelief when immersed in a compelling movie.

Where recipes are incomplete, it's usually because the recipes were apparently notes or checklists for people who already knew what they were about.

As E. R. Caley noted in his first English translation of Papyrus X (published as articles in the *Journal of Chemical Education,* 1926–1927), the recipes continue the ancient practice of naming products and minerals after place of origin. "Salt of Cappadocia" was likely common salt, though "stone of Magnesia" could have multiple meanings but generally meant magnetic iron oxide, or hematite. The word *alum* or *alumen* was another imprecise term but generally referred to iron and aluminium sulfates—ubiquitous to metal purification in the papyrus. While pitch and oils were added as reducing agents to molten metals, alum, crude soda ash, and common and other chemical salts also served as fluxes and solvents for impurities.

One product with multiple possible constituents was called "asem." It seems to have been a vital constituent. Generally speaking, it refers to silver, alloys of silver and gold (including the natural alloy of silver and gold, electrum), or a jewelers' alloy resembling these, suggesting that practitioners considered alloys that looked the same as identical, even if different in composition. Berthelot notes a facet of asem that might have suggested transmutation to later practitioners, for depending on

---

*Eutectic mixtures consist of measures of substances that when mixed, freeze or melt at temperatures lower than would the individual constituents.

the treatments undergone, the asem could provide what they called pure silver, as was thought, or pure gold. Recipe no. 5 gives one way—among many others—to make one kind of asem.

> Tin, 12 drachmas; mercury, 4 drachmas; earth of Chios [a kind of clay], 2 drachmas. To the melted tin, add the crushed earth, then the mercury, stir with an iron, and put (the product) in use.[20]

Other than electrum, which was seen on Egyptian monuments, asem also covered an alloy of tin and silver (a method of diplosis of silver); a tin amalgam (to simulate silver); and refined tin with a little mercury added.

Among the 111 recipes we find methods for purification and hardening of lead; the same of tin; coloration, augmentation, falsification, testing, and polishing of gold; making solder for working gold; writing letters in gold, doubling or "diplosis" (increasing volume of gold by adding another metal that didn't change its appearance), and preparing liquid gold; whitening of copper; making copper appear like gold; purification, coloring, testing, and gilding of silver; fixation and falsification of Alkanet (an herb whose roots make a red dye); and seven recipes for making very greatly valued purple dyes (only nobles could wear purple). The need for mordanting dyes to fabrics was well understood. Purple dyeing and mordant constituents occupy much more of the Stockholm Papyrus.

Recipe 89 is significant: a preparation for the "invention of sulfur water." The Greek *hydōr theion* can mean either "sulfur" or "divine" water, and alchemical texts play heavily on the nominal ambiguity of this vital substance. A handful of lime and one of fine powdered sulfur is placed in a vessel containing strong vinegar or infant's urine before being heated from below until the supernatant liquid appears like blood. The liquid should be carefully decanted to separate it from the deposit. It is in fact a preparation for calcium polysulfide.

Observing what sulfur water can do to metals made a big impression. It produces colored precipitates of black, yellow, and red, among other shades, and metal salts and oxides. Polysulfides can dissolve most metal sulfides, coloring metal surfaces with distinctive tints, and can even dissolve gold.

Regarding the use of symbols—a notable feature of alchemy as we know it—Caley noted how recipe no. 90 for diluting asem provides our first "evidence of symbolism in chemical arts."[21] Where you see the words *gold* and *silver,* these were denoted in the papyrus by special characters (that for gold being the same as the astrological sign for the sun, with the moon sign for silver).

> Having reduced the asem into leaves and having covered it with mercury and applied (it) strongly upon the leaf, one sprinkles pyrites upon the leaf thus prepared, and places it upon the coals, in order to dry it up to the point when the color of the leaf appears changed; for the mercury evaporates and the leaf softens. Then one incorporates in the crucible 1 part of gold, (and) 2 parts of silver. Having blended them, throw upon the floating scum some golden-colored arsenic, some pyrites, some salt of Ammon, some chalcitis, (and) some blue; and having ground with sulfur water, heat, then spread mercury upon the surface.[22]

The word *chalcitis* above referred to copper minerals and, according to Pliny, copper pyrites. The "blue" was, according to Caley, most likely a copper salt or mineral and may be identical to an "Armenian blue" that appears in the Stockholm Papyrus.

Coloring of metals occupied much of the practitioners' time. Applied mercury (also used in the alloys) gave a silvery look. Curious gilding methods included a blend of lead and powdered gold attached to an object followed by burning off the base metal. Gold amalgam for silver gilding is clearly explained. Varnishes and dyes were also used for coloring. One recipe engaging Caley's chemical interest is recipe no. 89, the only preparation of a chemical salt in the collection: a preparation (dissolving a solute into a solvent) of sulfides of calcium solution—the original lime-sulfur mixture.

The metals employed were gold, silver, tin, copper, mercury, lead, arsenic, antimony, and zinc, with antimony and zinc not being distinguished from their compound or metallic states. Caley noted that the use of compounds did not include reducing agents and wondered whether furnaces were adjusted or if practitioners placed wood or charcoal with fusible metals. Judging by the range of alloys available, it's likely the purpose was ornamental jewelry rather than what Caley calls "practical metals such as bronze or steel."[23] The papyrus's quantitative recipes for alloy manufacture are the earliest known. As a laboratory document alone, the Leiden Papyrus is important to history.

Chemist Caley accepted that "the papyrus is of the highest historical importance chemically in showing the real starting point of the alchemical ideas of the transmutation of metals."[24] This is not far from chemist Berthelot's understanding nearly forty years earlier of the papyrus's significance. Berthelot found the making and falsification of gold and silver materials "analogous" to transmutation, pointing out that the basic processes of Papyrus X were common to figures generally accepted as early alchemists, such as Zosimos of Panopolis (ca. 300 CE), pseudo-Democritus (ca. 50–100 CE), Olympiodorus (sixth century CE), and Moses of Alexandria (first and second centuries CE).[25] For Berthelot, Papyrus X proved—contrary to a prevalent idea that alchemy derived from chimeric imaginations—that the art was in fact based on real experiences and positive practices. So impressive were practitioners' skills in imitating gold and silver, and so convinced were onlookers of being in the presence of the real thing, that—as Berthelot speculated—alchemists may have been encouraged to believe they'd accomplished magical transformations. However, this whole issue, which we shall explore in another chapter, is vastly complicated by the fact that our current understanding of "substance," "element," and chemical change is distant from that of late antiquity.

There is also the linguistic or classification problem that the very word *alchemy* is an Arabic word (*al-kimya,* with "al" being a definite article added to a transliterated Greek word, *chēmeia* or "chymia") that postdates the seventh-century Islamic invasions, by which time, trans-

Fig. 1.5. Emperor Diocletian (284–305 CE); he ordered the destruction of all alchemical books in Egypt, according to John of Antioch. Museum of Archaeology, Istanbul (photo: G. Dall'Orto).

mutation of substance had become a primary way of seeing the potential of the art. The conundrum was to what extent the "unity of God" was reflected in the substantial hierarchy of creation: Was there a unifying substratum or principle in all metals (or "bodies") that could be affected by agents to change them substantially? However, our earliest evidence does not suggest that transmutation of lower to higher metals was an intention of the art in its earliest known forms. Nevertheless, it is possible to see such an idea developing within continued practice, especially if hard information was difficult to come by, while old methods were open to misunderstanding when experienced traditional practitioners, and reliable texts, were few and rare. Rarity of texts may possibly be accounted for in a detail from the tenth-century Byzantine lexicon *Suda* in which we find *Chēmeia* defined as "the preparation of silver and gold. Diocletian [emperor, 284–305 CE] sought out and burned books about this. [It is said] that due to the Egyptians' rebellious behavior Diocletian treated them harshly and murderously. After seeking out the books written by the ancient [Egyptians] concerning the alchemy of gold and silver, he burned them so that the Egyptians would no longer have wealth from such a technique, nor would their surfeit of money in the future embolden them against the Romans."* It has always been presumed that the rebels were obtaining hard currency from the art directly, but I should say that it is more likely that the art was so developed as to give them a lead in selling precious goods, which commercial advantage brought them requisite lucre.

It is also the case that numerous arts and sciences share tendencies to mystify practices, establishing distance between outsiders and core beneficiaries. Historians of science have little justification for denying the aspiration, however dreamlike, of ancient science any more than we should ridicule H. G. Wells for dreaming of a moonshot in 1901 without the practical means to achieve it. The dream comes first. It is arguable that wished-for transmutation of base to noble metals may be understood as a phase within the development of science. Our science as we know it may also be a phase in the development of a science we know not. The problem in the nineteenth century, when Berthelot was writing, was a belief that science represented progress from superstition (outmoded knowledge) and that alchemy belonged to superstition. It is as valid to say that superstition belongs to the history of science, declining with increasing knowledge, though purists may be keen to purify the record for reasons of ideological satisfaction. One thing is certain, these early records of alchemy were eminently practical and demonstrable, and for that reason, some historians of science have opined that they are therefore not really "alchemy." In that case, we could say that "alchemy" as commonly understood was a medieval and Renaissance phase of metallurgical chemistry, and the term does not belong strictly to late antiquity; it depends how you choose to cut it.

Furthermore, there was no absolute definition of *gold* during the late antique period. The word referred to the metal shown to contain no

---

*See the heading "chi," in the five-volume *Svidae Lexicon,* edited by Ada Adler and translated by Ross Scaife (Leipzig: Teubner, 1928–1938), 280.

obvious impurity, alloys with golden tint, gilded objects, and anything gold-colored, whether natural or contrived. Gold was not the only mineral to connote several substances. Egyptians applied the name *emerald* and *sapphire* to numerous precious stones and vitrifications. The possibility of extraordinary changes being subject to divine influence was disputed, as we shall see when investigating Zosimos of Panopolis. It should be recognized that the Greek word *daimōn,* outside of Christian usage at this time, referred to certain beings associated with *theos* (god), lesser deities or spirits, akin to Hebrew angels. Daimōnes were considered divine, invisible entities behind the workings of cosmic nature, with special knowledge appropriate to their role. However, Jewish and Christian teachings associated such intermediaries with malevolent beings and fallen angels, so by the third century, at least, there was a question over the wisdom of evoking them or invoking their assistance, even if the religion of the practitioners was syncretic, as the papyri suggest was sometimes the case. Nevertheless, there was also the idea of good and bad daimōnes, and help, by magic and prayer, from good divine beings (including daimōnes) was sought to ward off the activities of bad ones. Indeed such attitudes are prevalent in folklore throughout the world to this day.

Papyrus X, of course, has none of this magical element within its recipes, but that does not mean the recipes were not practiced within a general context of magical, religious consciousness. Today many monotheistic Muslims in rural districts in Egypt believe firmly in jinns.

Only one alchemist, Phimenas the Saite, is named as author of a recipe for asem. The name occurs in other alchemical literature as "Pammenes" (under which name an identical recipe for asem appears in the first-century pseudo-Democritus) and as Pamenasis and Pamenas.

The papyrus ends with ten recipes from Dioscorides's *Materia Medica,* possibly indicating an early crossover with medicine that, arguably, ultimately blossomed into making elixirs (an Arabic transliteration—*al-ʿiksīr*—of a Greek word for powder to dry wounds). Berthelot examined the minerals heading the ten extracts from

Dioscorides, as they inform us about the mineralogical knowledge of the papyrus. They are arsenic (our orpiment); sandarac (our realgar); misy (basic iron sulfate mixed with copper sulfate); cadmia (impure zinc oxide mixed with copper oxide, or even lead oxide, antimony oxide, arsenic acid, etc.); gold or chrysocolla solder (meaning both an alloy of gold and silver or lead, or malachite and various congeners); Sinope rubric (vermilion, or minium, or blood); alum (our alum and various other astringent bodies); natron (*nitrum* of the ancients, our soda carbonate, sometimes also soda sulfate); cinnabar (our minium and mercury sulfide); and mercury (the last of the 111 recipes).[26]

Interestingly, the mercury recipe contains the Greek word *ambix,* referring to the lid of a vase, on the surface of whose underside vapors of sublimated mercury condensed. This word, added to the Arabic article *al,* would give us the "alambic" (or alembic) familiar to accounts of "gold-makers" throughout history. The alembic and aludel (a pot or vase open at both ends so one could be placed atop another, with the bottom, where the material for sublimation would be placed, in the heat source) were thus familiar objects to fourth-century alchemists. It's also interesting that the Dioscorides extracts probably give us an earlier, as well as more correct, version of the *Materia Medica*— for whereas the oldest known version has a copyist ignorantly stating that mercury could be kept in vessels of glass, lead, tin, or silver lest "it gnaws away all other matter and flows away," the Leiden version correctly insists that only glass is appropriate as mercury attacks the other metals.

The Stockholm Papyrus

About 12 inches (30 cm) in length and 6 inches (16 cm) wide, the well-preserved Stockholm Papyrus is similar in size to Leiden Papyrus X, with between 41 and 47 lines of Greek capitals per page and containing 154 recipes. Nine concern metals, while around seventy assist in improving and imitating precious stones; the remainder

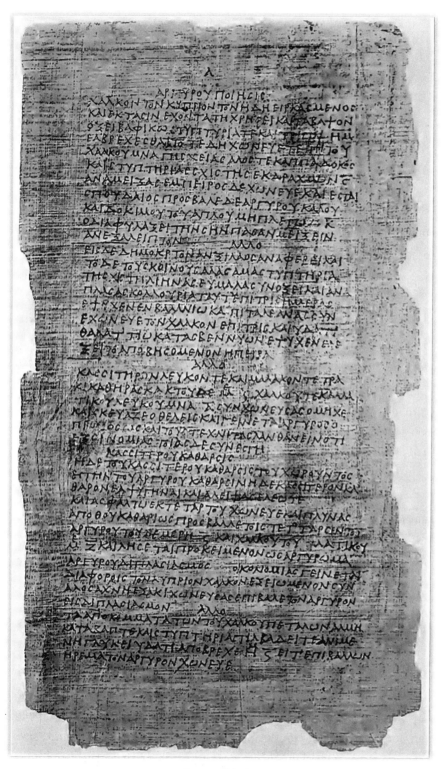

Fig. 1.6. The Stockholm Papyrus

deal with dyeing and mordanting cloth. The final part (154) is on a separate leaf from the recipes and appears to be a prayer, invocation, or incantation.

> Sun, Berbeloch, Chthotho, Miach, Sandum, Echnin, Zaguel, accept me who comes before thee. Trust thyself (to the God), anoint thyself and thou shalt see him with thine eyes.[27]

The deity name Berbeloch appears in the Greek Magical Papyri (PGM 5a.1). H. M. Jackson speculated it might be a variant for the important female deity Barbelo* of the Sethian Gnostics, referred to by heresiologists Irenaeus and Epiphanius.[28] Whichever way the names are understood—they are perhaps aspects of a single divine power— the piece provides more evidence for a definite link between chemical practice in this period and gnostic practice and cosmosophy. Caley saw it as indicating a connection with Egyptian priesthood, though Hermetic incantations of a similar kind might have been the practice of Hermetic lodges or dedicated groups, perhaps with a craft or guild basis, being independent or semi-independent of temples, like medieval lay confraternities, with a priestly connection and run as societies outside of official organized worship, even, if I may speculate a little, to compete (in providing special services) with Christian communities, whether orthodox or officially heretical.[29]

Briefly, the recipes often include variant ones for making and doubling silver; tin purification; pearl making and whitening; preparing amethyst, lychnis (ruby red according to Pliny, *Natural History* 37.103), chrysolite, chrysoprase, lapis lazuli, beryl, emerald, verdigris (for emerald), "green stone," and "sunstone"; emerald softening; softening, purification, and preservation of crystal; making ruby (from crystal); corrosion of crystal, stone, and "sunstone"; boiling and opening of stones; crystal bleaching; dissolving comarum

---

*See my *Gnostic Mysteries of Sex* for an investigation into the name Barbelo.

(plant); cleaning wool with soapwort; mordanting (to fix dyes to fabric) for Sardian, Silician, purple, genuine purple (note the word *purple* could also mean "red"); dissolving alkanet; cold-dyeing of purple, dark yellow, gold color ("Take safflower blossom and oxeye, crush them together and lay them in water. Put the wool in and sprinkle with water. Lift the wool out, expose it to the air, and use it"); dyeing in rose color or scarlet; orchil (red or violet dye from lichens) dyes for Phoenician color; dissolving orchil and alkanet; and dyeing of "madder" and, what the papyrus heralds as, Tyrian "Guaranteed Superior" purple.

Recipe no. 2 refers to a recipe of "Democritus" taught to "Anaxilaus" after him, while recipe 111 refers to a book of Africanus and no. 135 refers to Book III of Africanus: presumably a reference to well-traveled Christian historian Julius Africanus (160–240 CE), author of the five-volume work *Chronographiai.* A work, *Kestoi,* probably falsely attributed to him, dealt with medicine among other things, but with a credulity scholars think unworthy of the named author; our recipe keeper may have had access to such a pseudonymous text. Alchemical recipes attributed to Democritus were no less pseudonymous, as we shall see. Anaxilaus of Larissa was, according to fourth-century church historian Eusebius, banished from Rome in 28 BCE for practicing magic. Pliny cited him as a writer on the magical properties of minerals and herbs and drugs derived from them; his natural science knowledge enabled Anaxilaus to play tricks, which were taken for real magic: an interesting slant on the practices of some of those skilled in dyes of metals and fabrics perhaps.

Caley regards the recipes in the papyrus as being "empirical," with no hocus-pocus. Cleaning of stones, for example, usually means coating them with a glutinous substance and then peeling it off, though one suggests the stone should be eaten by a bird and collected from its rear on account, presumably, of an acidic stomach! References to *crystal* generally mean rock crystal or quartz. Surfaces were treated by heating and dipping them in oil, wax, or solutions of alum, native soda, common salt, and calcium sulfide in varying mixture to make the stones rough, porous, and receptive to dyeing with vegetable dyes and dyes of celandine, cedar oil, pitch, and numerous resins. The recipes in this and the Leiden Papyrus provide our earliest specific dyeing instructions: another boon to science.

Pseudo-Democritus

The name Democritus cropped up earlier. Ancient tradition asserted the man popularly accredited as first imaginer of the atom—pre-Socratic philosopher Democritus (ca. 460–370 BCE)—received deep wisdom in Egypt, so using Democritus's name as an authority for a text of Graeco-Egyptian alchemy came naturally. "Alchemical" writings attributed to Democritus certainly don't go back as far as the Greek philosopher, and our current authority on pseudo-Democritus, the remarkable Italian scholar Matteo Martelli, would date extant fragments of pseudo-Democritus's *Four Books* to circa 54–68 CE.[30] This makes the recipes in those fragments the oldest known texts of Graeco-Egyptian alchemy, even though our earliest known quotations were apparently extracted more than two hundred years later, while our earliest surviving Greek copies of those extracts derive from considerably later still (ca. tenth century CE).*

　　While the original *Four Books* remains lost, summary texts exist in two ancient treatises, *Physika kai mystika* (Natural and Secret Questions), and *Peri asēmou poiēseō* (On Making Silver). There is also a

---

*Following Berthelot and Ruelle's mighty labors, Joseph Bidez supervised efforts to describe all known Greek alchemy manuscripts (about 100 in number), resulting in the Union Académique International's 1924–1932 publication of eight volumes of the *Catalogue des manuscrits alchimiques grecs* (Brussels, collectively known as CMAG). The most important of these manuscripts being: (1) *Marcianus graecus* 299 (tenth to eleventh centuries, CMAG II 1–22; 2, originally Byzantine, now in Venice); (2) *Parisinus graecus* 2325 (thirteenth century, CMAG I 1–17); (3) *Parisinus graecus* 2327 (fifteenth century, CMAG I 17–62; a colophon indicates the copyist as one Theodoros Pelekanos of Corfu, who completed the copy in Crete in 1478). The latter two collections are now in Paris.

list of chemical substances known as *Katalogoi* (Catalog). Interestingly, the contents of the summary texts include some similar recipes and cover the same topics as the Leiden and Stockholm Papyri; that is, making silver and gold, artificially produced precious stones, and the dyeing purple of wool. This suggests that these were the four chief technical interests of our late antique alchemists and that the later emphasis on transmutation, which still dominates, and degrades, definitions of *alchemy,* represents a narrowing, even arguably a cul-de-sac, of alchemy's formative practices.

The one practice common to these activities is dyeing, or coloring, substances. It is interesting then that the most famous late antique alchemist, Zosimos, who often quoted Democritus as authority, lived some 62 miles north of Thebes, at Panopolis (ancient Greek *Chemmis; * Coptic *Khmin* or *Khmim*), which city, according to Greek sage Strabo (ca. 64 BCE–ca. 24 CE; *Geography* 17.41), was a notable producer of textiles, including dyed wools. It's perfectly possible that our alchemists were operating at the high end of this and related industry.

Oft repeated in extant texts is an aphorism usually attributed to pseudo-Democritus's alleged teacher, Persian sage Ostanes. It epitomizes the principle of universal sympathy and correspondence: "Nature delights in nature, nature conquers nature, nature masters nature." It could serve as rubric to the ouroboros image, the serpent swallowing its tail, whose epitome is usually inscribed as "Hen to pan"; that is, the One is All.

The first part of *Physika kai mystika* begins with recipes for purple dye but then switches to a story of how the author's master, Ostanes, died before transmitting secret knowledge. After an obstructive demon thwarted attempts to conjure the master from Hades, all the author received was the message: "The books are in the temple." At a feast in that temple's holy of holies, a column breaks apart, revealing the master's books, but the contents were unsurprising to the author, save the aphorism above.

Without a broken column to help him, Matteo Martelli assumed the grand task of reconstructing the original four books of pseudo-Democritus, the results being published in 2014. For the first time, Martelli edited and translated three Syriac manuscripts containing unique passages unknown to the extant Byzantine manuscripts. He also included a "dialogue between (alchemists) Synesius and Dioscorus," a commentary on the *Four Books* from the Byzantine corpus, and Synesius's "Notes on Democritus's Book." Martelli also posited convincing reasons for doubting the common ascription of the *Four Books* to third-century BCE Egyptian sage Bolos of Mendes.[31]

The traditional link of Democritus to Ostanes the Mede is more difficult to dislodge. The *Chronographica* of Byzantine churchman-historian George Synkellos (died 810) states:

Democritus of Abdera, the natural philosopher, was flourishing. In Egypt, Democritus was initiated into the mysteries by Ostanes the Mede, who had been dispatched to Egypt by the Persian kings of that time to take charge of the temples in Egypt. He was initiated in the temple of Memphis along with other priests and philosophers, among them a Hebrew woman of learning named Mariam, and Pammenes. Democritus wrote about gold and silver, and stones and purple, but in an oblique way.[32]

The second part of *Physika kai mystika* opens with the author's claim: "I too have come to Egypt to deal with natural substances, so that you may disregard many captious questions and the confused matter." It's not properly connected to the broken column story in which pseudo-Democritus is *already* in Egypt. Martelli concluded that the first part was the remains of the original fourth book, on purple, with the second part coming from the original first book on making gold, because the introductory claim is followed by thirteen recipes of *chrysopoeia,* or gold making, with processes for using solids and liquids for dyeing base metals yellow. Each recipe is followed by Ostanes's alleged aphorism.

Martelli reckons another book of the original four was that on making silver preserved in the second section of the *Codex Marcianus*. We have ten recipes for processing solids and liquids for the "whitening" of base metals; that is, making them silver. The Marcianus codex omits the original book on stones, which for Martelli suggests a narrowing of scope of alchemy over time. Was this down to a species of "gold fever"? The narrowing, by Byzantine times, Martelli observes as being attested in the tenth-century Byzantine lexicon *Suda,* in which we find the following entry:

Chēmeia: the preparation of gold and silver; Diocletian looked for the books on this subject and burned them . . . Look under the entry *deras* (i.e., fleece, vellum).[33]

The *Suda's* source was seventh-century chronographer John of Antioch during the Byzantine emperor Heraclius's reign, and the latter reference to the fleece is because John offered an alchemical interpretation of the myth of the Argonauts, again emphasizing that chēmeia meant exclusively gold and silver transmutation. For Martelli, this probably explains the broken nature of the *Four Books* in the *Codex Marcianus*. However, it's not all as simple as that, for the thirteenth-century *Codex Parisinus* (which shares its source with the Marcianus codex) does contain a recipe book devoted to the making of precious stones: *Deep Tincture of Stones, Emeralds, Rubies and Jacinths from the Book Taken from the Sancta Sanctorum of the Temples,* which suggests a rewidening of alchemical interest subsequently!

Martelli was pleased to find that Syriac and Garshuni manuscripts of pseudo-Democritus in three important collections kept in London and Cambridge were more complete than the Byzantine ones. The British Library holds the sixteenth-century Egerton 709 and Oriental 1593 Mss., while Cambridge University holds the fifteenth-century Mm. 629 Ms. (all Syriac). These manuscripts, probably dating from translations from the Greek made in the sixth century and the eighth to ninth centuries, had been partially edited and translated by Berthelot and orientalist Rubens Duval for their Syriac alchemy-devoted second volume of *La Chimie au Moyen Age* (1893).

The Syriac texts focus on the earliest Greek-language alchemists; namely, Zosimos and pseudo-Democritus. The Cambridge manuscript, in particular, includes three long sections from the original *Four Books*. The part on making silver includes a section perhaps lost to the Byzantine sources, and at fol. 96v we find recipe material from the two original books, *On Stones* and *On Purple,* in a third part titled *Again by Democritus: I greet you wise men.*[34]

As for the gold-making recipes in pseudo-Democritus, we can summarize a number of them as follows. A first instructs the operator to extinguish mercury by alloying it with another metal, or by uniting it with sulfur, or with arsenic sulfide, or by putting it by certain earthy materials. A resultant paste is spread over copper to whiten it. Add electrum or gold powder, and one obtains a colored metal in gold. A variant method has the copper bleached with arsenic compounds or decomposed cinnabar. As Berthelot observed, this is apparently a process of silver-plating copper before a superficial gilding.[35]

In a second recipe, the natural silver sulfide is treated with lead litharge—a polymorph of lead (II) oxide: bright yellow with tetragonal crystal structure—or with antimony to obtain an alloy, to be colored yellow by an undefined material.

A third recipe involves roasting pyrite, digested with sea salt solutions, and alloyed with silver or gold. An alloy of copper, tin, and lead with zinc, called "claudianon," is yellowed with sulfur or arsenic and then alloyed with silver or gold.

A fourth recipe begins with cinnabar, broken down by various treatments, which dyes silver into gold and copper into electrum.

A fifth features a golden yellow varnish prepared with cadmium, or veal bile, or turpentine, or castor oil, or egg yolk.

The sixth involves silver dyed by superficial sulfurization, obtained by means of certain pyrites, or by oxidized antimony, combined with sulfur water (calcium polysulfide) and sulfur itself.

The seventh requires preparing a copper-lead alloy called "molybdochalkos" and yellowing it to obtain a gold-colored metal.

The eighth uses an altered green couperose (vitriol) to dye copper and silver on the surface yellow, followed by a recipe for refining gold, reminiscent of the royal cement (see page 21).

The ninth recipe employs the aforementioned refinement recipe applied to superficial cementation, which gives the outer parts of the metal gold characteristics.

A small declaration on the nature of the science is followed by three varnish recipes, to dye in gold by digestion with mixtures of vegetable matter, saffron, chelidine, or safflower. The author concludes the section with the statement that "this matter of chrysopoeia accomplished by natural operations is that of Pammenes, which he taught to priests in Egypt."

Berthelot was struck by how the recipes using asem for making silver in pseudo-Democritus shed light on the thinking of third-century Egyptian practitioners as to the constitution of metals,[36] observing how asem might be made from some thirteen distinct alloys of gold, silver, copper, tin, lead, zinc, and arsenic.

In a first silver-making recipe, copper was bleached by volatile arsenic compounds; this sublimation action was assimilated to that of mercury.

In the second, sublimated mercury was extinguished with tin, sulfur, and various other ingredients; it was used to bleach (whiten) metals.

Similar to the second, the third recipe was applied to an alloy of copper, orichalcum, and tin. (Orichalcum, or aurichalcum, is mentioned as having been mined in Atlantis in Plato's *Critias* and, though now unknown, had been second only to gold. It might have been platinum or an alloy like bronze or brass.)

In a fourth recipe arsenic sulfide and sulfur were used to bleach and modify metals.

The fifth recipe describes preparing a white lead alloy.

The sixth consists of a simple superficial varnish to give copper, lead, and iron the appearance of silver; the varnish being fixed by decoction and coated without the action of fire.

The seventh recipe is an amalgamation tincture, and the eighth a simple varnish.[37]

What the recipes for asem had in common was a way to form a transition between gold and silver, for making silver objects. Berthelot reckoned such confusion facilitated fraud, eventually passing from processed products in operations to the minds of operators themselves; that is, they deceived themselves; such being, according to Berthelot, the beginning of the fantasy of transmutation. In this regard it's worth mentioning that by medieval times, processes of making the "stone" vital for transmutation had been repeatedly shown as being marked by a color-changing process. A key stage was whitening, yet it is apparent from the earliest known texts that whitening was concerned with making dyes for silver, where *white* meant silver, as *yellowing* meant the dye to render metals gold. As Berthelot maintained:

> The theories of the philosophical schools on the raw material being identical in all bodies, only receiving its present form from the addition of the fundamental qualities expressed by the four elements, encouraged and excited this confusion. [This philosophical conception is not supported by recipe evidence, and is unproven.] Thus, workers accustomed to making alloys simulating gold and silver, sometimes with such perfection that they themselves were mistaken, came to believe in the possibility of actually making these metals from scratch, with the help of certain combinations of alloys, and certain tricks of the hand, supplemented by the help of supernatural powers, sovereign masters of all transformations.[38]

Berthelot's confidence in assuming they believed the raw material of metals was identical in all bodies is unfounded (see the discussion on a so-called "unqualified substrate," pages 224–25.) It is difficult to conceive of such raw material, and there's no evidence they ever either obtained such, imagined it, sought it, or took such an idea as an operational assumption and practical priority.

Garth Fowden in our own time in his lucid *The Egyptian Hermes: A Historical Approach to the Late Pagan Mind* (1986) made a similar point, contradicting much inaccurate commentary on the alleged theory of alchemists. The earliest texts of alchemy contain nothing of the idea that metals would be undifferentiated, lifeless bodies without distinction being provided by soul (or active agents), related to the planets. The serious practitioners were not testing theories; they were refining practices.

Having now established a foundation of knowledge concerning our earliest records of Graeco-Egyptian alchemy, it's now time to investigate from extant evidence what can be reasonably known about the origins of alchemy in Roman Egypt and about the first alchemists themselves.

TWO

The Origins of Alchemy
in Roman Egypt

FIRST: THE TERM ITSELF—*alchemy;* as noted already, it's a latecomer. Early texts speak of the "sacred and divine art" (in Greek: *hē hiera kai theia technē*), otherwise, *chrysopoēia* and *argyropoēia*—literally Greek for "gold-making" and "silver-making," when specifically referring to those pillars of the art. Zosimos of Panopolis offers some of the earliest references to *chēmia,* or *chymia*—a variant of the Greek *chēmeia,* presumed origin of the Arabic *alkymia. Chēmeia* will eventually give us our "chemistry," of course, but it's not certain what its root denoted in late antiquity. Indeed, we may properly call practitioners of the "sacred art" *alchemists* only with some reserve, and more convenience.

If we knew more about the etymology, we might gain insight into where Egyptians received their knowledge from; that is, if we leave aside the idea that chēmeia came from a Greek view that the art's origin was Egypt, being a reflection on the Egyptian *kem-it* or *kam-it,* meaning the "black land," usually taken to refer to dark alluvial deposits conveyed by the Nile's annual inundation to fertilize Egyptian soil. The root *kem* or *kam* may just as likely refer to carbonization brought on by heat, whether artificial or by the sun in the south. The "blackening" may well be the chemical resultant of applied flames; that is, *chēmeia* may simply mean "the art of heat," or "roasting."

No early practitioner suggested the Egyptians themselves invented the art. Zosimos believed it was transmitted by angels (or daimōnes) who, according to the Jewish Book of the Watchers (second or third century BCE and found in I Enoch), quit heaven for lust of human women and corrupted human beings with illicit knowledge— illicit for humans, but which nonetheless came, like Prometheus's fire, from the heavens. Byzantine George Synkellos wrote how he found the following passage in a copy of Zosimos's "ninth book of Imouth."* It appears to be from a letter to female correspondent, Theosebeia.

> The Holy Scriptures, that is the books, say, my lady [Theosebeia], that there is a race of demons who avail themselves of women. Hermes also mentioned this in his *Physika,* and nearly every treatise, both public and esoteric, made mention of this. Thus the ancient and divine scriptures said this, that certain angels lusted after women, and having descended taught them all the works of nature. Having stumbled because of these women, he says, they remained outside heaven, because they taught mankind everything wicked and nothing benefiting the soul. The same scriptures say that from them the giants were born. So theirs is the first teaching concerning these arts. They called this the Book of Chēmeu, whence also the art is called chēmeia.[1]

A Syriac version of this extract from Zosimos held in Cambridge says it's from Zosimos's "eighth book."[2] It appears more complete, and adds to it (see pages 230–31), asserting that the angels provided a treatise divided into twenty-four books on dyeing copper, iron, and tin. No one seems to have noticed that there are twenty-four letters in

*Imouth or Imouthes, god of medicine, worshipped at Memphis; known to the Greeks as Asklēpios, presented in Hermetic tracts as a pupil of Hermes Trismegistos, to whom the Perfect Discourse (excerpt in Nag Hammadi Codex VI), known in its Latin version as *Asclepius,* is addressed.

the Greek alphabet, and that Zosimos is supposed to have written a series of treatises under the title of each letter from alpha to omega (of which only a few fragments, such as *Omega,* are extant). In this regard it's interesting that the Syriac version of the angels story has Zosimos complaining that later readers of the angelic-sourced treatise confined interest to dyeing base metals white or yellow (i.e., making gold and silver), whereas the art's true aim extended to many colors. This criticism perhaps originated in an allusion to Zosimos's lost alphabetic works (perhaps originally called the book [or books] of Imouth). As for the scope of arts angelically (or demonically) conveyed, Zosimos possibly had as authority a Greek translation of 1 Enoch 8:1: "Azael [leader of recalcitrant angels] taught men to make swords, weapons, shields, and breast-armours—instructions of the angels—and showed them metals and how to work them, armlets, adornments, [powdered] antimony, paint for the eyelids, all kinds of precious stones, and dyes."

Pseudo-Democritus apparently knows nothing of angels. Its author maintained that instruction in the art came via Persian sage Ostanes: a plausible epitome of what might have been the case, for the Persian king Cambyses II invaded Egypt in 525 BCE, leaving the country a Persian satrapy for 131 years, before it fell again to Persian rule from 343–332 BCE, a power displaced only by Alexander the Great at the dawn of the Ptolemaic or Graeco-Egyptian period. This picture of Egypt as a pivot of cultural cross-fertilization finds its reflection in some of the earliest names revered by Graeco-Egyptian practitioners of the art in late antiquity. As well as the Persian Ostanes, we find a woman with a distinctly Ptolemaic name, Kleopatra (meaning "glory of her father"), a highly inventive Jewish woman called Mariam (known to alchemical tradition as Mary the Prophetess), and an Egyptian priest called Pebichius. Early alchemy has something of a cosmopolitan, if not multinational and above all practical, rather than ideological air about it. This is in marked contrast, I think, to the more bookish, nationalistic, or patriotic conflict between rival claimants for highest antiquity pursued by learned Egyptians and Jews in the first century CE, when Egyptian grammarian Apion viciously disparaged Jewish history in favor of Egyptian, while later (ca. 80 CE) Jewish historian Josephus attacked Apion's writings and followers, insisting, contrariwise, that Egypt owed its science to Abraham, further insisting that the first man knew one only God, a belief only Jewish patriarchs had properly maintained. For its patriarch of science and wisdom, Egypt had Hermes Trismegistos; Jews had their own triad of Enoch, Moses, and Abraham. Where alchemy was concerned, the source may have been neither Jewish nor Egyptian.

Italian scholars Matteo Martelli and Maddalena Rumor have inquired into Near Eastern origins of Graeco-Egyptian alchemy.[3] The trail begins with pseudo-Democritus. Fourth-century alchemist Synesius believed the author of the *Four Books* to be the famous Thracian philosopher Democritus of Abdera, whose wisdom increased when initiated in a Memphis temple "with all the Egyptian priests by the great Ostanes. He [Democritus] took his basic principles from him and composed four books on dyeing, on gold, silver, (precious) stones, and purple. . . . For the philosopher himself (i.e., Democritus), in speaking about the great Ostanes, testifies that he did not make use of the Egyptian methods for applying and roasting (the substances), but he used to smear the substances on the outside and heat them to make the drug sink in. He said that the Persians were in the habit of working thus."[4] According to Synkellos, "Ostanes the Mede" had been "dispatched to Egypt by the Persian kings of that time to take charge of the temples in Egypt,"[5] while Pliny the Elder (*Natural History* 30.1–2) describes "magus" Ostanes accompanying the Persian king Xerxes (who ruled the Achaemenid empire 486–465 BCE) on his conquests, disseminating magic wherever he went.

While Ostanes was supposed to have influenced third- to second-century BCE Egyptian writer Bolus of Mendes (supposed author of lost works on natural marvels and remedies written under Democritus's name), no original writings of Ostanes survive. Numerous pseudepigraphical quotations from "him" survive and one pseudepigraphical treatise from the Byzantine corpus: *Ostanes the philosopher to Petasius, on the Holy and Divine Art.*[6] The art concerns making "divine water" to which miraculous properties are attributed (e.g., it "resuscitates the dead and makes the living die"), but anachronistic references to the persons of the Holy Trinity make it obviously pseudepigraphical. Enigmatic passages attributed to Ostanes by Zosimos in the Byzantine corpus, usually when citing pseudo-Democritus, are difficult to assess in terms of provenance, especially as Zosimos also took "Democritus" to be the fifth-century BCE philosopher. Following are several examples: the first referring to an untitled treatise by pseudo-Democritus's master, Ostanes, about the "affinity" of substances such as *magnēsia* and magnet, or mercury and tin.

> What does Ostanes mean when he talks about the combination of volatile materials with those that are not? "Pyrite stone has an affinity for copper." Ostanes did not speak of mercury, but of extreme decay; that is, of the condition in which pyrite does not give rise to any deposit, being completely liquefied. It is therefore necessary for you to understand, with regard to water and liquefaction, what the Philosopher developed in speaking of washing and delaying. About delaying, he said: so that the product becomes like water. The Philosopher again said, "Magnesia and the magnet have an affinity for iron." And the Master still says: "Mercury has an affinity for tin." The disciple says: "Mercury amalgamates with tin." He also says: "This whitens all kinds of bodies. Lead also has an affinity for pyrite; the Etesian stone, for lead." The Philosopher, in making these arguments, said about our art that nature charms nature.[7]

It's clear Zosimos took pseudo-Democritus at "his" word in giving authority to Ostanes. There may even have been a tradition from Ostanes about a miraculous stone, but it is uncertain as to whether, in the following passage from the Byzantine corpus for example, the explication of a metaphorical and enigmatic stone is not a much later commentary on a fragment of Zosimos.

It is on this subject that the very ancient Ostanes, in his demonstrations, said: Someone tells this about a certain Sophar [possibly "Sapor," a name shared by two late antique Sasanian kings of Persia], who previously lived in Persia. This divine Sophar expresses himself as follows: "There exists on a pillar a bronze eagle [mercury sign above this word], which descends into the pure fountain and bathes there every day, renewing itself by this diet." Then he says, "The eagle, whose interpretation we have given, is used to bathing every day." How, then, is he rejecting ablution and daily washing by saying the same thing in another way? It is necessary to (explain) exactly about this operation. Held in uncertainty because of the (ambiguous) doctrine of the philosopher, however, we must wash and rejuvenate the copper eagle for 365 whole days; as is fitting according to the rest of his treatise, for Ostanes expresses himself as follows: Press the vintage. [Berthelot thinks "vintage," as in grapes, refers to "poverty."] Below, he explains that this means washing by flow; by this mystery we must understand *ios*. He adds, expressing himself very clearly: Go toward the Nile current; you will find there a stone having a spirit; take it, cut it in two; put your hand in the interior and pull out the heart: for its soul is in its heart." By the expression: "Go toward the current of the Nile, you will find there a stone having a spirit"; it clearly designates the products washed by the currents (of water), during the maceration of our stone. This is how all copper ore is used for the generation of metals, as well as all lead ore. "You will find," he said, "this stone that has a spirit," which relates to the expulsion of mercury.

6. It is for these reasons that my excellent (master), Democritus, distinguishes himself and says: "Receive this stone which is not a stone, this precious thing which has no value, this polymorphic object which has no form, this unknown which is known to all, which has several names and which has no name: [sign of cinnabar above in *Codex Marcianus*] I mean aphroselinon." For this stone is not a stone, and while it is very precious it has no market value; its

nature is unique, its name unique. However, he has been given several names, I do not say absolutely speaking, but according to his nature; so that if one calls him either: being that flees from fire, either: white vapour, or: white copper, one does not lie.[8]

The style of the latter paragraph, predominant in the cryptic manner of much Byzantine and medieval Western alchemical discourse, seems distant from surviving epitomes of pseudo-Democritus. Nevertheless, Zosimos may have had access to other works attributed to Democritus in which the author was keen to cite Ostanes as ultimate authority.

Another interesting reference to Ostanes, coming from an eighth- to ninth-century alchemist called the "Anepigraphos Philosopher" when writing on gold-making, may confirm Synesius's view that Ostanes taught a Persian method of dyeing.

12. Exposing these things to the Persians, he [Democritus] said, This man accomplished this by his own wisdom; having employed suitable species, he coated the substances outwardly, and deeply imbued them with the action of fire. He says it is customary for the Persians to do so. This is why, in all inscriptions on steles, he transmits to the vulgar the precept of dyeing thoroughly by plaster; he also shows how to avoid failure. Because often, the preparation being overabundant, the coatings were not fully absorbed and did not produce their specific effect. We have said that fire, when activated by the bellows with too much force, determines the loss of the spirit and, consequently, does not produce the desired effect.

13. Ostanes also uses the same method, saying at the end of his treatise: It is necessary to dye metal leaves in liquors and thus to coat a preparation; because in this way it will easily receive a dye. But I tell you in my turn, and I remind you of the practice of goldsmiths and of all those who know how to dye gold with couperose, salt, and ocher. By each proceeding in his own way, they purify gold, according to the aforementioned means and in a thousand other ways. By

sprinkling and relaxing, they make the brilliance of some jewels disappear. Their species are subject to the action of the bellows; they exhaust the action of the bellows, and they endeavor to make the proper shade penetrate the whole depth.[9]

An anonymous recipe book on making precious stones in the *Codex Marcianus* relies on a source attributed to Ostanes for the use of animal gall and copper rust to manufacture emeralds and an herb called "yakinthos" and woad for making blue stones.

> With regard to the manufacture of emeralds, according to the opinion of Ostanes, this universal compiler of the ancients, (the species used are) copper rust, biles of all kinds of animals and similar materials. For hyacinths (amethysts), we use the plant of the same name (hyacinth) and the isatis root, decoction with it. For the snare, it's the orcanet and the dragon-blood. . . .
>
> Thus Ostanes, for emeralds, took the biles of animals and the rust of copper, without adding the marine color. For hyacinth, he took the plant of the same name, the black Indian and the root of isatis. For the ruby, the orcanet and the dragon-blood, Mary [the alchemist] took, on her side, the rust of copper and the biles of marine animals. As for the stone that shines at night, it is that stone which scientists call hyacinth. . . . When the dye is completely developed, objects project a glow like the rays of the sun.[10]

The Syriac tradition gives us a translated letter from Egyptian alchemist Pebichius to one "Osron," Persian magus. The first letter describes Pebichius's discovery in Egypt of Ostanes's hidden, divine books. As they were written in Persian, Pebichius asks Osron's help with the alphabet, for which favor he sends a description.

> I (i.e., Pebichius) opened Ostanes's book and I found every art: astrology and astronomy and philosophy and philology and magic

and the art of sacrifices and that art that is terrible for many people, but absolutely necessary, that is, the making of gold. . . . And the whole book (included also) the stones and the purples and the divine dyeing of glasses. I transcribed it in Egyptian and Greek alphabet.[11]

The letters possibly date to the first century CE, as Pebichius is counted an early alchemist, often cited by Zosimos. Contents resemble the *Four Books,* but with additional material. Martelli notes that the indirect references to pseudo-Democritus and Ostanes share interest in baths for dipping metallic leaves and stones, as well as in affinities between substances. This may simply mean that "Ostanes" means pseudo-Democritus, though the Pebichius letters might suggest otherwise.[12]

Sadly, we've no evidence to tell whether bathing metals in liquid tinctures was originally Persian practice, but Martelli and Rumor cite a Middle Babylonian tablet (1500–1000 BCE)* concerning pebbles being dyed to make them into precious stones.[13] According to Martelli and Rumor:

> The two processes described therein involve the use of liquid media: in the first recipe a certain pappardillu stone is to be mixed with honey, milk, red alkali, wine, and another ingredient not yet identified; the mix is to be poured into a bowl that will be sealed with a dough-like material and then heated for a whole day. The second part of the tablet—and probably a separate recipe—instructs one to dip some other material (the text is broken, but we can expect here a stone) in a liquid [the verb used here is *labāku,* "to soften by soaking in a liquid"], and to boil it into vinegar and alum. The text

---

*Martelli and Rumor describe this as "Photograph Bab. K 713. A more precise dating is difficult to establish, as the original tablet is lost. The transliteration, published by L. Oppenheim in 'Mesopotamia in the Early History of Alchemy' [*Revu' d'Assyriologie e' d'archéologie orientale*], 60 (1966): 30–31, is based on the surviving photograph."

finally advises to steep "it" in a lapis-colored liquid, and to place it on the fire so that one may obtain the artificial version of the dušû stone. To date, this tablet is the only text that preserves a recipe for the dyeing of pebbles, yet it testifies to the practice of dipping stones in coloring baths at the end of the second millennium in the land of the Chaldeans, a practice that coincides with what we know about Ostanes' later teachings. After Ostanes allegedly handed it on to his Greek pupil, the same technique became standard in Greek "alchemy" to the point that it is regularly employed in the recipes collected in the alchemical papyri.[14]

Furthermore, in the anonymous recipe book cited above, Ostanes is the authority behind a dyeing bath of copper rust and the "bile of mongoose and vulture." *Mongoose* and *vulture* are most likely cryptonyms for other substances, and at this point Martelli and Rumor notice something intriguing about the possible source for these otherwise absurd choices for bile (bile being bile whatever animal is involved). Could the Akkadian (Babylonian) language hold a clue?

The Akkadian for "mongoose" is *šikkû,* homophone of *šikku* (*šīku*). That latter word denotes a kind of poor-quality copper, so the expression may encode an old ingredient term, afterward forgotten. As to "vulture," the Akkadian word for a bird of prey is *erû*. The usual English translation is "eagle," but "vulture" would often better fit the context. The word is exactly homophonous to the Akkadian word for copper: also *erû*. A knowledgeable practitioner would have recognized the pun, whereas a copyist without requisite knowledge would not have seen the puns, especially if the terms were crossing cultural borders. Furthermore, the Sumerogram (cuneiform word) "ti8.mušen," meaning bird of prey, or vulture, also appears as a reference to a copper alloy in a Middle Babylonian text for making artificial stones with colored glass![15]

That Ostanes is described as a "magus" could easily put him in Mesopotamia, as there had long been Zoroastrian wise men (*magoi*) there, and by the first century, the words "Chaldaean," "Babylonian," and "magus" were often loosely employed by Greek and Roman writers. Babylon was conquered by Persia in 539 BCE. That stone and metal dyeing techniques in Middle Babylonian and Neo-Assyrian tablets parallel third-century Greek alchemical papyri was first noted by anthropologist Adolf Leo Oppenheim in the late 1960s,[16] convincing him that Graeco-Egyptian technology for treating stones and metal existed in Mesopotamia in the thirteenth to seventh centuries BCE. Publishing Neo-Babylonian tablet BM (British Museum) 62788* from Sippar in 1979, Erle Leichty revealed eight Mesopotamian recipes for dyeing wool blue and purple.[17] Thus, we have the possibility of raw material for pseudo-Democritus's *Four Books,* as conveyed by his master, magus Ostanes. The idea that Ostanes brought skills to Egypt from that region cannot be discounted and, since it's asserted in the tradition itself, seems probable, though we may also see a blending of technologies as the Egyptians had been working in related arts and crafts for centuries. What is interesting perhaps is the move in first-century Egypt to a systematic gathering of the knowledge and, given the number of recipes, the amount of experimentation going on there. I suspect the Roman conquest of Egypt with Marc Antony's death in 30 BCE was a factor amid increasing trade and social and economic adjustments.

However, according to Martelli and Rumor, some systematizing of related arts and crafts may already be discerned in a Sumerian lexical list—whose forerunners began in the Old Babylonian period—compiled to preserve the Sumerian language from extinction. In a twenty-four-tablet series known as the Ur5-ra [Sumerogram] = *ḫubullu* [Akkadian for "interest-bearing debt"], the last third of the eleventh tablet holds some twenty-five lines of names deal-

---

*Martelli and Rumor say of this tablet: "The tablet, BM 62788, is dated to the sixth century BC and has recently been joined to another fragment, BM 82978. I. Finkel is going to publish a new edition of the entire tablet." Martelli and Rumor, "Near Eastern Origins," 50.

ing with hides, dyes, metals, raw material for "primary glass" (used to make artificial stones), cosmetic coloring substances, and other tincture-useful chemical and mineral substances. Farther on, there are about one hundred lines concerning copper-based metals, and further tablets listing iron, silver, gold, animals, meat cuts, stones, plants, fish, wool and clothing, towns, countries, mountains, provisions, and men.

What links the twenty-five names above is the idea of dyeing, and thus the list might be seen as a distant relative of the conception of alchemy in pseudo-Democritus and the Stockholm and Leiden Papyri. As Martelli and Rumor suggest: "It is thus plausible that these lists might reflect an early association, or classification, of the same tinctorial arts that later form a part of the technical core of the most ancient Greek alchemical works (pseudo-Democritus, Ostanes, Papyri [sic]), on the basis of which Zosimos interpreted the Book of Enoch and described the revelation of the Book of Chēmeu."[18]

Akkadian Origin of Chēmeu?

Martelli and Rumor save perhaps their best shot for the end of their paper on possible Near Eastern antecedents to Graeco-Egyptian alchemy.

When Zosimos explained to Theosebeia that their art derived from rebel angels imparting knowledge gathered into a "book of Chēmeu" (apparently taking "Chēmeu" as the name of the art's patriarch, supposing it the origin of the Greek chēmeia), he may have been demonstrating his ignorance of history. A better idea might be Martelli's where he suggests a possible link between the Greek word and the Akkadian verb kamû/kawû in its second meaning, "to bake, to roast," noting how the same root, "KM/W(*Y?)," is present in the Aramaic verb "to burn"—to me at least, an explanation both lucid and plausible, though it can also work in Egypt's favor. The Egyptian for "black" is km, pronounced "kam" or "kem." Other than the black of

Egyptian fertile soil, *black* also suggests, as we noted earlier, something exposed to intense sun or flame, burnt or carbonized, which process of blackening is perhaps the most obvious physical transformation of all, and is of course implicit to the later tradition that the process for producing the alchemist's stone begins with a so-called *nigredo*. If we wish to relate the root *km* to a historical or legendary name, we don't need to look as far as Zosimos's rather isolate "Chēmeu" (which "name" may be a copyist's error anyhow). Noah's second son, Ham or Cham (in English), is written חם (hm) in Hebrew. The Hebrew also means "heat" or "to be hot." The Hebrew Bible uses the word to denote people in Egypt (Psalm 78:51), and Egypt itself (Psalm 105:23). We thus suggest once more that the Greek chēmeia, and the proper meaning of the art would be *the art of heat,* involving heating, burning, roasting, blackening: a decidedly "black art," were it not for the fact that out of the black, or apparent death of substance in the flame, the successful practitioner brought forth color, value, and thus, an appearance of life, rising in evaporate vapor toward a startling transformation: arguably a visual analogue for transmigration of soul (cf: the ascension of Jesus in Acts 1:9 when "a cloud received him out of their sight"—the apparently corporeal became incorporeal.)

Heat and Glass

An interesting variant on the etymology of *chēmeia* occurs in Marco Beretta's fascinating book *The Alchemy of Glass* (2009) in which Beretta notes the Egyptian for "obsidian" (natural black glass) is *aner chem* (black stone), with *chem* meaning "black," of course.[19] This leads him to consider whether this material, and glassmaking in general, should be recognized as significant to our understanding of the art, for as he maintains, gold was not the most valuable commodity known to late antiquity. Precious gems and lapis lazuli were minerals cherished by some even more, and one of the best ways of imitating the real thing was with glass. Egyptians made imitation lapis lazuli from powdered glass, with copper oxide or cobalt.* The Egyptian for *lapis lazuli* meant "to be blue, to shine like heaven." Chrysopoeia may have blinkered us as much as the Byzantines to the original scope of the art.

Long before the art of glassblowing appeared in the first century BCE, Egyptian priests found divine presence and religious meaning in minerals. During the 18th Dynasty (ca. 1500–1292 BCE), Egypt produced and traded both real and artificial lapis lazuli. A thousand years later, Egyptian priests would direct Greek scientific interest to glass's special properties. Beretta believes the ability to imitate lapis (stone) lazuli led to reflection on the nature of matter and the question as to whether a counterfeit was also a replica. He also notes that glassmaking, like alchemy, represented a cross-cultural fusion with an intimate link to what was considered sacred. Minerals corresponded to the spirits of the gods on earth, and the knowledge of how to manipulate minerals was likewise of divine origin, requiring binding rites and authority.

Glassmaking appears to have originated in Mesopotamia around 2500 BCE. Interestingly, Leo Oppenheim described a surviving Mesopotamian recipe to make "zukû-glass which has the look of gold."[20] Indeed, the analogy with minerals was close: the Akkadian for "glass" was *ba῾slu abnu* (molten stone). Fifth-century BCE Greek historian Herodotus calls glass *líthos chytē*, which means the same thing, and Beretta sees significance in the shared idea of melting and fusing between glass (consisting of sand, limestone,† and sodium carbonate) and minerals, suggesting that glass may have been seen as a natural stone subject to heat treatment.[21]

---

*According to A. Lucas and J. R. Harris's *Ancient Egyptian Materials* (London: Edward Arnold, 1962 [p.189]), cobalt compounds are alien to Egypt, except as traces in other minerals, suggesting that Egyptian glassmakers were familiar with glassmakers elsewhere.
†Ancient glassmakers did not see the value of lime, being content with silica and alkali, with which lime came inadvertently.[22]

Having found its way to Egypt circa 1400 BCE, Egyptian ingenuity extended glass technology's range, with glass and glazed pottery treated rather like contrived stones, especially since mineral stones were also glazed. Beautiful results were obtained by Egyptian glassmakers by adding iron and manganese oxides, producing superb copies of ruby, topaz, emerald, and crystal, which precious stones were classified, according to Beretta, with gold, electrum, and silver, not only on account of value but also by the kinship of technology employed to imitate them—their being subject to melting enabling fusion.[23] Beretta asserts that the value of imitation lapis lazuli would have suffered were its nature perceived to be different from what it replicated. It's possible, then, that *some idea* of transmutation was implicit to the art. To transform sand into precious stone is analogous to the common idea of transmuting lead into gold. Besides, you received more money (silver or gold) for glass than for sand! The artist had performed a godlike function. Beretta insists boldly that "color, destined to play a central role in Alexandrian alchemy, was of crucial importance for Egyptian craftsmen in order to recognise a body's chemical essence. The ability to change this color, not only on a body's surface but in its entirety, was evidence that matter could be transformed and transmuted."[24] I am not sure we need to load the art as practiced in ancient Egypt with an idea of transmutation in an attempt to involve it with later definitions of alchemy, which are themselves under question. It is enough to say that Greeks, like Egyptians, associated metals with extracted minerals on the basis of meltability and solubility, including glass.

The range of colors open to glassmakers positively exploded with the timely arrival of glassblowing in the first century BCE, the first known evidence of which comes from Jerusalem, interestingly enough. The glassblowers' sand of choice was collected on the Syro-Palestinian coast, near Tyre and Sidon. The introduction of air from the mouth via a pipe to melted glass created a marvel of pliability, and the range of possible imitations massively increased with parallel development of furnaces that could raise temperatures above 1000°, producing glass liquid.

Around the time glassblowing began to revolutionize manufacturing in the civilized world, Roman historian Diodorus Siculus, who died in the same year as Marc Antony, at the dawn of the Augustan age, left an apposite account of Arabian mineral resources in his *Bibliotheca historica* (2.52) in which he directly relates production processes of minerals in nature to the production of "false gold" by human beings.

> In these countries are generated not only animals which differ from one another in form because of the helpful influence and strength of the sun, but also outcroppings of every kind of precious stone which are unusual in colour and resplendent in brilliancy. For the rock-crystals, so we are informed, are composed of pure water which has been hardened, not by the action of cold, but by the influence of a divine fire, and for this reason they are never subject to corruption and take on many hues when they are breathed upon. For instance smaragdi and beryllia, as they are called, which are found in the shafts of the copper mines, receive their colour by having been dipped and bound together in a bath of sulphur, and the chrysoliths, they say, which are produced by a smoky exhalation due to the heat of the sun, thereby get the colour they have. For this reason what is called "false gold," we are told, is fabricated by mortal fire, made by man, by dipping the rock crystals into it. And as for the natural qualities of the dark-red stones, it is the influence of the light, as it is compressed to a greater or less degree in them when they are hardening, which, they say, accounts for their differences.[25]

Given Marco Beretta's compelling case that development of glass technology is intrinsically related to aspects of first-century CE alchemy, especially in the production of precious stones and development of effective furnaces, it is surprising that glass or glass-blowing does not appear in pseudo-Democritus's *Four Books,* especially in those parts dealing with stones (unless we take it that some of the "stones" or "crystal" to be dyed were products of glass-craft, which is possible). It is even more remarkable when we consider that the momentous, and highly profitable revolution involved in glassblowing was well into its stride when the *Four Books* are supposed to have been composed (late first century CE), which rather makes one wonder whether glassblowing had a different organizational, or possibly exclusive, guild structure to that of the dyers, say, of Panopolis, and that the mysteries of one craft were professionally closed to the other, despite technical crossovers. It is also possible that a tradition seen at the time as stemming from the "authority" of Ostanes the Mede had *already* conditioned a classification and limits of the sacred art to metals, stones, and purple dye.

Exploring what made the Roman period so critical to the development of alchemy, Zosimos specialist Shannon L. Grimes concluded that what was new was not that Egyptian practitioners were turning to Greek philosophy—familiar territory for centuries—but rather that it was "the rise of trade guilds in this era, which disrupted traditional temple economies and created new networks for the exchange of materials, ideas, and techniques."[26] While maintaining that the "sacred art" originated exclusively, even secretly, under the wing of priests with metallurgical skills engaged in making temple paraphernalia, Grimes regards the rise of trade guilds in the Roman period as the reason "craft secrets began to circulate more freely." These economic shifts, she believes, provide "the best explanation for the emergence of alchemical texts in Roman Egypt."[27] This explanation might also account for why glass-craft appears absent from those texts; that is to say, if glass-craft had not been an art regarded as confined to the temple priesthood from which the guilds may have taken their lead. Such would have been predictable results of the collapse of the Ptolemaic dynasty with Cleopatra VII's suicide in 31 BCE and the transfer of power and authority that inevitably followed Octavian's absorption of Egypt into the Roman Empire and the imposition by him of Roman governor Gaius Cornelius Gallus; that is to say, the once protected priesthood lost power to organize Egyptian society, and with the long advance of Christianity, lost respect, and doubtless mystique as well.

THREE

The Pioneers of Graeco-Egyptian-Jewish Alchemy

THERE ARE FEW INDICATIONS in the works of Zosimos of Panopolis to support Shannon L. Grimes's thesis that early development of the "holy art" was a privilege of the Egyptian temple priesthood. Zosimos, in his *On the Apparatus and the Furnaces* (Berthelot and Ruelle, *Collection des Anciens Alchimistes Grecs,* vol 2, 3.47, 216), mentions a visit to an "ancient sanctuary" (temple structure) in Memphis, where he looked in detail at a furnace, only to conclude: "I acknowledged that it had not been perfected by people introduced to sacred things. Good health." We may also recall from chapter 2 how a Syriac source preserved in Cambridge has one Pebichius, perhaps a priest, writing to Persian magus Osron to help him decipher books by Ostanes found hidden in Egypt (most likely in a temple). "Hidden" could, of course, be a euphemism for unwanted, neglected, or forgotten. Zosimos counted Pebichius among the most ancient practitioners, and Pebichius (sometimes "Epebichius"[1]) has been tentatively dated to the first century CE. Zosimos often references Pebichius's advice, so he must have had access to writings attributed to him.

One text attributed to Zosimos deals with the question of whether the "work" should be carried out at a particular or propitious time. The work appears connected with making divine water or sulfur water. Pebichius is cited along with Mary (the Prophetess), Democritus, and Hermes.

Pebichius also said on this question: "Share the preparation in two parts, and put half in a terra-cotta vase and the other half on copper"; wanting to make this sound in one (word): cooking, by (the vase) of terra-cotta, and iosis, by copper. Now he spoke previously of bleaching, saying that copper is burned in laurel wood; that is, native sulfur (with copper) in the presence of laurel leaves. You can thus know the merit of the ancients, how clearly they explained all things. By appearing to hide all things, they said clearly: "First, upon light flames, so that the sulfur water may be absorbed at the same time."[2]

The author concludes that summer is the most opportune time because of the practical benefit of light, adding that dyeing purple also requires a special period for its dissolutions and cooling. In another treatise, *On that which the Art has spoken concerning all the bodies in treating of a unique dye,* Pebichius, in company with "Chymes" (in a quote much akin to one attributed to Cleopatra's axioms on chrysopoeia), Mary, Africanus, and Agathodaimon contribute to the question on whether a single dye can be applied to all materials with the words "By means of the four bodies." The four elements are here intended with practical reference to solids, liquids, and spirit (vapor), as being constituents of copper, as of man. "Chymes declared it with truth, quotes the author, 'One is the Whole, and it is through him that the Whole has come into being. One is the All, and if the All did not contain everything, the All would not have been born,' adding: 'You must therefore plan the Whole, in order to make the Whole.'"[3]

Writing *On the body of Magnesia and its treatment,* Pebichius is quoted by Zosimos to praise the action of "divine" or "sulfur water" in breaking down the "bodies" (metals) until they become "intangible": "But what other substance works well without the help of fire, if not divine water? It is from her that Pebichius (says) that she is more powerful than any fire. In the Chapter of the Sulfurous it is said that it acts without the help of fire."[4] Perhaps this chapter was accorded to Pebichius, or maybe it was Mary, for her ideas dominate the section.

The paragraph before Pebichius's words is concerned with "transmutation." According to Berthelot: "In the Greek text the author opposes the words *strophē* and *ekstrophē,* and the corresponding verbs. These words still seem to mean converting the inner nature of a metal into gold or silver, by transmuting or extracting the former nature, which was that of copper, lead, tin or iron." "Strophē" means a turn. Combined with "ekstrophē" it suggests a "turning inside out," possibly of something otherwise hidden within. While translated as "transmutation," this is uncertain if taken to indicate—as Berthelot and Ruelle too enthusiastically did—a complete transition of one definite substance to another. Attributed to Zosimos, the passage reads:

> Thus, to convert and transmute in these authors means to give a body to the incorporeals; that is to say, to the fleeting matter. By their transformations one obtains the molybdochalkos [alloy of copper and lead], the black lead, which must be treated with mercury, and become the body of magnesia. They do not mean, as some do, that the mutation applies to converting and transmuting mercury. But when the fleeting [or disappearing] materials have taken on a body, the conversion takes place for all the bodies, by their dye in white or yellow. Indeed this conversion is called transmutation, after the incorporeals have taken a body, by the effect of art. In the retrograde conversion accomplished by fire—that is to say, in bleaching or yellowing—the strongly diluted materials associated with fire are again rendered fleeting and become incorporeal. At this moment they are reduced to the last degree of division. Sublimated steam, the first of the incorporeal materials, thus leads to supreme art.[5]

Cleopatra

Another early practitioner with a literary, albeit slight, link to Egyptian priesthood, and one of several notable women at the art's cutting edge, was "Cleopatra the wise [*sophē*]"—not in all respects to be confused with

Elizabeth Taylor. Alchemical tradition credits Cleopatra with knowledge of the philosopher's stone, the secret of transmutation—though as we've just observed, "transmutation," where it is discernible in the older texts, seems to refer to the breaking down of metals (bodies) into liquid (deemed mercurial because subject to change), then into an incorporeal state (evaporation) associated with vapor, before becoming visible again as something else after distillation and (presumably) condensing on an appropriate surface (alembic), where a change of color was deemed the principle sign of transmutation.

Cleopatra's name is most prominent in an anonymous first- or second-century CE text known as the "Dialogue of Cleopatra and the Philosophers."[6] Her reputed teacher there, Komarios, is described as "high priest," and the dialogue occurs in the *Book of Komarios*. Its author includes Ostanes in the dialogue, and this may dispose us to consider the possibility that the art was initially developed either in, or in association with, Egyptian temple and priesthood structure. The content of Cleopatra's dialogue is expressed as sometimes delightful allegory, with pseudo-Democritan or Ostanist motifs, employing symbolism to cover, lightly, chemical processes. We are enjoined, for example, to descend to the Egyptian sea, and there amid the sand, to extract natron: the *natron* (sodium carbonate decahydrate) being *the point*. It was vital to effective mordanting of textiles.

Ostanes rather points to the essence of the matter when he says to Cleopatra: "In thee is concealed a strange and terrible mystery. Enlighten us, casting your light upon the elements." Cleopatra responds with attractive and suggestive visual analogues much repeated and embellished beyond bounds in much later alchemical tradition, analogues such as those between plants and distillation; the union of bride and bridegroom as nature rejoices in nature; the nourishing of ingredients in the fire, like the nourishing of the mother's womb for the child to be (the work) when the time comes; the apparent consigning to the tomb (Hades) of ingredients that after a time, mount from the flames of Hades like the child from its mother. Such rich death-resurrection symbolism envisioned in what would become known as "Cleopatra's glass" (or vase) would fascinate Christian alchemists, seeing in it an eternal recounting of the mystery of the faith, and for some mystics, the key to the spiritual working of the universe.

Following is a taste of the work, and if you read carefully these words attributed to Cleopatra,* you should see a person involved in preparing and cooking materials for effective dyeing.

> Now listen and understand and judge correctly what I say. Take from the four elements the highest arsenic and the lowest arsenic and the white and the red, equal in weight, male and female, so that they are joined to each other. Just as the bird hatches and brings to perfection its eggs in warmth, so you, too, must hatch and polish [or bring to perfection?] your work by taking it out and watering it in the divine waters and [warming it] in the sun and in burned places, and you must roast it in a gentle flame with the virgin milk and hold it [away] from the smoke. And enclose it in Hades and move it in safety until its structure becomes more solid and does not run away from the fire. Then you take it out of it, and when the soul and spirit have joined each other and become one, then you must throw it on solid silver, and you will have gold [of a quality] that the storehouses of the kings do not have.[7]

---

*Curiously, this particular passage was omitted by Berthelot from *Collection des Anciens Alchimistes Grecs* (CAAG), vol. 3, 4.20, page 283, with a note that it could be found in the section on Zosimos. It appears there as an alleged quotation from "Stephanus" in the context of a treatise attributed to Zosimos on "Lime" (CAAG, vol. 2, 3.2, 122–23). Berthelot's note on page 123 informs us that the paragraph was missing from the *Codex Marcianus* and is taken from Greek alchemical collection *Paris gr.* 2327 (Codex "A"), copied in 1478 by one Theodore Pelekanos. Berthelot adds that he's conserved it in his Zosimos translation to show how fragments of Zosimos have suffered augmentation by alien pieces. Berthelot then adds that the name of alchemical writer and philosopher Stephanus of Alexandria (ca. 580–640), applied to the author of a piece *in fact taken from a treatise of Komarios,* also "merits attention because it proves that the confusion highlighted in [Berthelot's] *Introduction* [p. 182], between the works of these two authors is very ancient." Berthelot rather adds to this confusion!

The mystery perhaps is that you may also feel you have seen a mystical truth in what might otherwise have appeared merely technical. The secret belongs to *who can see it.* "Go up," enjoins Cleopatra, "to the highest peak, to the bushy mountain, in the middle of the trees, and see: (there is) a stone at the top; take the arsenic (extracted) from this stone and use it to whiten divinely." "Behold, in the midst of the mountain, below the arsenic, is his wife"—that is, when arsenic is combined in the flames with natron and other materials, "the male and the female have become one." Where Jung projected his conception of *mysterium coniunctionis,* or divine copulation, we can now see that the "middle of the mountain" is the pile of ingredients, and the arsenic has participated in a chemical union. And, of course, one can see that the thinking alchemist envisioned in all this a microcosm of the *whole system of life:* itself a perfect analogue of spiritual growth and change. As Hermes intoned: "As above, so below."

"Here," Cleopatra declares,

> is the mystery of the philosophers, that which our fathers swore to you not to reveal or divulge; this is the mystery concerning the divine species and the divine action. Indeed, it is divine that, by the union of divinity, makes the substances divine [probable pun for sulfur]; by which the spirit takes a body, mortal beings acquire one another, and, receiving the spirit that comes out of the substances, are dominated and dominate each other [the Ostanes motif]. The dark spirit, filled with vanity and softness, when it dominates the bodies, prevents them from being bleached and receiving the beauty and color that the creator makes them put on. In the same way the body, the mind and the soul are weakened, because of the shadow on them.

As the speech goes on, we might easily forget this is all a peroration on a chemical operation to produce an effective dye.

But when the dark and fetid spirit is rejected, to the point of leaving no smell or dark color, then the body becomes luminous and the soul rejoices, as well as the spirit. When the shadow has escaped from the body, the soul calls the body now luminous, and said to him: Awaken from the depths of Hades and rise from the tomb; wake up from the darkness. Indeed, you have assumed the spiritual and divine character; the voice of the resurrection has spoken; the preparation of life has entered into you. For the spirit [above this word is the sign for cinnabar] rejoices in its turn in the body [in *Codex Marcianus* (a.k.a. "M") above this word is an abbreviation for lead], as well as the soul in the body where it resides. He runs with a joyful rush to embrace him; he embraces him and the shadow no longer dominates him, since he has reached the light [above the word "light" is the sign for native sulfur]; the body does not bear to be separated from the spirit forever, and he rejoices in the dwelling [in "M" above this word is the sign for gold] of the soul, because after the body has been hidden in the shadow he found it filled with light [the sign for native sulfur above the word]. And the soul has been united to her, since he became divine in relation to her, and dwells in her. For he has put on the light of divinity (and they have been united), and the shadow has escaped from him, and all have been united in tenderness [In Codex "A" in the margin, mercury is expressed by its sign, surmounted by a Greek "m" (*mu*), possibly referring to an amalgam of lead]: the body [above is the sign for gold], the soul [above is the sign of mercury] and the spirit [above is the cinnabar sign]. They have become one; it is in this (unity) that the mystery has been hidden. By the fact of their reunion the mystery has been fulfilled. The house was sealed, and (then) stood a statue full of light and divinity. For the fire [above is the native sulfur sign] has united and transmuted them, and they came out of his womb [in "M" the sign for ios of copper is above the word "womb"].[8]

Indeed, without the alchemical signs added to the manuscript, one might easily take it as a quote from a Gnostic gospel. Such interpenetration of idea we shall investigate in chapter 12. A note by Berthelot on Cleopatra's speech also recognized theological discourse redolent of "the old gnostics" (second century CE) yet inherent in the manipulation of materials: "These vague and symbolic phrases had a meaning for the adepts, which is revealed to us by the signs placed above the words in M. Their date is uncertain; but they seem to go back, at least in origin, to the old gnostics, commented later by Stephanus and by the contemporary Byzantines of Heraclius [emperor, ca. 610–641]. In any case, they are the starting point of the mystical galimatias [confused and meaningless talk] of the Arab and Latin alchemists."[9]

One can, I think, detect a theosophy, or unified process-structure of nature and spirit, here stemming from a syncretic "all is one" principle at the core of Indian advaitism and pre-Socratic Greek philosophy, shaded by an arguably Zoroastrian dualism of dark and light natures in tension. As such assumptions are presented as essentially privileged knowledge for initiates, we touch on the conception of a gnosis, a redemptive knowledge, permeating the account. That the substances must give birth to something, to release something to a higher plane has an *imperative* sense about it intriguingly reminiscent of the roughly contemporary apocryphal text, the Gospel of Thomas (saying no. 70): "If you bring forth what is within you, what you bring forth will save you. If you do not bring forth what is within you, what you do not bring forth will destroy you." And more startlingly perhaps, these lines attributed to the savior at the conclusion of the Gnostic Apocryphon (secret book) of John, also from the Nag Hammadi library (discovered some 37 miles south of Panopolis in the Thebaid in 1945: "I entered into the midst of darkness and the inside of Hades, since I was seeking (to accomplish) my task. And the foundations of chaos shook, that they might fall down upon those who are in chaos and might destroy them. And again I ran up to my root of light, lest they be destroyed before the time." The analogy is fairly plain.

Cleopatra is also credited in most Greek alchemical collections with a *Treatise on Weights and Measures,* and Berthelot extracted from it a list of the old Egyptian months with Latin and Coptic equivalents. This seems a case of simply using "Cleopatra" as a name of authority, which might also be said of "her" role in the *Book of Komarios.*[10]

Another text copied for the *Codex Marcianus* is a treatise on making asem, and we find reference to what has been considered Cleopatra's invention of an alchemical vase or crucible: "After obtaining the asem, if you want to purify it, throw into the crucible of Cleopatra's glass and you will have pure asem."[11] Inventiveness distinguishes the best known female alchemists. Mary is credited with inventing the air-tight (hermetically sealed) vessel for vapor collection (*kērotakis),* the *tribikos* (an alembic with three arms, for collecting distilled material), and what we know today as the "bain-marie" (after Mary the alchemist)—all this being just one reason why I want to qualify the idea of a male temple priesthood context for alchemists in the early Christian era. The setting seems to me much more the world of elite product industry, especially textiles and decorative or private sacred wares. Such cutting-edge processes were expensive, and one can perhaps speculate on a picture of temple priests *outsourcing* requirements or even moonlighting in lay guild associations.

Cleopatra's name also appears in an unusual treatise entitled *The Eight Tombs: On the divine and sacred art of the philosophers.*

As for us, having written in riddles, we leave you, who have this book in hand, to work diligently and search for the subject of the mystery. Indeed the Philosopher [pseudo-Democritus] says that men have written, but daimons are jealous of it. It is doubtless in the kingdom of heavens that there are those who have been judged worthy (to understand). As for you, conforming yourself to Cleopatra's short explanation, you will bring to light the dark object of discovery and you will render service: "Rise, said this one, to the highest point of the house."* And: which lies between the two luminaries, I mean the sun and the moon, there exists the egg with the appearance of alabastron. It is certainly not a bird's egg; but its shape resembles that of the egg.[12]

While Berthelot relates this treatise to a "commentary on Zosimos's *Concerning the action* and the sayings of Hermes and some philosophers" attributed to Olympiodorus—chiefly because of that treatise's reference to the "tomb of Osiris" (where Osiris is principle of "all liquidity" operating the "fixation in the spheres of the fire"[13])—Osiris isn't mentioned in the "Eight Tombs" treatise. The third tomb (of eight) is "the second calcination," or purification by intense heating of solids to remove volatile materials, oxidizing mass, or bringing to powder (from the Latin *calcinare,* "to burn lime"). That the Olympiodorus commentary was written by Olympiodorus the Younger (ca. 495–570 CE)—one of the last Alexandrian pagan Neoplatonist teachers—is extremely doubtful. As to the reference to Cleopatra in *The Eight Tombs,* I should note that "her" instruction in the *Book of Komarios* to mount the bushy mountain with "the stone" atop it has apparently here been changed from a mountain ascent to rising up a house. This, coupled with the reference to the "kingdom of the heavens," suggests the passage may allude to John 14:2 where Jesus says that in his Father's house are many houses (or mansions). Such might suggest a sublimated Christian gloss on an earlier text, but whether orthodox, heretical, or syncretic we'll probably never know. Berthelot compared the eight tombs with Gnostic systems of syzygies constituting an Ogdoad of divine emanations, itself derived from the eight primordial gods whom ancient Egyptians worshipped at Hermopolis.

---

*This is a reference to Cleopatra in the *Book of Komarios,* where she enjoins the philosophers to rise to the highest point of the bushy mountain to find a stone; see pages 66–67 and 271. I would add that this is the winged object formed by the four elements—Berthelot thinks this an allusion to the winged uraeus as well as to the egg of the world, created by Ptah, whence the sun and the moon are derived.

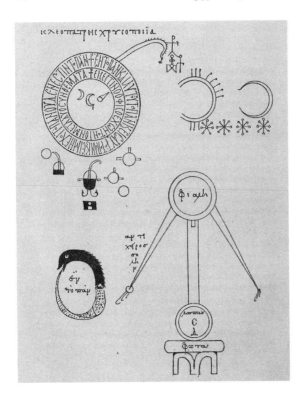

Fig. 3.1. The *Chrysopoea of Cleopatra*, with practical and mystical or magical elements (*Codex Marcianus*, fol. 188v; eleventh century, Bibliotheca Marciana, Venice)

Like so much of the Graeco-Egyptian alchemical fragments, the work evinces a tolerant syncretism. Whether this represents the position of any authentic "Cleopatra" is impossible to say.

The same question would go over a drawing of the *Chrysopoeia of Cleopatra* (fig. 3.1 on pg. 72) in the *Codex Marcianus*. It shows some practical elements, and those Berthelot calls "mystical and magical."[14] We see (top left) two concentric circles (possibly an alembic lid seen from above), the outer with "One is the all and by him the all and toward him the all; and if the all does not contain the all, the all is nothing" inscribed around it, with signs for gold, silver, and mercury within. Around the center is inscribed "The serpent is one, he who has the venom, after the two emblems." A serpent extends out of the circles, the head touched by a magical sigil, below which is an incomplete circle linked to a lunar or silver sign by four eight-rayed stars. Five aspects

Fig. 3.2. The same type of apparatus as figure 3.1, with characteristic variants. (*Codex Parisinus Graecus 2325, thirteenth century*)

Fig. 3.3 (below). Concentric circle, alembic and vase and attachment, derived from figure 3.1, much modified, relating to posterior practice (*Codex Parisinus Graecus 2327, fol. 220, 1478*)

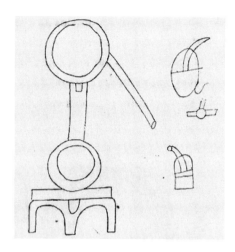

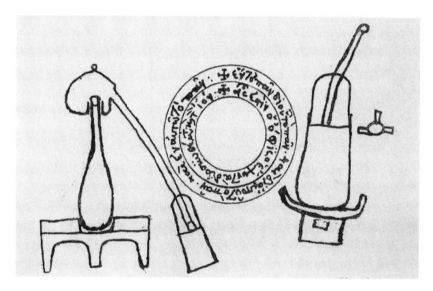

of a laboratory operation are depicted beneath the concentric circles, the center one according to Berthelot concerned with fixing metals, the apparatus poised on a bain-marie with two splayed legs over a furnace. A curved tube for escaping vapor comes from the bain-marie. Below these diagrams is a famous image of the ouroboros, with a black head section and a tail divided into three and apparently spotted with stars (the *heimarmēnē*, or "night-cloak" of the universe), within which are the Greek words "Hen to pan." To its right is a laboratory furnace (with the word *phōtas,* "fires") on which sits a flask (*lōpas*) connected by a perpendicular tube to a *phialē* (kind of cup) with two conical tubes suspended down from it that appear to emit vapor.

The principle of unity (One is All), with the four classical elements relating to each one of the others dominantly and submissively, seems emblematic of the Cleopatra tradition.

Jewish Chemistry

Judging by the works of Zosimos and other sources, Jewish metalworkers held a highly respectable position of esteem alongside Egyptians in Egypt. This should not surprise us. By Zosimos's time, the Jewish community had been influential in Alexandria for centuries, and everyone is familiar with the story of Jesus being taken by his father to Egypt to avoid Herod the Great's political wrath; Jesus's family felt assured of a welcome and, presumably, a livelihood. Jewish philosopher Philo graced Alexandria before Jesus's birth and died there some thirteen years after the crucifixion (which I date to 37 CE according to unbiased analysis of evidence; see *The Mysteries of John the Baptist* by this author).

Jews had to live, and metalwork and related trades were acceptable, forward-looking, and presumably lucrative, though we may seriously doubt whether Jews would have contributed to servicing what their religion dismissed as idolatrous temples. This constitutes another reason for doubting the placing of early alchemy too intimately within priestly organizations. The setting, as I assess the fragmentary evidence, is almost certainly *commerce* and industry and, hypothetically, the protection of commerce and its trade secrets by forms of initiation, reserve, exclusivity, code, and, quite likely, appropriate ritual. Indeed, such a notion of independent settings would complement a possible *sitz im leben* of the Hermetic philosophical corpus exceptionally well—and yes, it may not be altogether illegitimate to see some analogy here in behavioral terms, with what little we know of Freemasonry *before* the development of London's Grand Lodge after 1716, which overtook special assemblies of freestone masons and master masons intimately joined to the commercial arts of architecture, sculpture, and construction (and who, incidentally, claimed Hermes as patron).

The Byzantine Greek alchemy corpus includes two treatises under this title: *True Book of Sophē the Egyptian*. The first is subtitled *and of the divine lord of the Hebrews (and) of the powers Sabaoth* (hosts), *Mystical Book of Zosimos the Theban;* the second, *and of the divine master of the Hebrews (and) of the powers Sabaoth*. Berthelot footnoted that *Sophē* was a form of the Greek name for Khufu, "Cheops" (an Egyptian pharaoh), whom Herodotus identified as the builder of the Great Pyramid. However, *Sophē* was also given as a distinction to alchemist Cleopatra: *the Wise* (or Sage), so the treatise is perhaps linked to her. After a substantial quotation from a work of Mary, the first treatise's second section begins:

> It is cooked; for even if it does not contain mercury, it must be cooked; whereas before the action of the fire, there is no dye. It must be made to undergo the purifying action by the (suitable) materials to ascertain that it is pure. Try, or melt. If you know the two steps, those of the Jews and of . . . , don't be afraid of trying all the things in detail that I've exposed to you.[15]

A distinct method of purification is attributed to "the Jews," carrying a suggestion of privileged knowledge communicated thanks, it seems, to Mary. If followed correctly, the treatise promises practitioners will overcome poverty, for "thousands of books teach how copper is bleached and yellowed properly. It is only fit to be allied by diplosis if it is changed to ios. It can be treated methodically by a thousand (means); but it is only made clean to the alloy by one way, becoming our true copper; that is the whole formula."

The second treatise begins with a positively solar panegyric on Jewish creative genius.

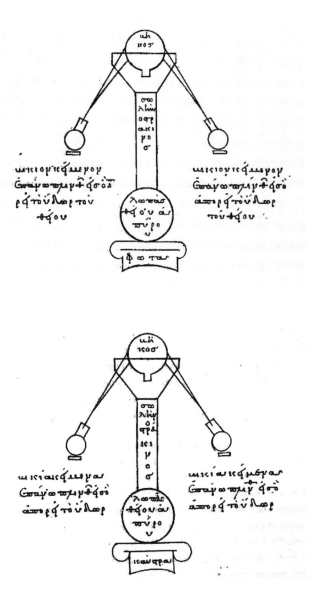

Fig. 3.4. Alembic with two recipients (dibicos), with variants to figures 3.2 and 3.3, from *Codex Marcianus*, folio 193v. The ascending tube has the Greek inscription *solēn ostrakinos* (clay tube); the marquee or chapiter is called "bēkos" (*bikos* = amphora). The Greek by the two globular flasks tells us the "balloons" are placed above the rectangular tablet, into which flows the water of sulfur. The figure is repeated in *Codex Marcianus* but with slightly different wording.

There are two sciences and two wisdoms: those of the Egyptians and those of the Hebrews, which is made more solid by divine justice [an allusion perhaps to balanced scales of justice held by the Egyptian goddess Ma'at or by Isis]. The knowledge and wisdom of the best dominates both; they came from the ages of old. Their generation is destitute of a king, autonomous, immaterial; it seeks nothing of material bodies or corruptibles; it operates without submitting to (foreign) action, supported now by prayer and (divine) grace. The symbol of chymia is drawn from creation (in the eyes of its adepts), who save and purify the divine soul chained in the elements, and above all which separate the divine spirit confounded with flesh. As there exists a sun, flower of fire, a heavenly sun, right eye of the world; so also copper, if it becomes a flower (that is, if it takes the color of gold) by purification, then becomes a terrestrial sun, which is king over the earth, as the sun is king in the sky.[16]

This rather gnostic speech, intended for an ideal, transcendent race of wisdom's offspring, is essentially one in praise of divine wisdom (*Sophē*), which rules over and above both peoples. Jews and Egyptians who so choose may identify themselves with this race that has no kingdom on earth, is discriminating of body and soul, and is essentially a unity. The Septuagint had long before identified the Jewish *ḥokhmah* (or "hokma" = wisdom) with the Graeco-Egyptian Sophia. In Sophia (Lady Wisdom in Ecclesiasticus 1:4–10) was a divine, feminine principle that offered to Jews and Egyptian sages a common door of understanding. This may also explain the title, with just a hint that *Sophē* is still somehow Egyptian, though revered in the wisdom of the Jews, with such wisdom then to be valued highly. This delicacy, or syncretic cultural tact, may reflect eirenic responses to longstanding disputes in Alexandria between Jewish and Egyptian scholars as to the primacy of their respective traditions.

Shannon L. Grimes has observed how scholars have wondered whether Zosimos, in favoring Mary and Jewish methodology so frequently, considered Jewish expertise to lie especially in distillation (perhaps

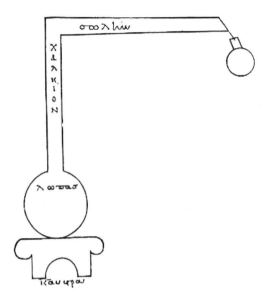

Fig. 3.5. Distilling apparatus, without dome or superior condenser, with one recipient (also in Ms. 2325), a copper neck (*chalkion*), and a single tube (*solēn*) (*Codex Marcianus*, fol. 194v)

techniques related to superior blown-glass equipment, see page 84), while a "Democritan" school was more advanced in fusion and cementation, with Zosimos favoring the former, and as Ms. Grimes puts it—when reflecting on Robert Multhauf's suggestion that Zosimos in fact intended to *synthesize* the two schools[17]—"tending to convert (Bolos) Democritus's cementation processes into distillatory processes, using apparatus associated with Maria, and although Democritus mentioned distillation briefly in *Physica kai mystika,* with a claim to have written on it more extensively elsewhere, we not only lack any such work but find that where Zosimos refers to (Bolos) Democritus in connection with distillation he usually does so in an attempt to show him to be in agreement with Maria."[18]

A vital Jewish place in early alchemy is testified elsewhere in the Byzantine corpus. One of divers lost treatises attributed to Zosimos is headed *Chapters of Zosimos to Theodore.* Bearing no indication who Theodore was, it begins with a statement that it concerns the "summer stone"; "that is to say, composed of the All, as a summery stone, and by that of great utility. In effect, in treatments it appears in divers colors, the one in a kerotakis treatment, the other in a fusion operation to the state of oilseed liquid: to know a yellow color and a black color."[19] Berthelot cites Claudius Salmasius's (Claude Saumaise's) very rare *Plinian Exercises, the Polyhistory of Caius Julius Solini* (Venice: Johan van de Water, 1629, vol. 2), a massive tome about the known world, which apparently assimilates the summer stone "to pyrite and chrysolith (magnesium iron silicate), porphyry and androdamas [silver marcasite; variety of hematite or bloodstone; according to Pliny (*Natural History* 38) it is diamond-hard, attracts silver, copper, and iron and produces a red liquid: a liver disease remedy]."*

The sixth section refers to knowledge found in the "Jewish scriptures" concerning an "inexhaustible mass":

It has not been called only by a masculine, feminine, and neutral name; but it has also been given a diminutive form, such as the small copper water; others, say the water of the small mass: now the mass is copper. This is why in the Jewish scriptures and in every scripture there is talk of an inexhaustible mass† that Moses obtained according to the precept of the Lord. Now this word, corrupted by time, has become a small mass. Others draw it from the phanos, which are used to draw water and which carry nipples. [The author plays on the word μαζυγιον, which he draws sometimes from μαζα, "mass"; sometimes from μαζος, "nipple."][20]

Berthelot further notes that the chemistry of "Moses" also refers to *maza* (mass), a reference to which may be found in the treatise *Chymia of Moses,* subtitled "Good Manufacturing and Creator success; Work success and Long Life."[21] Section 17 is a distillation recipe for the "manufacture of water extracted by distillation."

---

*Berthelot cites in a footnote: "*Salmasii Plinianae exercitationes,* 776, *b, D.* Le *Lexique* (pp. 6, 7, 13, 16)." However, I have checked this reference and could not find any reference to "summer stone."

†According to Berthelot's footnote, this passage seems to relate to the production of a metallic ferment, one that, interestingly, appears in Leiden Papyrus X as the "inexhaustible mass" (recipe no. 7).

Taking egg whites, throw in a pound of whites, 1 ounce of our lime, and after scrambling, break whole eggs at will and leave them until they drain from below, for 7 days. On the 7th day, after removing from the mass (the purest part), place in the distillation apparatus prescribed by art, with vinegar, in proportion to the eggs. Lute [spread sealant] the bottom (of the vase) carefully, cook and melt on a horse-dung fire. Read the bottom for distillation. This water is "black, pure water."*[22]

While the supposed author of this long treatise, Moses of Alexandria, or Moses the Alchemist, or even "Moses the thrice happy"[23] (perhaps a playful skit on the Egyptians' Thrice-Greatest Hermes), has been considered a Jewish alchemist, the name has inevitably led to confusion over whether the Moses of Exodus was an alchemist, or even author of chemical works ascribed to the name. The biblical Moses, after all, melted the idolatrous golden calf and mixed the melt with water. Nominal conflation is assisted by the opening lines of the *Chymia of Moses,* an altered version of Exodus 31:2–5 (traditionally attributed to Moses). The alchemist opens his treatise with:

And the Lord said to Moses: "I have chosen the priest named Benelel, of the tribe of Judah, to work gold, silver, copper, iron, all stones good to work, and bowls good to fashion, and to be the master of all the arts."†

---

*This three-word quotation is very like "And a spirit most black, humid, pure," attributed to Apollon in the treatise *Manufacture mainly that of the whole;* Berthelot and Ruelle, CAAG, vol. 3, 4.7, 266.

†The King James Version reads: "See, I have called by name Bezaleel the son of Uri, the son of Hur, of the tribe of Judah: / And I have filled him with the spirit of God, in wisdom, and in understanding, and in knowledge, and in all manner of workmanship, / To devise cunning works, to work in gold, and in silver, and in brass, / And in cutting of stones, to set them, and in carving of timber, to work in all manner of workmanship."

Because the name Moses was given to authorship of numerous apocryphal works in late antiquity, it is not surprising they were familiar to the compiler of Leiden Papyrus W. The pseudepigraphical status of the name does cast doubt on whether there was actually an alchemist called Moses, though the possibility itself is perfectly reasonable. The recipes' compiler was almost certainly Jewish. Anyhow, the *Chymia of Moses* is a no-nonsense recipe series, dated to the first or second century, some of which are taken from pseudo-Democritus while most wouldn't appear out of place in Leiden Papyrus X. The work is quoted in the Byzantine corpus, sometimes in association with Pebichius or Chymes. Berthelot concluded it most probable that "these were collections of practical processes, formed from different sources, by goldsmiths and craftsmen who transmitted them to each other as a secret tradition, enlarging them from time to time with new recipes. The Leiden Papyrus, pseudo-Democritus, the processes of Iamblichus, the Chemistry of Moses represent some of these notebooks that have come to us."[24]

Mary the "Prophetess"

The earliest testimony to Mary being "first" of "ancient" practitioners of the art comes from Zosimos in a treatise called *On the Measure of Yellowing*.

> Mary (places) in the first line molybdochalchos and manufacturing (processes). The burning operation (is) what all the ancients advocate Mary, the first, says: "The copper burned with sulfur, treated with natron oil, and resumed after having several times undergone the same treatment, becomes an excellent gold and without shade. This is what God says: Know all that, according to experience, by burning copper (first), sulfur produces no effect. But when you burn (first) the sulfur, then not only does it make the copper without stain, but again it brings it closer to gold." Mary, in the description

Fig 3.6. *Maria the Prophetess* (also known as Maria the Jewess); a fanciful engraving of her from early seventeenth-century doctor and alchemist Michael Maier's *Symbola Aurea Mensae Duodecim Nationum* (1617)

below the figure, proclaims it a second time, and says: "This was graciously revealed to me by God; namely, that copper is first burned with sulfur, then with the body of magnesia; and one blows until the parts that are left have escaped into the shadows: (then) the copper becomes without shadow."[25]

While there's some ambiguity about whether Mary was first—that is, earliest or greatest—of the old adepts, or that she was simply first to advocate the operation described, there's no doubt that Zosimos held her work in high, possibly highest, esteem among authorities on the art. Only the Philosopher (as he calls pseudo-Democritus) is up there with her. We can also see from this extract how she came to acquire the sobriquet "Prophetess." She evidently believed she was guided by God into the right paths of chemical processing.

Mary had mastered several distillation procedures and may have perfected vital apparatus, such as the sealed, copper-topped kērotakis.

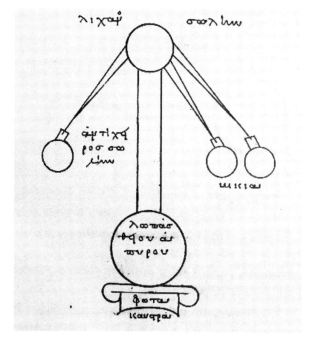

Fig. 3.7. Alembic with three recipients (tribicos),
Codex Marcianus, fol. 194v. Two Greek words are
superimposed over the furnace: *kaustra* (place of
combustion) and *phōta* (literally "lights,"
meaning flames).

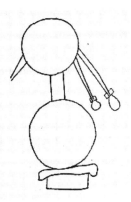

Fig. 3.8. Tribicos (*Codex
Parisinus Graecus,*
Ms. 2325, fol. 84)

Zosimos credits her with the first description of the tribikos, while the double-boiler vessel to limit the temperature of one liquid to the boiling point of another, called a bain-marie by medieval alchemist Arnold Villanova, was apparently named after her. Here, in Zosimos's *On Tribicos and Tube,* he quotes Mary's description of the copper construction of the tribicos:

> Make three tubes of rolled and thinned copper the thickness of which is this: it shall be about that of a skillet of brass, to cook the cakes; the length shall be a cubit and a half. Make three tubes under these conditions, and also make one (large) tube, of about one palm in diameter with an opening proportionate to that of the copper vase. The three tubes will have a suitable mouth at the neck of the small vessel, by means of a pin, through the thumb tube; so that the two forefinger tubes fit laterally to both hands. Toward the end of the copper vase, there are three holes, fitted to the tubes and well connected. They are welded in an eccentric way to the upper container, intended to receive the volatile part. The copper vase is placed over the terra-cotta flask that contains the sulfur. After having luted the joints with flour paste, adapt to the ends of the tubes of glass containers, large and strong, so that they do not break due to the heat of the water that trains the distilled material.[26]

In his *On the Apparatus and the Furnaces,*[27] Zosimos says Mary described "a great number" of apparatus constructions, not only those for manufacturing "divine (sulfur) water," but many kinds of kerotakis and furnace. Zosimos refers first, interestingly, to a glass vessel (remember the importance of glassblowing), with its "earth tube," the flask "udcoé" (?), and the narrow-necked vessel into which the tube entered in correct proportion to the opening of the glass vessel. The first dateable evidence (50–40 BCE) for glassblown vessels (including open-ended tubes) surfaced in Jerusalem, with Nahman Avigad's excavation in the Jewish Quarter of the Old City in 1971, so it's possible Judaean products were

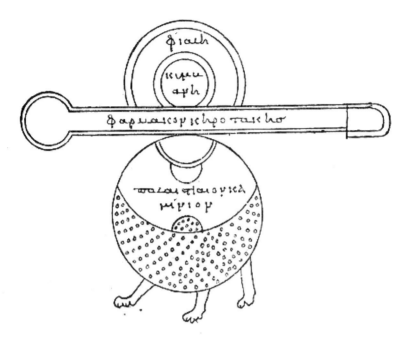

Fig. 3.9. A bain-marie (double boiler) to kerotakis (pallet for softening
metals); *Codex Marcianus*, folio 195v. The digester drawn here is as
long as a palm (*palaistiaion kaminion*); it seems riddled with holes,
unless that is superficial decoration. We see a bath of ashes, or
of sand. The pallet of preparations, *pharmakon kērotakēs* (*sic*)
is very large, heated only in the middle. There are two lesser
cups, placed immediately under the kerotakis, one big,
surmounting a smaller one; they receive the meltable
materials. The sublimated products are collected in
two superior concentric and successive condensers:
one called "flask," the other "mug."

acquired by a Jewish community in Alexandria, to be applied to industry. Such would suggest a revolutionary development in the art, its inception marking the apparatus formation as Zosimos understood it. And it
was perhaps a Jewish woman called Mary who was instrumental in the
development. Given this insight, we can see that the later Byzantine idea
of Mary as Democritus's contemporary was so misleading, and we may

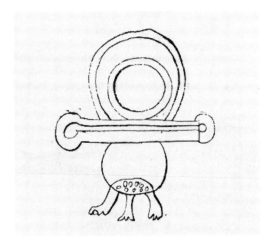

Fig. 3.10. A bain-marie to kerotakis; from *Codex Parisinus Graecus* 2325, derived from *Codex Marcianus* (see figure 3.9)

accept what most scholars today accept; that is, that Mary lived in the first century CE, in arguably a golden age of industrial progress, if you happened to be in the right place to witness it.

Mary's contribution to Zosimos's chemical knowledge is copious and repeatedly acknowledged. In the treatise *On the Body of Magnesia and its Treatment*, Zosimos credits her with correct understanding of the processing of molybdochalkos, or "black lead."

> This is what Mary sets out liberally and clearly concerning what she calls the loaves of magnesia. The first degree in the truth of the mystery is explained in these (passages). Thus Mary wants this to be the body of magnesia; she proclaims it not only in this passage but also in many others. In another place, she says, "Without the help of black lead, one cannot produce this body of magnesia, of which we have specified and accomplished the preparation." "Such are," she says, "the doctrines"; and without getting tired, teaching for the second and third time, she names body of magnesia the black lead and molybdochalkos; on this subject, she speaks of cinnabar, or lead, and of the summer stone. It is this body that produces the simultaneous fusion of all materials cooked and golden in power. It cooks the raw matter, and so works its diplosis. It produces, she says, in power all the golden materials by

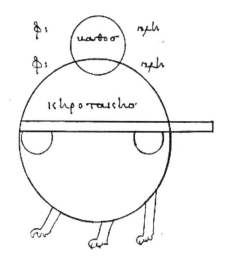

Fig. 3.11. Another bain-marie to kerotakis (*Codex Marcianus*, fol. 196). The pallet carries two inferior cups toward its extremities. In the superior cup (flask, *phialē*) is the word *bathos* (cavity or chamber).

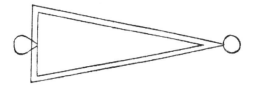

Fig. 3.12. Below the above bain-marie, we see the kerotakis, or triangular pallet: a singular form, distinct from those in figures 3.9 and 8.5.

cooking; for it is not yet in action. On this (point) I will write another speech; but for the moment let us take care of our subject.

It was thus exposed by Mary that the body of magnesia is the black molybdochalkos; for it has not yet been dyed. It is this molybdochalkos that you must dye, projecting the motaria [?] of the yellow sandarac [resin from a small cypress tree], so that cooked gold no longer exists (only) in power, but in action. Thus (expresses) Mary, after having named the body of magnesia loaves.[28]

It was Mary who is most identified as having named "fixed and not fleeting things" *bodies*. Thus, Mary says that "the body of the magnesia is the secret thing that comes from lead, from the summer stone, and from the copper."[29] The "body" comes from lead *to* magnesia, which is not otherwise a body, for in section 9 of the treatise we are informed that magnesia, pyrite, mercury, and chryso-colla (a blue-green crystal with high copper content) and their likes are "incorporeals." The *bodies* are copper, iron, tin, and lead. They don't evaporate in the fire. However, when a body is mixed with an incorporeal, according to Mary, the bodies become incorporeal and the incorporeals body. In a corresponding axiom of Mary, she declares in this context: "If two don't become one; that is to say, if the vola-tile (materials) don't combine with the fixed materials, nothing will happen of what is expected."[30] It is vital that the bodies become incorporeal by becoming one with the incorporeals, so that, "reduced in spirit," they can rise as sublimated vapor, and become bodies again.[31] This is of course the distillation process that so impressed Zosimos and for which blown glass was such a boon.

Mary, with feminine intuition practically directed, famously likened the body and the incorporeal materials to male and female: "Join the male with the female and you will find what is sought." The union is effected by fire, suggestive of passion: "Do not touch with your hands for it is an igneous preparation."[32] Indeed! So . . . what once seemed hopelessly enigmatic, or exceedingly mystical or para-doxical, I hope now makes sound industrial sense. As Zosimos would say, "Good health!"

FOUR

Zosimos I

Clearing the Decks

HIS NAME MEANS "SURVIVOR," and while it may be a nom de plume—and the more intriguing if so—his name has indeed survived as the first recognizable *personality* in the history of alchemy. In Zosimos, alchemy reaches its classical point, even in its relative youth. We have more written testimony from Zosimos of Panopolis than any other early alchemical writer, and his ardent brilliance shines forth across the roughly 1,700 years that separate us from him. His influence, which is remarkable, is easily traceable throughout the centuries. If alchemy requires piety and renunciation, whether in the Byzantine period or in the Renaissance, we are hearing the warnings of Zosimos against false paths; the eager genius of Panopolis stands upright at the crossroads pointing upward.

Zosimos never leaves us in any doubt that we are listening to *him,* and he knows his chemical onions. More, he is creative; he is philosophical; he is polemical; and he is, without doubt, spiritual, succeeding in bridging the spiritual and theoretical with the practical and the useful. A pontifex twixt earth and heaven, he clearly wished to be seen and be respected, as such.

It would of course be rewarding to know more about him, but while he always appears to speak from the heart and mind with determined consistency, he tells us little about himself. He wraps his soul in his beliefs, for his beliefs offer most to his soul. He is called the Panopolitan—though the *Suda* puts him in Alexandria. We may not unduly suppose him to have had dealings with both centers. Was he pure-blood Egyptian? We know not. He is highly respectful of the monotheist cause, and of Hebrew technology and prophecy in particular. He is no less respectful of Greek philosopher Democritus and of Greek poet Hesiod. He believed Democritus provided a literary rock of purity in the art of chēmeia. There are strong indications of acquaintance with a form of gnostic Christianity with a clear theological analogue to his supra-cosmic, universe-friendly vision of the art—for alchemy may appear consistent with ultra-pneumatic gnosis as well as "two natures in one undivided substance" orthodoxy.

Fig. 4.1. Marble bust, third century CE, with Greek inscription "Zōsimos." Who this particular person was, we know not; provenance of this bust is presently unknown (image thanks to Rvalette).

Above all, as Garth Fowden wrote so convincingly nearly forty years ago in *The Egyptian Hermes,* Zosimos is perhaps the best known early devotee of the spiritual vision of the philosophical tractates attributed to Hermes Trismegistus and known generally as the *Corpus Hermeticum.* Zosimos understands them intimately; his thought is wedded to them, and he sees them as inseparable from his chemical practice. As Hermetic studies pioneer A. J. Festugière noted, Zosimos was "father of religious alchemy," the first alchemist to portray alchemy in terms of salvation, as a technique of dual purpose: purifying metals and purifying human souls.[1] Thus, he was arguably the first theologian of alchemy, or first promoter of theological alchemy: a holy pursuit that, if it was to bear potential fruit, had to be practiced as both spiritual discipline and transformative art, offering spiritual vision of all created existence and man's privileged potential within the total divine scheme.

For Zosimos, the universe is a tangible mirror image of incorporeal being, the image coalescing, even coagulating on the physical plane. It was, he believed, fashioned by and sustained by two emanations of the unknowable Father: two "sons" of God: the cosmic fashioner (demiurge) and the holy spirit-mind (*Logos* and *nous*). In the chemical process, Zosimos felt privileged to see—once mind (*nous*) was purified—revelation of God's creative and redemptive processes. For Zosimos, alchemy is divine analogy, and more than that, it is a means both to initiate and prefigure divine redemption and ultimate salvation through sacrifice, purification, and ascent to the One. Zosimos's conception of alchemy is, as scholars Garth Fowden, Daniel Stolzenberg, and Shannon Grimes have maintained, a form of theurgy. Theurgy would normally entail ritual practices for purifying the soul and identifying with divinity, as favored by Zosimos's contemporary, Neoplatonist Iamblichus (245–325 CE), whose thoughts on theurgy may be found in his *de mysteriis.*[2] However, Zosimos is adamant that the pure art is not *magic,* and he requires no ritual impedimenta whatsoever, only a pure intention to practice with propriety. For Zosimos, the art relies solely on natural processes. Only the earth/body-bound involve magical practices and supplication of daimons. Zosimos's alchemy is a natural, divine path to God, in which pious practitioners are called to identify with all elements and transformations, so as to experience harmonious union, or "gold": most divine dye that raises soul and is the soul raised to its goal. The "metal" (body) must be willing to suffer the process.

It may be argued that Zosimos transfigured an industrial process into the beginnings of a discreet, and discrete, spiritual movement, and for such an achievement canonization might seem appropriate. The Survivor has survived.

Was Zosimos an Egyptian Priest?

As to whether Zosimos was Egyptian, rather than Jewish, as has been speculated, his treatise On the Apparatus and Furnaces; Authentic Commentaries on the Letter Omega refers to "the first man, [who] is called Toth among us," meaning Egyptian tradition and Hermetic writings, while among "them," meaning the Jews, he is called "Adam," so that makes it reasonably likely he identified most with the country, although it doesn't offer certainty since he perhaps considered himself an adopted son of "Poimandres" (Mind of sovereignty, who initiates Hermes Trismegistos in Corpus Hermeticum libellus I), for example, or that he was simply expressing solidarity with a universally minded Hermetic group, guild, or "lodge."[3]

The question of whether Zosimos was a priest is rightly disputed. Shannon Grimes, for example, seems to favor a picture of Zosimos as Egyptian priest, master craftsman, and overseer of craft work associated with temple worship, with duties like making religious statues for Egyptian temples. "Zosimus was a master craftsman, a teacher of teachers," Grimes asserts in her doctoral thesis.

> He served as an advisor to his colleagues, Theosebeia and Neilos, who taught the alchemical arts to groups of disciples. If Zosimus was a priest, he would have been a priest of fairly high rank, since he describes other master craftsmen as "prophets," a high-ranking

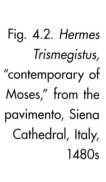

Fig. 4.2. *Hermes Trismegistus,* "contemporary of Moses," from the pavimento, Siena Cathedral, Italy, 1480s

class of priests. The high priest of the Temple of Ptah at Memphis, a renowned center of metallurgy and other crafts, bore the title of "Greatest of the Masters of Craftsmen," which is further evidence that master craftsmen were priests of high rank.[4]

One problem with this picture of high priests at Memphis is that it is almost certainly anachronistic to the period in which Zosimos was operating. The system referred to had been anciently operative in pre-Ptolemaic days and still obtained under the Graeco-Egyptian Ptolemies, too, but after Cleopatra's death and Roman occupation, the picture is unclear. In fact, the last in a long list of names of high priests of Ptah at Memphis is Psherenamun II, son of Psherenamun I and Taneferher. The stele referring to him is dated 27 BCE.[5] The date is significant: only three years after Roman assumption of government. During the ensuing 330 years to Zosimos's period, we have no certainty that the old system survived in Memphis in any manner like the way it functioned before Egypt was annexed to the empire. Indeed, Zosimos's own writings suggest it did not, as we shall see shortly.

In the same thesis, Grimes's picture is somewhat beefed up by Zosimos's reference to a lady he sometimes calls "sister," one Theosebeia, to whom he addresses copious quantities of advice and warning, especially over her taking alchemical instruction from a priest, one Neilos. Zosimos shows scant respect for this priest, whom he accuses of numerous sins of low magic and worshipping statues of gods—hardly unusual activities for Egyptian priests! Zosimos gives no indication of being a worshipper of the traditional Egyptian pantheon, and while the Hermetic philosophical corpus is mostly henotheist, Zosimos shows no devotional interest in polytheism. As for Theosebeia, her "sisterhood" could be a case of them both belonging to a sodality, or it may be a Christian greeting, or indeed, she may have been Zosimos's sister! At one point he dignifies her as one who wears purple, which was generally confined to nobility, but this might have been a mutual jest that she'd acquired pretentious "airs and graces." But this is speculation.

Theosebeia means "Godfearer" or "God worshipper," and if we consider the former, it was that name given by Jews to uncircumcised gentiles who respected the biblical God. This would mitigate against any idea of her serving in a pagan temple. That such a one would take advice from a priest on a professional basis might mean Neilos was offering specialist knowledge that Theosebeia wanted, or she was interested in his religion or magic. It's really pointless to speculate further. When Zosimos describes priest Neilos's interests in Egyptian magic and temple devotions, he is scornful, though he speaks with knowledge of traditional temple practice, and may, perhaps, have once been associated with it in some capacity. Grimes asserts of Theosebeia: "She was either a priestess or the leader of a craft guild (or perhaps both), since Zosimus mentions that she formed an assembly of disciples and established oaths among them to protect the secrets of their art."[6]

The Syriac passage in question does not link the idea of an assembly or disciples to any temple context, being Zosimos's fraternal admonishment of her having members sworn to secrecy, which Zosimos abhors. A difficulty here is whether secrecy was maintained for industrial or commercial reasons or out of some kind of gnostic exclusive community rule. Anyhow, Zosimos is against it on the Christian principle (I suggest) that if alchemical knowledge is necessary for human welfare, it should be shared ("Ask and ye shall receive," Matthew 7:7–8). He elsewhere regards secrecy as being on a par in iniquity with fools flaunting knowledge by attaching their names to commentaries on existing books held by priests, who themselves condemned the braggers but lacked power to stop them (which was not the case before Roman rule). Zosimos says he wants nothing to do with such disputes, accusing protagonists of "poverty of spirit" (perhaps misunderstanding Matthew 5:3 that if by "poor in spirit" Jesus intended "humble" when he said the poor in spirit would enter the kingdom of heaven—perhaps Zosimos here shows the eclectic character of his religious compass).[7] When Zosimos writes of how "the ancient priests" used to deliberately secrete cryptographic stelae in the darkest recesses of their temples, it is *not* with approval, but with a certain irony that those who got their knowledge thanks to the temples losing control of their secrets were now *repeating* the folly of holding them as secrets requiring oaths—and these weren't even secrets worth knowing![8] Interestingly, he says the Jews did not hide the secrets entrusted to them, on the Solomonic principle that for wisdom's sake one would give up all one had. Those who used secrets for themselves, without giving riches away first, would suffer destruction for the riches they held, thanks to the jealousy of worldly powers.

Grimes reinforces the idea of Zosimos as priest more pointedly in her paper "Secrets of the God-Makers: Rethinking the Origins of Greco-Egyptian Alchemy," where Zosimos's role, she writes, "seems to have been that of a master craftsman, in charge of collecting, interpreting, and translating recipes for the lower-ranking artisan-priests that were overseen by this branch."[9] Zosimos's text reads: "As we have said, the various symbols of priests have been explained by the ancient masters and the various prophets, whose names have become famous, and who have prevailed with all the power of science."[10] The reference to ancient masters and prophets who interpreted alchemical texts might just as well refer to distinguished past practitioners and even to Hebrew prophets, such as Moses. In other words, what Egyptian priests hid from the eye, others (especially Jews) have brought to light with distinction.

In Zosimos's treatise *The Final Account* (or *Quittance;* Olivier Dufault prefers "Abstinence"; the Greek is vague) we find passages that I believe on close inspection make it highly unlikely that Zosimos was in any way a protagonist for the temple priestly system.[11] Olivier Dufault's painstaking chapter on Zosimos in terms of a "client and scholar" relationship, in *Early Greek Alchemy, Patronage and Innovation in Late Antiquity,* bypasses the notion of Zosimos as priest and instead envisions him as an independent scholar with Theosebeia as his client. An academically qualified private informant keen to stress solid, established traditions of literary learning (such as Democritus), he is thus focused on demolishing ungrounded ideas that have come Theosebeia's way through priest Neilos as well as "virgin" alchemist Paphnutia. Zosimos's argument is intended to be devastating, and he pulls no punches in a disturbing onslaught on the competition—a polemic that Dufault examines.[12]

It should first be said that in my own purview, Zosimos's polemic against Theosebeia's unnatural propitiated tinctures pursues the myth referred to earlier where he used the Enochic story of the "Watchers" who lusted after human women—he calls them both "daimons" and "angels" (the latter following Genesis 6, and the apocryphal I Enoch)—to explain both the origin and ambiguous status of chemical knowledge in the world, for it was knowledge wrested from its proper place and abused by daimons—and subsequently by men and women. Indeed, Zosimos's own account of the lustful recalcitrant beings begins with the statement that "holy scripture" tells of daimons who have "commerce with women," and who "direct them."[13] He is saying even "noble" Theosebeia is vulnerable, and particularly so, for she craves knowledge. She is in danger, for there are, Zosimos tells her in *The Final Account, two* kinds of propitious tinctures.

One kind depends on specific times. Here, Zosimos perhaps refers to the daimons of the decans, who each occupy ten degrees of the zodiac, according to contemporary astro-magical lore. Producing the dyes at allegedly propitious times involves, he warns, direct appeal to daimonic beings. Such beings—apparently alluding to the Watchers condemned by God in 1 Enoch not to return to heaven, as well as the discarnate souls of the giants the Watchers sired on human women—Zosimos describes as *hoi kata topon ephoroi,* which means "local overseers"; confined, they operate in particular places. They are also described as *perigeioi,* or "terrestrial" (when this word appears, the Byzantine manuscript copyists have added a large *d* to indicate daimonic presence). Overseers watch over *slaves.* Now, Zosimos insists that true knowledge relies on God, who is *everywhere all the time,* being consistent with the idea of the "All" (Pan), as Mary also insisted, so it's bad news propitiating local daimons, however much one might think they know; they're woefully limited. Such contact is impure, and results will reflect it. Zosimos calls such tinctures *kairikai,* meaning "of the moment" (*kairos*), also suggesting the negativity of things ephemeral and transient. These tinctures are controlled by will of the overseers, and, critically, *these "overseers" gave them to the priests.* Well, not exactly *gave;* no, for the price of these tinctures is worship, maintenance of statues, feeding the pride of parasitic beings under divine censure, and *this* is the kind of unnatural thing Neilos and Paphnutia are involved in. Don't trust the priests!

We may now get an idea of why the treatise is called *The Final Account* (or *Quittance*), for in 1 Enoch, Enoch is chosen by God to pronounce final judgment on the Watchers. Their leader, Azael (in the Greek version), makes a plea for survival, and they're apparently permitted to haunt low and obscure places until the end of time. The end-time to which Zosimos seems to be alluding—either as having in some manner begun already or as something imminent—is not clear, but then, neither is the precise fate of the Watchers in 1 Enoch.Dufault, however, takes a rather parallel meaning and suggests that Zosimos calls for a

"Final Abstinence"; that is, one must finally abstain absolutely from appealing for daimonic help to obtain alchemical success. Zosimos feels humankind has entered a new era, with daimonic power left only to haunt the earthbound who have not reached beyond the fixed stars of astral fate to the noetic realm.

In section 7 of the treatise, Zosimos says that in former times, powerful men kept the overseers from taking over altogether, and the mighty men enjoyed access to the second kind of tincture, the "natural" (*physikos*) tinctures that did not carry risk of daimonic interference. However, asserts Zosimos, the overseers, begrudging the existence of the natural tinctures, hid them, replacing knowledge of them with non-natural tinctures. The allusion here seems to be both to the Watchers and to the hiding of secrets in the dark recesses of the temples, with priests keeping them from view. The overseers asked for sacrifices so that use of the tinctures would be successful. In other words, instead of realizing the divine bounty of the whole of divine nature and natural processes, would-be adepts were compelled to resort to a magical system that was corrupting, enslaving and, when it came down to it, unnecessary.

Those who brought (the colors made by unearthly [non-natural, or supernatural] means?), being thus set aside, advised considerable numbers of people to act against us all, the savants, operating by natural actions. They did not want to be set aside by men but to be supplicated and adjured to yield what they had made, in return for offerings and sacrifices. They therefore kept hidden all the natural processes, those that give the results without artifice. It was not only out of jealousy against us but also because they were concerned about their existence and did not want to expose themselves to being beaten with rods, driven away to starvation, censuring the offerings of sacrifices. They hid the natural processes and put forward their own, which were of an unnatural order; they exposed to their priests that the mass of the people would neglect their sacrifices if they no longer had recourse to the unnatural (or supernatural) processes, to address those who possessed this supposed knowledge of vulgar alloys, this art of making water and washing. Thus, by the effect of custom, law, and fear, their sacrifices were greatly followed. They did not even respond to their false advertisements. When their sanctuaries were deserted and their sacrifices neglected, they still obtained men who remained (with them), and they devoted themselves to the sacrifices, flattering them with dreams and other deceptions, as well as with certain councils. They kept going back to these false and supernumerary promises to please men who were friends of pleasure, miserable and ignorant. You, too, O woman, they want to win you over, through their false prophet [Neilos?]; they flatter you; being hungry, (they covet) not only sacrifices, but also your soul.[14]

This speech, aimed straight at Theosebeia in the first instance, may stand as a no-holds-barred, iconoclastic condemnation of priestcraft and of all magical associations with daimons, with a plea for reliance on a superior revelation of nature. That revelation has come to Zosimos through knowledge of Jewish monotheist prophecy, Christian Gnostic liberation from daimonic causation, and from the vision of the divine creation in the writings attributed to Hermes. It is, in its way, a plea for pure science within the terms of the epoch. Thus, it must, to my judgment, be a rank absurdity to imagine Zosimos as anything remotely like a pious member among the ranks of Egyptian temple priesthood. By 300 CE, any knowledge the temples once had was well and truly *out,* and temple worship, for those who still respected the old gods, a cultural tradition or custom, not the sole path to knowledge, as had been the case in the old Egypt. Indeed, I should say that underneath this polemic is some sense of the message of the Christian epistle to the Hebrews, written with the idea in mind that "the veil of the temple was rent" and the last and greatest "high priest," in Jerusalem at any rate, was both sacrificer and sacrificed, and with his coming, an end to the temple cult was inevitable. The sense one gets is that Zosimos saw

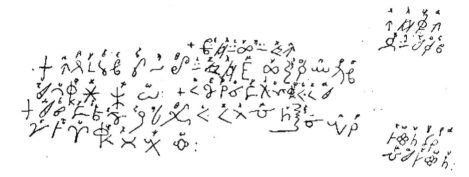

Fig. 4.3. Two magical or cryptographic alphabets, formed from misformed Greek words; cryptographic not hieroglyphic (*Codex Marcianus*)

Theosebeia as one slipping back to the old ways, impervious to the new freedom of the natural tincture, operating by universal providence in nature, open to the pure-hearted: *science,* in fact.

Put another way, Zosimos was attempting to put the "fear of God" back into the "God-fearer." Whether or not he succeeded, he might yet put it back into us.

FIVE

Zosimos II

Alchemical Yoga

PSYCHOLOGIST CARL JUNG was fascinated by a series of "dream lessons" left by Zosimos, apparently taking their contents as genuine dreams. How could he not?—believing, as he did, that alchemists experienced their "unconscious" projected onto the phenomena of alchemical processes. According to Jung, unconscious contents were "constellated" when alchemists (unconsciously) perceived something analogous in the chemistry. From Jung's perspective, alchemy's truest function was to induce vision.

According to Jung:

> Zosimos had a mystic or Gnostic philosophy of sorts whose basic ideas he projected into matter. When we speak of psychological projection we must . . . always remember that it is an unconscious process that works only so long as it stays unconscious. Since Zosimos, like all the other alchemists, is convinced not only that his philosophy can be applied to matter but that processes also take place within it which corroborate his philosophical assumptions, it follows that he must have experienced, in matter itself, at the very least an identity between the behaviour of matter and the events in his own psyche. But as this identity is unconscious, Zosimos is no

more able than the rest of them to make any pronouncement about it. For him it is simply there, and it not only serves as a bridge, it actually *is* the bridge that unites psychic and material events in one, so that "what is within is also without." Nevertheless, an unconscious event which eludes the conscious mind will portray itself somehow and somewhere, it may be in dreams, visions, or fantasies.[1]

Had Zosimos's "dream" narratives been genuine dreams, there might have been something in Jung's rather too influential approach, but it is evident from exploring the "dreams" with real chemical processes in mind that these narratives were not spontaneous effusions from Zosimos's rich imagination or unconscious but rather contrived teaching devices with literary precedents, laden with specific allegorical equivalents, while Zosimos had full control over what he was expressing and knew what he meant to express. Zosimos didn't find the content either in his unconscious or through its bubbling up to awareness—though he may have been more in touch with the psychic underworld and overworld than most—because he didn't need to. Zosimos found the content in practical furnace and dye work alloyed to his quite consciously grasped philosophy of creation, which he saw mirrored by analogy with dye production. Had he read Jung's interpretation of his alleged "inability to pronounce," the chances are Zosimos would have suspected that Jung's "unconscious" was a daimonic, terrestrial or sub-terrestrial mimicking of the capacities of the *nous,* because for Zosimos, being *is* consciousness (or seeing), and ultimate consciousness is identification with ultimate being. As the climax to the first Hermetic philosophical tractate maintained, it was those ignorant of nous who were asleep and ignorant; Zosimos was fully awake, and the dream device was consistent with the convention that revelation of truth could come in that manner. Zosimos might further suggest that *our* modern problem (which Jung so ably addressed) is bound to the idea of the "unconscious"—that is, for Zosimos, unconsciousness of the noetic realm—and corresponding imprisonment in matter and the bonds of mundane rationality deprived of higher *nous*. In that dichotomy, Jung and Zosimos would surely have agreed, but I doubt if Jung had anything to teach Zosimos, for whom *nous* was already sovereign.

Practical Dreaming

First, we'd better track down Zosimos's dreams. Unfortunately, getting them in proper order is difficult, as not only were Zosimos's treatises subjected to an ulterior order within the Byzantine alchemical corpus and Syrian manuscript collections with little interest in original sequences, but Berthelot and translators Ruelle and Duval, when they made their collection, also imposed an order of their own, mixing Zosimos's works with later commentaries on them, while separating coherent works into a weave with chemical procedures interspersing them. Some thirty years ago, philologist Michèle Mertens attempted to catalog Zosimos's work into four more appropriate groups: *Authentic Memoirs,* including *On the Apparatus and Furnaces; Authentic Commentaries on the Letter Omega* and *On Excellence* (or *Virtue*), which contains Zosimos's five dreams or visions; *Chapters to Eusebia* (this title appears in the *Codex Marcianus* contents and seems to be either a confusion with Theosebeia or with the later Greek historian also called Zosimos, who wrote about Constantinople's empress Eusebia); *Chapters to Theodorus* (short summaries); and a group made of *The Final Account* enclosed between two extracts from a *Book of Sophē.*

Mertens's French translation of *Authentic Memoirs* was published in 1995 in *Les Alchimistes Grecs* (edited by H. D. Saffrey; Budé series). Mertens's ordering is not definitive, however, and new translations are still required (134 years seems a long time to wait—since Berthelot and Ruelle—and *still* no definitive English translations!). There is also the abiding problem of what is missing; Zosimos mentions numerous works now lost, and some of the surviving texts probably were once part of a larger work, such as a twenty-four-book grand work by Zosimos mentioned in the *Suda,* apparently based on each letter of the Greek alphabet, of which only a fragment (*Omega*) survives.

Zosimos's first "lesson" (alpha) is titled *On Virtue* (or "Excellence") in the *Codex Marcianus,* to which Paris manuscript 2327 adds: *"and the composition of the Waters,"* as the treatise opens with those words, followed by a general picture of the work of separating metals from volatiles such as sulfur and arsenic, "and the fixation of the spirit [dye] on the body; operations that are not the result of the addition of foreign natures drawn from the outside, but which are due to the proper nature, unique, acting on itself, derived from a single species, as well as (the use) of hardened and solidified ores, and liquid extracts from the tissue of plants; all this uniform and polychrome system includes the manifold and infinitely varied search for all things, the search for nature, subordinate to the lunar influence and the measure of time, which regulate the term and increment by which nature is transformed."[2]

The section that follows introduces the dream, or rather nightmare, narrative.

> When I said these things, I fell asleep and saw a priest standing before me, on the top of an altar in the form of a flask.* This altar had fifteen steps to go up. And there stood the sacrificer, and I heard a voice from above saying unto me, I have accomplished the work of descending the fifteen steps [later we hear only of seven steps], walking in the darkness, and the work of ascending the steps, going into the light. It is the sacrificer who renews me, rejecting the dense nature of the body. Thus consecrated priest by necessity, I become a spirit.

---

*The Greek *phiale* (literally "phial," or "vial") occurs in the *Cleopatra* kērotakis illustration (see figure 3.1, page 72). It appears as a dome-shaped cover over the top of the distillation tube.

Fig. 5.1. Seven steps in alchemy: the dream tradition of
Zosimos finds a new manifestation in Raphael Custo's
engraving "Middle: Conjunction" for Stephan Michelspacher's
Cabala: Mirror of Art and Nature, in Alchymia, 1615.

And when I heard the voice of him who stood upon the flask-shaped altar, I asked him who he was. And he, with a hail voice, answered me in these words: I am Ion,* priest of the sanctuaries, and I suffer intolerable violence. Someone came in the morning in a hurry, and he assaulted me, beating me with a sword, and dismembering me, following the rules of the combination. He took off all the skin from my head, with the sword that he held (in his hand); he mixed the bones with the flesh and made them burn with the fire of the treatment. This is how I learned, through the transformation of the body, to become spirit. This is the intolerable violence (that I suffered).[3]

Despite the startling, indeed horrific, incidents in the lesson (which may have amused and educationally alerted listeners), we can easily detect chemical operations of distillation, sublimation, and cutting accompanied by grills, effervescences, and color changes in what ensues. As for Zosimos's literary form of address, it is highly reminiscent of *Corpus Hermeticum* 1.

Once, when thought came to me of the things that are, and my thinking soared high and my bodily senses were restrained, like someone heavy with sleep from eating too much or bodily toil, an enormous being of unbounded size seemed to appear to me and call my name and say to me: "What do you want to hear and see; what do you want to learn and know from your understanding?"

"Who are you?" I asked.

"I am Poimandres," he said, "mind of sovereignty; I know what you want, and I am with you everywhere."[4]

Needless to say, Zosimos knew the text very well and shared its import with Theosebeia, advising her to hasten to that revelatory *Mind*

---

*The "L" (ca. 1460) manuscripts have "I am the one who is."

Fig. 5.2. Hermes Trismegistus in Dr. Everard's 1650 English translation of the *Divine Pymander* (14 libelli of the *Corpus Hermeticum*). Most imagine Hermes is the figure standing, but in the first treatise, Hermes is dozing when the divine Poimandres ("Sovereign Mind") appears to him.

as palliative to being misled (the Zosimos text may be corrupt or more accurate, having "Poimenandres," where our earliest Greek copy of the first Hermetic tract has "Poimandres" (often, but uncertainly, taken to mean "shepherd of men" from *poimēn,* a shepherd).[5]

Zosimos continues lesson alpha as follows:

And while he yet talked with me, and I compelled him to speak with me, his eyes became as blood, and he vomited out all his flesh. And I saw him (changed into) a small counterfeit man, tearing himself with his own teeth, and collapsing. Filled with fear, I awoke and thought, "Is this not the composition of the waters?" [Later seen as the white and yellow sulfurous waters; the Greek for "sulfur," *theion,* also means divine being.] I was persuaded that I had understood; and I fell asleep again. I saw the same altar in the form of a flask, and in the upper part of it was boiling water, and many people went without ceasing [in which Berthelot detected an allegory of distillation of vapors in an upper vessel]. And there was no one I could ask outside the altar. I then went up to the altar to see this spectacle.

And I perceive a little man, a barber [literally, "razor-working man"; in those days barbers let blood for health; blood here being synonymous with "spirit" or "color" extracted from metals], washed clean by the years, who says to me, "What are you looking at?" I told him that I was surprised to see the water's agitation and that of the burned and living men. He said to me, "This spectacle you see is the entrance, and the exit, and the mutation." I asked him again: "What mutation?" And he answered me: "This is the place of the operation called maceration; for men who desire to obtain virtue come in here and become spirits, after having fled the body." So I said, "Are you a spirit?" And he answered me, "Yea, a spirit and a keeper of spirits." While we were talking, the ever-increasing boiling, and the people howling lamentably, I saw a man of copper, holding in his hand a tablet of lead. [Berthelot recognizes an allegory here for molybdochalchos placed on the kērotakis, or the constituent.] He said the following words to me, looking at the tablet: "I command all those who are subjected to punishment to calm down, each one to take a lead tablet, to write with his own hand, and to hold their eyes up in the air, and their mouths open, until the harvest is come [or grapes are ripe]." The act followed the word and the master of the house said to me: "You have beheld, you have stretched out your neck towards the height and you saw what was done." And I said unto him, I saw, and he said unto me, "He that thou seest is the copper man: he is the chief of the priests, and he that vomiteth his own flesh. Authority was given to him over this water and over the punished people."[6]

The reference to ordering calm may be an imperative toward calming passions (which bind the spirit to the body), a regular instruction of Hermetic discipline, and something Zosimos urges on Theosebeia: an obvious analogy of chemistry and spiritual enlightenment. Shannon Grimes makes a diverting point by taking "maceration" as "embalming," leading to the idea that the priest urging the sufferers to open their mouths might allude to the Egyptian ritual of the "opening of the mouth" performed on corpses in the process of mummification (to enable the soul to use the body in the afterlife) and to attract divine being into sacred statues.[7] However, given what we know of Zosimos's view of statues, the "opening of the mouth" might be more in tune with the Gnostic belief that *pneuma* (spirit) is conveyed and received by open mouth to open mouth (hence the significance of kissing in Gnostic writings applied to Jesus and close disciples). The "salvation," or transformation to a more spiritual state, comes from on high, where participants should look and prepare to receive.

Indeed, the imperative to *receive* is underlined in the fourth part of the narrative where the speaker awakes to see the resultant "divine water" and erupts into something like a prosaic hymn of praise as he realizes inwardly that the cosmos is an unbounded, holistic synthesis of infinite giving and receiving, sympathy and attraction, antipathy and separation, of transformation and becoming, where every duality may be inverted and balanced.

> And when I had this apparition, I awoke again. I said unto him, "What is the cause of this vision? Is this not white and yellow bubbling water, divine water?" And I found that I understood correctly. I say that it is beautiful to speak and beautiful to listen, beautiful to give and beautiful to receive, beautiful to be enriched. How does nature learn to give and to receive? The copper man gives and the liquefied stone receives; the mineral gives and the plant receives; the stars give and the flowers receive; the sky gives and the earth receives; the lightning strikes give the fire that surges. In the altar in the form of a flask all things are intertwined, and all are separated: all things are united; all things are combined; all things are mixed, and all things are separated; all things are wet, and all are dried up; all things flourish, and all of them are defloering. Indeed, for each one it's by the method, by the measure, by the exact weighing of the four elements that the interlacing and dissociation of all things takes

place; no connection occurs without method. There is a natural method to blow and to suck in, to keep grades stationary, to increase and decrease them. When all things, in a word, agree by division and union, without the method being neglected in anything, nature is transformed; for nature, being turned on itself, is transformed: it is the nature and the bond of virtue in the whole universe.

5. In short, my friend, build a monolithic [of one stone] temple, similar to ceramic and alabaster, having neither beginning nor end in its construction [circular?]. Let there be inside a source of water very pure, sparkling as the sun. Look carefully on which side the entrance to the temple is, and take a sword in your hand; seek then the entrance, for it is narrow where the opening is. A serpent lies at the entrance, guarding the temple. Take hold of him, and kill him first, and strip him, and take his flesh and his bones, and divide his limbs; and gather the limbs and the bones together at the entrance of the temple, and make a stepping-stone of him, and go up, and come in: there thou shalt find that which thou seekest. The priest, this man of copper, whom you see sitting in the spring [or source], gathering (in him) the color, don't look at him as a man of copper; for he has changed the color of his nature and he has become a man of silver. If you want it, you will soon have it (as a) man of gold.[8]

The latter, rather enchanting image of the man of copper, turning silver, and then, if one wishes, to gold, apart from having an air of an astral journey encounter, obviously suggests color changes by which the creative process of dyeing might be mapped: blackening, whitening, yellowing. In 1938, A. J. Hopkins published "A Study of the Kerotakis Process as Given by Zosimus and Later Alchemical Writers," in which he saw in Zosimos's work the inception of a kērotakis process requiring the roasting of a copper-lead alloy with sulfur. The alloy is "attacked" by the sulfur and vaporizes it while its corrosive action leaves a blackened residue, which is then purified with "sulfur water" (a sulfur and lime powder solution dissolved in vinegar). This agent draws out excess sulfur. Zosimos's white and yellow waters might indicate the sulfur water, or the alloy's whitening and yellowing by means of ingredients such as mercury, or silver and gold leaf dissolved in a solution of arsenic. The priest is sacrificer and copper alloy being sacrificed so he may attain to be silvered, and ultimately made golden.[9]

That may do for the dyeing process, but Zosimos's allegories suggest a spiritual scale of values no less progressive or useful to the soul than to furnace work. It isn't difficult to see the torments of the figures as those suffered by souls, not in hell but in *this world,* not knowing their destiny, souls chained to bodies and the sense of foreboding as flesh senses its vulnerability to destruction. The operation of the sacrificer makes it possible for them to ascend yet, though they must undergo the fire for the sake of spirit's release and transformation.

The instruction to build a temple of one stone, with attendant instruction to find the right way to enter it because the entrance is narrow, and withal guarded by a serpent, is intriguing. It could almost be a passage omitted from the book of Revelation's heavenly city, for this temple has a source of pure water "glittering like the sun,"

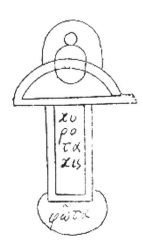

Fig. 5.3. Vase to kerotakis. The word *kurotakis* (kerotakis) is inscribed on the vertical part (probably an error). There is no digestion vase; the action of fire is direct (*Codex Marcianus*).

and it has neither beginning nor end—curiously reminiscent of the Christ of Revelation who is alpha and omega, beginning and end, despite the apparent contradiction. Is the serpent an ouroboros, with no end or beginning, swallowing its own tail in heavenly cycles? Are not the bones and flesh of this creature, at least as portrayed in the *Chrysopoeia of Cleopatra,* the *heimarmēnē,* the "night-cloak" of the fixed stars that govern fate below? And is it not Zosimos's repeated refrain to declare the spirit superior to fate, unlike the natural body, which has its role but is subject to necessity? And is the alchemist not to make of this serpentine guardian embodying the truth that the One is All, another unity, another stone: a stepping-stone from the realm of fate into the higher realm and home of spirit, to become one with God, and then see all?*

Mount this stone, find ingress through the narrow entrance, then find all one seeks, says Zosimos, as does Matthew 7:14, for "strait is the gate, and narrow is the way, which leadeth unto life, and few there be that find it," a message inwardly consistent with the climactic scenes of the first Hermetic tractate (1.25–26), where having passed through the seven zones, or bindings, of cosmic passions,† Hermes passes into the Ogdoad (or "eighth": the fixed stars), where he "has his own proper power," and hears voices from an even higher level whither he will rise. Having risen "into god," Poimandres charges him with the task of teaching his "race," but, on seeing them, he is saddened by the blind procession of the intoxicated, who care not for immortality and rush

---

*Note also that the serpent is to have its anatomy separated—that is, "analyzed"—before it is recombined. The alchemist must understand each part of the work and separate the elements before reconstituting them, first breaking the apparent unity of the All, then fulfilling it at a higher level as the One.

†The seven negative impulses of the cosmic framework are probably in Zosimos's mind when he writes of the seven steps to the altar, which steps may also allude to the planetary spheres: moon (corresponding to silver), Mercury (cinnabar), Venus (copper), sun (gold), Mars (iron), Jupiter (tin), Saturn (lead). Incidentally, Jung took the temple of one stone as a symbol of complete fulfillment, psychic and spiritual harmony, or as he called it, "individuation."

headlong into more suffering, more corrosion, thinking themselves wise, ignoring *nous,* and as though drunk or asleep.

This first lesson Zosimos has to teach is the primary lesson; the remaining lessons (beta and gamma) are subsidiary. Besides, how can you top the top?

It is interesting that lesson beta begins with Zosimos trying to repeat the experience but getting "lost." One of the problems of high spiritual experience is that it so transcends ordinary rational memory processes that although one knows one's experienced an unforgettable completion, or gilding of understanding, one forgets, as it were, the detail, or the way to how it happened, or the internal, substantial flavor as it was experienced at the time (with time transcended or not experienced). Perhaps the absence of ordinary temporal sense affects the capacity to memorize the experience, for the core of the experience cannot find a shape in memory, only a residual memory that something happened. This sense perhaps informs an aspect of Zosimos's next lesson, which otherwise denotes a suggestive, allusive allegorizing of chemical art.

1. At last I was seized with the desire to ascend the seven degrees and to see the seven punishments; and as was fitting, in one of the (fixed) days I effected the path of ascension. When I went back several times, I crossed the path. On the way back, I did not find my way back. Plunged into great discouragement, not seeing how to get out, I fell into sleep.

During my sleep, I perceived a certain little man, a barber in a red robe and royal clothing, standing outside the place of punishment, and he said to me, "What are you doing (there), O man?" And I answered him, "I stop here because being myself deviated from the way, I find myself lost." He said to me: "(Then): follow me." And me, I came and followed him. And it came to pass, when we were nigh unto the place of chastisement, that I saw him who led me, this little barber, enter into the place, and his whole body was consumed with fire.

2. When I saw it, I went away, and trembled with fear; and I awoke, and said to myself, What do I see? And again I drew my reasoning to the light and I understood that this barber was the man of copper, clothed in red clothing, and I (myself) said: I've well understood, it is the man of copper. It's necessary he first enter the place of punishment.

3. Again my soul desired to rise to the third degree. And again, alone, I followed the way; and while I was near the place of chastisement, I went astray again, not knowing my way, and stood in despair. And again, similarly, I saw an old man whitened by the years, turned completely white, of blinding whiteness. His name was Agathodaimon [Good Daimon*]. Turning around, the white-haired old man looked at me for an hour, and I asked him, "Show me the right way." And he turned not back to me, but hastened to go his own way. And I came and went from here and there, and hastened to the altar. And when I was come up to the altar, I saw the white-haired old man enter into the place of chastisement. O demiurges of the celestial natures! How it was immediately ablaze! What a frightful story, my brothers! For, as a result of the violence of the punishment his eyes were filled with blood. I (to him) addressed the word and asked him, "Why are you lying down?" But he opened his mouth and said to me: "I am the man of lead and I suffer intolerable violence."† Upon this, seized with great fear, I awoke and sought in myself the reason for this fact. I reflected again and said to myself: What I understood by that is that it's necessary to reject lead; the vision is really about composition of liquids.[10]

---

*Agathodaimon was a popular protective deity in Graeco-Roman Egypt, associated with good fortune and good harvests. He appears as a teacher of the art in Zosimos's works, and as a familial colleague of Hermes Trismegistos in the Hermetica. As we learn Agathodaimon is the "man of lead" a little later, the white hair "whitened by the years" may not only imply a whitening process, but also Saturn, "bringer of old age" whose metal is lead.

†Berthelot thought this might signify calcination of the white litharge (natural mineral form of lead oxide), which changes it into a red minium (naturally occurring form of lead tetroxide). Maybe it's also about cupellation (metallurgical refining process).

That last phrase suggests by its abruptness that it's an interpolation, for in the Berthelot-Ruelle running order, the first and second lessons are interrupted by "explanations" in not very apposite style, where the different figures are taken directly as mineral processes, probably added later, and almost certainly not by Zosimos. They seem a little too *specific* (and prosaic) to be true, and are most likely speculative. It's obvious Zosimos was *alluding* to process, but why bother to create such interesting narratives merely to follow them with recipe information? Why not just put the recipes down? Well, the obvious answer is that he wanted readers to gain more understanding by blending in startling fashion mythical, symbolic elements with physical ones to show an underlying unity and spiritual purpose to the art, which could easily be otherwise missed. "What is the true import of what we do here?" he is asking, and puts himself in the position of someone confused or in the dark who needs enlightening. And a classic way to attain enlightenment or guidance is to bypass daily consciousness and receive dream messages. Indeed, it is Zosimos's continual complaint that the deeper and higher meaning of the art—and of life itself (which the art mirrors)—is neglected or perverted by those wishing to deceive either themselves, or buyers of wares, and who in staying in the sublunary or terrestrial realm merely encourage deception by daimons of limited knowledge. They are, as it were, not prepared to sacrifice, or make sacred, their part in the art and are therefore not transformed by it. They cheapen the processes and themselves, and far from rising to the golden and the pure, descend to the leaden and a blackness from which they have, by their conduct, eschewed hope of release.

Here beginneth lesson gamma:

Again I noticed the divine and sacred altar in the form of a flask, and I saw a priest clothed in a white (robe) falling to his feet, who was celebrating these frightful mysteries, and I said: "What is this?" And he replied, "This is the priest of the sanctuaries. It is he who has the custom of bloodying the bodies, making the eyes clear, and raising the dead." Then, falling again (to the ground), I fell asleep again. And it came to pass, as I went up the fourth degree, that I saw (someone) coming from the east, having a sword in his hand. Another, behind him, carried a circular object, of a dazzling whiteness, and very beautiful to see, called Meridian of Cinnabar. [In Paris manuscript 2327 this is represented by a circle with a point in middle, like the sun and, later, gold.] As I approached the place of chastisement, he told me that he who held a gladius must cut off his head, sacrifice his body, and cut his flesh into pieces, that his flesh might first be boiled in the apparatus, and then they were carried to the place of punishment.

When I woke up again, I said (to myself): I understood correctly; it concerns liquids in the art of metals. He who carried the gladius said again, "You have accomplished the ascent of the seven degrees." The other resumed, at the same time that he allowed all the liquids to dissolve the lead (?)*: "Art is accomplished."[11]

It is possible that the "fourth degree" refers to the fourth "planet," the sun, as it was observed to move fourth fastest in its "sphere," after the moon (the speediest), Mercury, and Venus. As the sun's metal is gold, the allusion would be to Zosimos's approach to completion. This would chime in with the "Meridian of Cinnabar," the meridian being the point when the sun is at its height. It may be that in the red of the cinnabar (mercury sulfide) we see a stage of reddening, and in the sun at its meridian we move to the yellowing. The two characters may represent a copper-lead alloy that is to be treated and made gold. The figures come from the east, where the sun rises: doubtless symbolic of an approach of noetic light. The planets also appear in the east and having risen to the meridian, descend: the metals risen must descend

---

*Berthelot thought this might refer to absorption of molten litharge through the sides of the flask. The text may be corrupt.

into the blackness as the sun rises. For Zosimos, the art is cosmic and supra-cosmic; an analogy of eternal redemption. Like the ouroboros, the process is cyclic and is repeated, for the priest at the end who is to be beheaded is the one who appeared in the first lesson, describing his having been flayed and burned in fire. So the narrative returns to its beginning: alpha to omega, which is alpha again; the beginning and the end is the beginning—art is accomplished.

SIX

Zosimos III

From Omega *to the* Final Quittance

THE BULK OF WHAT SURVIVES of the Survivor consists of Zosimos's advice to Theosebeia, most of it purely practical. He is very keen to correct anyone she may have been taking instruction from, particularly, as we have seen, priest Neilos and female practitioner Paphnutia the virgin. In doing so, he equates the perfect dye with perfection of the spirit, inner peace, knowledge of God, and liberty from self-deception or deception by unnatural, daimonic contact, or just ill-informed methods, which he demolishes by resorting to the works of Mary, "Democritus," Moses, Cleopatra, Chymēs, and Pebichius, whom he insists are genuine, anciently established authorities, coupled with his own extensive experience. To demonstrate that Zosimos is anything but habitually allegorizing, symbolizing, or given to obscurity, let's hear some extracts from his treatise *On the Action of Yellowing.*

3. Mary (places) on the front line molybdochalkos [alloy of copper and lead] and the (procedures of) manufacturing processes. The burning operation (is) what all the elders advocate. Mary, the first, said: "Copper burned with sulfur, treated with natron oil, and taken again after having undergone the same treatment several times, becomes excellent gold and without shadow. This is what God says:

118

Know all that, according to experience, if you burn the copper first, sulfur produces no effect. But when you (first) burn the sulfur, then not only does it make copper spotless, but it brings it closer to gold." Mary, in the description below the figure, proclaims it a second time, and says: "This has been graciously revealed to me by God, to know that copper is first burned with sulfur, then with the body of magnesia [white mineral: magnesium carbonate]; and one blows it until the sulfurous parts escape with the shadow: (then) the copper becomes without shadow."

4. It's thus that all burns. Thus in Moses's chemistry [Greek, *maza;* see page 79] one burns with sulfur, salt, alum, and sulfur (I mean white sulfur). Thus again Chymēs burns in many places, above all when he operates with celandine [yellow plant of the buttercup family]. Thus in Pebichius, the operation of burning in laurel wood is revealed enigmatically and by periphrase; his laurel leaves signifying white sulfur. Such is the explanation concerning measures to be taken.

5. Here is what Mary said, here and there, in a thousand places: "Burn our copper with sulfur, and after having been revived, it will be without shadow." Not only does she know how to burn it with white sulfur but also to whiten it and make it without shadow. It is also with the (sulfur) that Democritus burns, whitens, and renders without shadow. And again, "they not only burn the yellow sulfur, but they make the metal without shadow and yellowing." Here is what Democritus says: "Saffron has the same action as steam; as well as casia compared to cinnamon." In Moses's chemistry, toward the end, similarly, there is this text: "Sprinkle with native sulfur water; it will become yellow and without shadow"; that is, obviously, burnt. . . .

7. Such is the act of burning the bodies; such is the explanation concerning the actions. The burning action is called bleaching [whitening]; for sulfur, this act is called bleaching and destruction of the shadow. Bleaching is even called iosis and refining is also a bleaching. The act of burning is again called yellowing; the

destruction of shadow, yellowing; and iosis, yellowing. The prophet Chymēs, exclaimed enthusiastically: "After the projections [adding ingredients], we must make it yellow and without shadow." Then we shall explain the process relating to divine water and to iosis or decomposition.[1]

Sometimes fragments in the Byzantine and later alchemical codices contain material whose attribution to Zosimos is uncertain. Titles of treatises can be intriguing, only to fizzle out or reappear in another manuscript codex without attribution. For example, *Authentic memoirs on Divine Water* does not appear under Zosimos's name in the *Codex Marcianus,* but it does appear in Paris manuscript 2325 (thirteenth century), where it immediately precedes mystical axioms on the "All" derived from the *Chrysopoeia of Cleopatra.* For some reason, Zosimos scholar Michèle Mertens used the title *Authentic Memoirs* to group together *On the Apparatus and Furnaces; Authentic Commentaries on the Letter Omega* and *On Excellence* (or *Virtue*). As *Authentic Memoirs on Divine Water* is positioned in Berthelot's collection (vol. 2), these Zosimian memoirs contain a mere eleven lines, and while perhaps not authentic, they are striking, for the polyvalent focus on the "divine mercurius" will become a principal theme of spiritual and practical alchemy, also discernible in certain Gnostic apocrypha.

1. This is the divine and great mystery; the object we seek. This is the All. From him (comes) the All, and through him (exists) the All.* Two natures, one sole essence [Greek, *duo phuseis, mia ousia;*

---

*This phrase is startlingly similar to logion 77, Gospel of Thomas: "Jesus said, 'It is I who am the light which is above them all. *It is I who am the all. From me did the all come forth, and unto me did the all extend.* Split a piece of wood, and I am there. Lift up the stone, and you will find me there" (translated by. Thomas O. Lambdin; my italics). The Christ-Mercurius-Lapis (Stone) identification emerges as a significant motif in late medieval and Renaissance alchemy; it is perhaps lodged in early alchemical tradition, or was inferred from it (see chapter 10).

see pages 253–55 on Hermetic source of *homoousios* (same substance, or same essence) in post-Nicene trinitarianism]; for one attracts one; and one dominates one. This is silver water [indicating, according to Berthelot, philosopher's mercury and ordinary mercury], the hermaphrodite, which always flees, which is attracted to its own elements. It is the divine water, which everyone has ignored, whose nature is difficult to contemplate; for it is neither a metal, nor water always in motion, nor a (metallic) body; it is not dominated.

2. It is the All in all things; it has life and spirit and is destructive. He who understands this possesses gold and silver. The power has been hidden, but it is recovered [drawn back?] in erotylos* [Greek, *anachaitai de tōi erōtulōi*].[2]

There's much to learn about late antiquity from Zosimos. For example, whence might we think practitioners obtained ocher pigments?

---

*Berthelot adds that *Erotylos* appears in Leiden Papyrus W (predominantly magical and Judaeo-Gnostic); see CAAG, vol. 1, introduction, p. 17. But the word has no capital *E* in the Greek in Zosimos's treatise and is therefore not a name! Berthelot improperly capitalized the word in the French translation: quite an error. According to Emilio Suárez de la Torre ("Pseudepigraphy and Magic," in *Fakes and Forgers of Classical Literature: Ergo decipiatur!* Edited by Javier Martínez, 249 [Leiden: Brill, 2014]), in a text from "Leiden Papyrus J 395," attributed to Moses, three "Orphic" names are used "to reinforce the efficacy of a magical invocation to have a "systasis" [union] with a god"—Orpheus, Erotylos (author of *Orphika,* according to PGM 13, 933–47), and Hieros (PGM 13, 954). This is a blind alley. In fact, the erotylos is a gem valuable to divination according to "Democritus (page 129)" in William Borlase's *Observation on the Antiquities, Historical and Monumental, of the County of Cornwall* (Oxford: W. Jackson, 1754), 173. More pertinently, Pliny's *Natural History,* ch. 58, refers to gemstone the *erotylos* (possibly meaning "love stone"), also known as *amphicomos* (fine-haired) and *hieromnemon* (skilled in sacred matters) as one highly praised by Democritus for utility in divination. I suspect this stone is what is being referred to and what was confused in the Leiden Papyrus text with an imagined author, for there exists no other reference to a writer of the name, whereas the context of Democritus and stones is entirely apposite. The likelihood is that erotylos was a stone from which mercury could be extracted, possibly by heating a sulfide ore with air combining with the sulfur to form sulfur dioxide, with mercury liberated at a temperature above its boiling point (compare "lift up the stone and you will find me there," Gospel of Thomas 77).

Zosimos tells us, but first you have to realize he uses the same word, *ocher,* both for what ocher pigment came from and what it was called, which can be confusing. In ancient times, the orange pigment was derived from realgar, the arsenic sulfide mineral. It's also helpful to know that when he discusses the "rubric," though we naturally think of a "heading," in fact our word *rubric* comes from the Latin for "red chalk" or red ocher (*rubrica*) because red-colored letters were used to head new sections of manuscripts. Zosimos also makes it clear that readers of recipes should be aware that words do not always mean what they appear to mean. To say the art suffered from "terminological exactitude" at this stage in its development is an understatement! Hear Zosimos *On the Preparation of Ocher.*

1. The preparation of ocher is done in the (neighboring) mountain of the Adriatic Sea. There are crevices in the mountain; through the crevices one sees layers of ocher [realgar] in plates. Ocher is also produced in Babylon in the mountains. We see the ocher in the cracks; we remove it and we cook it: we thus obtain the rubric, which we still call minium of Sinope [because minium, or lead tetroxide, is a vivid red]. We do not use this rubric, or this minium of Sinope. But the ocher indicated above is the real dye; unless the metal proposed to be dyed is the body of the magnesia, or the black lead [probably lead].

2. As to what rank is to be assigned to it, apart from the subjects of tinctures, all the writings explain themselves on this point. If you therefore want to rank it, that is where you will find the desired result; especially if you follow Mary and the Philosopher [Democritus]. The Philosopher mentions pyrites, cinnabar, claudianon, cadmia, androdamas, chrysocolla. He says that it is appropriate to get things done on molybdochalkos, cinnabar, or the body of magnesia, a substance that is called black lead. If now you come to the chrysopoeia, you will see which (substances) break down tin, iron, or copper: they are cinnabar and white litharge [possibly basic

lead carbonate: hydrocerussite]. In your turn, understand what you are looking for: by magnesia, understand molybdochalkos; by lead, it is (again) molybdochalkos. When they talk about argyropoeia [silver-making] or chrysopoeia [gold-making], they hear molybdochalkos; that's the product they process, then submit (to dye). At the right time, they fix it, after having broken it up; then they bleach, or yellow, the hardened metal with them.[3]

Zosimos expatiates a little more on this theme in *On the Treatment of the Metallic Body of Magnesia* before launching a full-scale tirade at Theosebeia and what he perceives as her ignorant instructors as compared with the infinitely more reliable "elders" or "ancients."

2. Did we not recall in the seventh book [presumably one of Zosimos's lost works], when speaking of red cobathia [*cobathia,* Greek word for the poisonous smoke of white arsenic oxide when arsenic ores were roasted in air; "red cobathia" is an arsenical compound], that we must first learn of what magnesia the philosophers speak? If it is simple (magnesia) from Cyprus or compound magnesia obtained by our art? Indeed, by moving away from simple magnesia, they want to speak of the compound [molybdochalkos: lead/copper compound]; but at the same time they heard the simple. It is in this way that the art has been hidden by the double sense attributed to denominations.

7. But you, O blessed one, renounce these vain elements, whose ears are disturbed; for I say that you converse with Paphnutia the virgin and certain men without instruction. The things you hear them say are vain, and you begin to make meaningless reasoning. Renounce the society of people who have a blind mind and too fiery an imagination. We must pity these people and listen to the language of truth, from the mouths of men worthy to proclaim it. These people do not want help; they cannot bear to be instructed by masters, flattering themselves to be masters (themselves). They claim

to be honored for their vain and empty (meaningless) reasoning. When one wants to teach them the degrees of truth, they do not support the knowledge of art, and they do not digest (it). They want gold rather than reason. Heated by extreme dementia, they become incapable of reasoning and cannot wait for wealth. Indeed, if they were guided by reason, gold would accompany them and be in their power: for reason is the master of gold. He who attaches himself to it, who desires it and joins himself to it, will find the gold placed before us, in the midst of the twists that keep it hidden.

8. Reason is the indicator of all the goods, as was said somewhere. Philosophy is the knowledge of the truth and reveals the things that are. Whoever accepts reason will see by it the gold placed before (his) eyes. But those who do not support reason constantly walk in emptiness and undertake the most ridiculous acts. Thus did Nilus provoke laughter, this priest your friend, who cooked the molybdochalkos in a field oven (as if he had baked bread), working with cobathia [smoke] for a whole day. Blinded by corporeal eyes, he did not think that his process was bad, but he blew; and leaving (the product) after the cooling, he showed only ashes. When asked where the bleaching was, embarrassed, he said he had penetrated into the depth. He put on copper, he dyed the slag; for the copper being stopped by no solid, passed over and disappeared in the depth. Similarly for the bleaching of magnesia. Having heard these things (from the mouths) of his adversaries, Paphnutia was turned into a laughingstock; and you shall be, too, if you fall into the same dementia. Embrace for me Nilus, the one who cooks with cobathia, and be fully edified on the economy of the body of magnesia.[4]

Zosimos's highly informative harangues on Theosebeia's straying from the path occupy much of the remains of his treatise *On the Apparatus and Furnaces,* but in the order we've inherited, we're first greeted by a paragraph referring to its title extension: *Authentic Commentaries on the letter Ω* (omega). Omega is the last letter of the Greek alphabet, and this may once have been the opener for a book for Theosebeia divided into sections, taking each Greek letter as title and associative guide. The Byzantine *Suda* compendium asserts such a work was accomplished; we don't know if it ever was or whether completion was assumed on account of the survival of several Zosimos treatises that fit the description. We also have numerous Zosimos treatises in Syriac with Syriac single letters added to their titles (or subtitles).

On the Apparatus and Furnaces, Authentic Commentaries on the letter Ω may once have been two separate works. As it stands, it opens thus:

> 1. Element Ω is round, formed of two parts: it belongs to the seventh zone, that of Saturn in the language of corporeal beings; for in the language of the incorporeals there is another thing that must not be revealed. Nicotheus alone knows (it), he the hidden character. Now, in the language of corporeal beings, this element is called the ocean, the origin and seed of all the gods. Such are the fundamental principles of the language of bodily beings. Under the name of this great and admirable element Ω, one understands the description of the apparatuses for divine water, that of all simple and engineered furnaces, that of all, absolutely speaking.[5]

Berthelot notes, "This multiplicity of mystical languages, in which the same meaning is expressed in different words, while the same sign has several meanings, is found in Leiden Papyrus V [about occult properties of plants]. The Cabbala is also based on similar conventions."[6] As omega is the last letter of the alphabet, so Saturn is the last of the planetary spheres surrounding Earth before the Ogdoad (fixed stars), as discussed in chapter 5 (page 112). According to Garth Fowden, Nicotheus—"apparently of Jewish-gnostic background"— is mentioned in Porphyry's *Life of Plotinus* (16) as alleged author of one of a series of "revelations" produced by people who claimed (improperly, according to Porphyry) to be followers of Egyptian

Neoplatonist philosopher Plotinus. Apart from Nicotheus, the other revealers named by Porphyry were Zoroaster, Zostrianus, Allogenes, Messus, and "other people of this kind."[7] The Nag Hammadi library of Gnostic writings includes works titled *Zostrianos* and *Allogenes* ("Another Race," or "Seed," or "Alien"), while "Messus" may be identical with Nag Hammadi text *Marsanes,* which is certainly akin to the other two ascent discourses, purportedly revealing beings beyond this world, whose content fits what Zosimos is getting at; namely, that the life of such incorporeals is known only through privileged revelation. This gives further insight into Zosimos's personal syncretic, gnostic eclecticism, which, infused into his alchemy, has enjoyed extremely long-lasting consequences.

On Destiny, Fate, Worldly Thought, and Noetic Understanding

In attempting to guide Theosebeia into producing the right dyes profitably, Zosimos reveals a great deal about his beliefs, beliefs that he really *sees* reflected in the chemical processes. The essence of this simultaneous two-dimensional or two-world practice seems to come from devotion to the works of Mary, notably in her distinguishing "bodies" from "spirits," and applying these conceptions to developmental processes, particularly distillation. As a general rule at the time, that which partook of invisibility was spiritual, and because the invisible could be made manifest (in condensation, for example), then the visible and invisible worlds were bound as one, even though body and spirit were distinct in quality and virtue when in those states. The ideal of late antique philosophy in Alexandria was to flee, and be willing to flee, the perishable world altogether and to return to pure spirit, back home with the divine ideas. The same kind of aspiration, for Zosimos, was to be applied to the making of perfect dyes. For him, the issue was one of truth, and truth came from God.

2. Zosimos (addressing himself to) Theosebeia, expresses this to her in good will. (The exposure of) suitable dyes, O woman, has made a mockery of my book on furnaces. Indeed, many (writers), filled with benevolence for their own genius, mocked the proper dyes, and they looked at the book on furnaces and appliances as not being true. No speech can persuade them of the truth, if it is not inspired by their own [self-assessed] genius. By a fatal destiny, what they had received, they turned it to evil in their language, to the detriment of art and their own success, the same words being unfortunately turned in two (opposing) senses. It was with difficulty that, compelled by the necessity of demonstrations, they granted some point, even about the things they had previously understood. But such authors must not be approved, neither by God nor by philosophers. For the times (of operations) being designated in the last detail, and after the Genius has favored them in the corporeal order, [in the operation of regenerating metallic bodies] they refuse to grant another point, forgetting all the obvious things that precede. Everywhere they had to obey destiny, for things already said and for their opposites, without being able to imagine anything else, relative to corporeal beings; (I say) nothing other but the fatal order of destiny. The men of this species, Hermes, in the treatise on the Natures, called them fools, fit only to carry out destiny, but unable to understand anything of the incorporeal things, or even to conceive the destiny that leads them with justice. But they insult his teachings on corporeal beings, and they indulge in imaginations alien to their own happiness.[8]

The Hermetica provide ample support for those last two sentences. Indeed, much of what Zosimos has to say stands as a kind of commentary on the texts attributed to Hermes Trismegistos, such as the following passages in tract no. 4 in which Hermes speaks of those attached exclusively to the corporeal.

These people have sensations much like those of unreasoning animals, and, since their temperament is willful and angry, they feel no awe of things that deserve to be admired; they divert their attention to the pleasures and appetites of their bodies; and they believe that mankind came to be for such purposes. But those who participate in the gift that comes from god, O Tat [Hermes's disciple], are immortal rather than mortal if one compares their deeds, for in a mind of their own they have comprehended all—things on earth, things in heaven, and even what lies beyond heaven. Having raised themselves so far, they have seen the good and, having seen it, they have come to regard the wasting of time here below as a calamity. They have scorned every corporeal and incorporeal thing, and they hasten toward the one and only. This, Tat, is the way to learn about mind [nous], to (resolve perplexities) in divinity and to understand god.[9]

Zosimos's argument against fruitless practice hinges on the word *destiny,* for the works of the corporeal world fall under the sway of zodiacal powers, whereas the true philosopher is superior to fate, not because he or she transgresses fate—the "way of the world"—but because the true philosopher's mind is governed by spiritual *nous,* which is outside of the self and of the heavenly realms, partaking in uncorrupted truth. The essence of the art, Zosimos has explained, came originally from heaven but was corrupted, as we heard him explain elsewhere, when purloined by priests in thrall to daimons. So Zosimos is saying that the bad exponents Theosebeia has been listening to presume results require propitiation of the "times," that is, daimonic agents of the Fate-world—the zodiacal powers. Bad exponents abandon thereby both natural reason's accord with simple, natural processes, *and* the higher reason (*nous*) that inspires truth. One can see what it was in Mary's writings that appealed to Zosimos; she learned from God—fate or destiny being for the corporeal dimension only. One could say Zosimos is a dualist, but if so, it is not radical dualism but rather holistic, and the spirit, being higher, must dominate those desirous of rising beyond the realm of mixed fortune. This theme he now elucidates further:

3. Hermes and Zoroaster declared that the race of philosophers is superior to destiny. Indeed, they do not enjoy the happiness that comes from it. Dominating its pleasures, they are not afflicted by the evils she causes; living always in their interior, they do not accept the fine gifts she offers, because they see the unhappy end. It is for this reason that Hesiod [*Works and Days,* verse 86] presents Prometheus, giving advice to Epimetheus: "What happiness do men consider the greatest of all? A beautiful woman, they say, with a lot of money." He says that he receives no gift from Jupiter Olympian; but he rejects them, teaching his brother that he must reject, in the name of philosophy, the gifts of Jupiter; that is, the gifts of destiny.[10]

The joys fate apportions are fleeting and make the inevitable evils of fate harder, or even impossible, to bear. Worldly success and worldly failure are, as Rudyard Kipling wrote of triumph and disaster in his poem *If,* "two imposters" to be equally scorned. Security, like the sun, rises elsewhere.

5. Look at the picture that Cebes* drew, as well as the three times great Plato and the thousand times great Hermes; see how Thoth interprets the first hieratic word, he the first man, interprets all beings, and denominator of all bodily things. Now the Chaldeans, the Parthians, the Medes, and the Hebrews call him Adam, which means virgin land, bloody land, igneous land, and fleshly land. These things are found in the libraries of the Ptolemies, deposited

---

*Cebes of Thebes, philosophical devotee of Socrates; "his" work *Pinax* is considered a pseudonymous work of the first or second century CE.

in every shrine, especially at the Serapeum; (they were placed there) when Asenan, one of the chief priests of Jerusalem, sent Hermes,* who interpreted the entire Hebrew Bible into Greek and Egyptian.[11]

6. Thus the first man is called Toth among us, and among them, Adam; the name given by the voice of angels. It is symbolically designated by means of the four elements, which correspond to the cardinal points of the sphere, and saying that it relates to the body [formed by union of the four elements]. Indeed, the letter A of its name refers to the East (*Anatolē*) and Air (*Aēr*). The letter D denotes the setting of the sun (Δυσις = Dysis), which lowers because of its gravity. The letter M shows the Midday (*Mesembria* = meridian); that is to say, the fire of the cooking that produces the maturation of the bodies, the 4th zone and the middle zone. Thus the fleshly Adam, in its apparent form, is called Thoth; but the spiritual man contained in him (bears a proper name) and appellative. But we ignore for the present what this proper name is; for Nicotheus, this character that one can't find, alone knew these things. As for naming the appellative, it's this: φως (*phōs*, "light, fire"): this is why men are called φωτες (*phōtes*: "light-people," or human souls before entering the world).

7. When he was in Paradise in the form of light (*phōs*), subject to the inspiration of destiny, they persuaded him, taking advantage of his innocence and his incapacity for action, to put on the (persona of) Adam, the one who (was) subject to destiny, the one who (answers) to the four elements. He, because of his innocence, did not refuse; and they boasted of having enslaved (in him) the outer man. It is in this sense that Hesiod [compare *Theogony*, verses 521, 618] spoke of the chain with which Jupiter attached

---

*According to Berthelot, "Hermes" is intended here in its "generic meaning," according to which he was the author of all Egyptian works. The Greek translation of the Bible is explained otherwise than in the familiar story of the Septuagint (where seventy wise Jews fulfilled the task); Zosimos favors Egypt.

Prometheus. Then, after this chain, he sends him another one; (that is,) Pandora, which the Hebrews call Eve. Now, Prometheus and Epimetheus, he is one and the same man in the language of allegorics; it is the soul and the body. Prometheus is sometimes the image of the soul; sometimes (that) of the spirit. It is also the image of the flesh, because of the disobedience of Epimetheus, committed with regard to Prometheus, his own (brother).

Our intelligence says: The Son of God, who is almighty, and who becomes everything when he wants, manifests himself as he wants to everyone. Jesus Christ added himself to Adam and brought (him) back to Paradise, where mortals previously lived.[12]

The last two lines may be a later Christian interpolation to bring the meaning more in line with post-Nicene orthodoxy. On the other hand, the section following (8), which also refers to a redemptive theology of Jesus Christ, seems thoroughly imbued with the docetic strain of Christian gnosis that was decried by orthodox church fathers ("docetic" meaning that Christ only *seemed* to suffer, for his *inner being* was divinely impervious to suffering and corporeality). Furthermore, section 7 itself, which is leading up to 8 thematically, is *already* a conflation of the Hermetic story of the fall of man taken from *Corpus Hermeticum* 1 (12–14) with the more radical Christian Gnostic view of vicious archons enslaving man through jealousy of man's hidden spiritual potential (which the archons conspire to blind him to).

In the Hermetic myth (*Corpus Hermeticum* 1), God makes man with loving pride and introduces his beautiful creation to the demiurge or craftsman-mind who has made the universe below. The divine man looks down through the spheres, and seeing himself reflected in the waters far below, and being enamored of his own perfect reflected image in the corporeal water, breaks through the boundary vault, sinks down to created earth, whereupon the powers of nature fall in love with him in the manner of Narcissus, divesting man of power to return, for coming to earth involves a kind of amnesia regarding his true origin; *passion* is his undoing.

In Gnostic writings such as the Apocryphon (Secret Book) of John and the Second Treatise of the Great Seth, and other texts, the fall is considerably less harmoniously depicted, and something of these second- and third-century horrors Zosimos knows, for does he not here recount the cruel *boasting* of "they" who trick the light-man into being enslaved? In the aforementioned Sethian text, we read: "For Adam was a laughingstock, since he was made a counterfeit type of man by the Hebdomad [rulers of the seven spheres]." Indeed, one might speculate that Zosimos and "sister" Theosebeia may have been (or once had been) members of a Sethian community, or living in a context where the Sethian viewpoint was current. The "Great Seth" implies Jesus was a manifestation of the original, eternal Seth, righteous son of Adam, born to undo the horror of Cain and Abel. The "seed" (or race) of righteous Seth may easily have been identified with the Hermetic race who heeded the famous call to baptism in the free bowl of *nous* in *Corpus Hermeticum* 4.

Zosimos identifies the inner man, the "light," with the original spirit, which is not subjected to fate. When man "receives," or becomes aware of, divine spirit-mind, he or she awakes and sees the predicament of mortal men. The first thing to be recognized is how the great number of human beings live under the dominion of fate, and *that,* according to Zosimos, is the position of Theosebeia's advisers, and it is one from which Zosimos is determined to identify, isolate, and free her. The next section reveals the core of Zosimos's learned doctrine of spiritual liberation from fate and the earthly Adam.

8. He [the Son of God] appeared to men deprived of all power, having become man (himself), subject to suffering and beatings. (However), having secretly stripped his own mortal character, he felt (in reality) no suffering; and he had seemed to trample

on death and to push it back, for the present and until the end of the world: all this in secret. Thus stripped of appearances, he advised his followers also secretly to exchange their mind (or spirit) with that of the Adam which they had in them, to beat him and to put him to death, this blind man being led to compete with the spiritual and luminous man: it's thus that they kill their own Adam.[13]

It is somewhat staggering to read this flagrantly Gnostic interpretation of the Passion in the context of an alchemical treatise. In the Coptic Second Treatise of the Great Seth (second or third century CE), Jesus says he "visited a bodily dwelling." *That* was the sum of his relationship with the corporeal: *just passing through.*

I did not succumb to them as they had planned. But I was not afflicted at all. Those who were there punished me. And I did not die in reality but in appearance, lest I be put to shame by them because these are my kinsfolk. I removed the shame from me and I did not become fainthearted in the face of what happened to me at their hands. I was about to succumb to fear, and I "suffered" according to their sight and thought, in order that they may never find any word to speak about them. For my death, which they think happened, (happened) to them in their error and blindness, since they nailed their man unto their death. For their Ennoias did not see me, for they were deaf and blind. But in doing these things, they condemn themselves. Yes, they saw me; they punished me. It was another, their father, who drank the gall and the vinegar; it was not I. They struck me with the reed; it was another, Simon, who bore the cross on his shoulder. It was another upon whom they placed the crown of thorns. But I was rejoicing in the height over all the wealth of the archons and the offspring of their error, of their empty glory. And I was laughing at their ignorance.[14]

"*They nailed their man unto their death*," to which we may add Zosimos's "*it's thus that they kill their own Adam*" and see the meaning of the riddle, at least to Zosimos. We find the same message in the Apocalypse of Peter, also from the Coptic Nag Hammadi codices, where "Peter" envisions events of the Passion in the company of the "living Jesus."

> When he had said those things, I saw him seemingly being seized by them. And I said "What do I see, O Lord? That it is you yourself whom they take, and that you are grasping me? Or who is this one, glad and laughing on the tree? And is it another one whose feet and hands they are striking?"
>
> The Savior said to me, "He whom you saw on the tree, glad and laughing, this is the living Jesus. But this one into whose hands and feet they drive the nails is his fleshly part, which is the substitute being put to shame, the one who came into being in his likeness. But look at him and me."
>
> But I, when I had looked, said "Lord, no one is looking at you. Let us flee this place."[15]

No one was looking at the living Jesus: in Zosimos's terms, they were under thrall of the corporeal vision, not the incorporeal vision. This division of corporeal and incorporeal is at the root of Zosimos's polemic to Theosebeia and of the philosophical Hermetica.

In the next section we learn that "these things are done" until the demon "Antimimos" comes. This idea of a counterfeit son of God recalls doctrines associated with Persian Manichaeism, which was gathering pace in the late third century: something else to add to the eclectic mix of burgeoning encratism, or hatred of the body, growing in the religious culture of the late third century. This Antimimos is jealous of those who've abandoned their outer "Adam" for the true Son of God, who've immolated their "mortal spirits" and belong where they were before the world's creation. We learn that Antimimos will come out of

Persia, directing men according to destiny with discourses "full of errors and fables." In section 10 we're informed that "these things are spoken only by the Hebrews, as well as by the sacred books of Hermes on the luminous man and on the son of God, his guide: on the earthly Adam and on Antimimos his guide, who says to himself, by blasphemy and error, the son of God."[16]

What next follows posits a problem, for the discourse we have returns suddenly to the account begun in section 7 regarding the Greek "earthly Adam Epimetheus" (as against the allegorical inner light or fire of Prometheus chained), which account was apparently interrupted by that next paragraph referring to Jesus, Son of God: the one that felt like an interpolation.

Could the entire Gnostic, arguably "Sethian," section be an alien interpolation? Or is it internally consistent?

It's very hard to be certain, because the Sethian analysis does explain at another level alleged antipathy between the inner being and the corporeal "coat" that relates to the *heimarmēnē* (zodiacal destiny) and all created, fated life below. The problem is that it is a big thing to see Zosimos, father figure of alchemy, as a Sethian Gnostic or something very much like it. And while the Sethian interpretation of the Passion, for example, is consistent with some aspects of the philosophical Hermetica on things spiritual and things of the body, it has been much more acceptable to see Zosimos, as Garth Fowden does, as a Hermetic luminary rather than "tainted" directly by the condemnation of "heretic," because Hermes, despite being a pagan prophet, found supporters in the orthodox communion, such as church historian Lactantius, whereas the Sethian Gnostics were, and are, outside the blessing of both orthodox fathers and good Platonists like Plotinus and Porphyry. Nevertheless, the possibility must be considered, especially in the context of the plethora of eclectic syncretism pervading both Alexandria and the Thebaid in the third century, of which Zosimos of Panopolis was such an imaginatively cardinal exemplar. One thing is certain: if there was an alien interpolation, it certainly did *not* come from the pen of an orthodox cleric-scholar of the Byzantine period. It is certainly contemporary to the late third and early fourth centuries.

Be that as it may, our text picks up on Zosimos's criticism of earthly Adam Epimetheus, who neglected his brother's advice to refuse Jupiter's gifts but resolves all with repentance and access to the "happy region" and those "who have a spiritual understanding. But those who have only a corporeal understanding belong to destiny; they admit or confess nothing else."[17]

Section 11 returns to the central issue of dyes, asserting that those who succeed "by chance" or the fortunes of Fate simply gabble, and attributes success to the horoscope of the practitioner, which makes some more fit than others. Zosimos observes that in all arts success may go to people who have the same equipment but are differently equipped in intelligence. A less intellectually gifted person may find success. This is another bugbear of Zosimos: that which makes him critical of Aristotle on the basis that Aristotle's learning was, for all its impressive scope, worldly, blind to the spiritual and higher dimensions of truth that transcend the reason of the world. Worldly brilliance may make for a fool.

Zosimos's cure is to follow the good books, even *his,* for even an inexperienced doctor may mend a leg by following rigidly a very good book on the subject. Just as no one is resigned to die for lack of a priest with medical skills, so no one should succumb to the "incurable disease" of poverty if they trouble to learn and practice the proper technique with furnaces. If they did so; they would triumph over poverty—which, Zosimos says amusingly, brings him to his subject, which is furnaces, about which Theosebeia had written to him for information. And with furnaces we are properly reminded that the purpose of the dyes, apart from gaining spiritual insight, was to make a good commercial living, and thus obtain gold and silver. Even so, Zosimos strikes a modest, realistic, and funny closing note.

I was surprised to see that you write to obtain from me the knowledge of things that are not to be known; have you not heard the Philosopher, when he said: "These things I have purposely ignored, because they are amply described in my other writings"? Yet thou wilt learn them from me; believe not that my writing is more trustworthy than that of the elders [ancient authorities], and know that I could not (surpass them). But so that we may hear all that has been said by them, I will tell you what I know. This is what it is.[18]

The First Book of Zosimos the Theban's Final Account

This remarkable work opens with promise: "Here finds itself confirmed the book of Truth. Zosimos to Theosebeia, hail!" All the realm of Egypt depends, Zosimos reminds her, on two arts: suitable dyes, and minerals. Here is blatant confirmation that we are looking, if darkly, into an industrial setting, not a sacerdotal one. Zosimos says that like the liberal arts, these arts have required guardians to survive. Without kings, learning would not have been preserved. Hence, he argues, that learning was not without strict controls: a minter of coins could not mint for himself. "Likewise also, under the Egyptian kings, the craftsmen of the art of cooking [furnace work], and those who had knowledge of the ways, did not work for themselves; but they did work for the kings of Egypt, and worked for their treasures. They had particular leaders placed at their head, and great was the tyranny exercised in the art of cooking, not only in itself but also in regard to the gold mines. Because as far as the search is concerned, it was a rule among the Egyptians that a written authorization was required."[19]

The secrets of the tinctures were not exposed, and there was a technical distinction between "suitable dyes" and working on minerals. Those running the city markets and who collected royal taxes could have executed anyone who manipulated the tinctures without proper authority. Only in Democritus, among the ancients, had Zosimos found anything clear about the substances required for manufacturing appropriate dyes, but even there, a great deal was not explained about the products of treatments, especially with regard to yellowing, or the body of yellow magnesia, and of yellow mercury. Zosimos says Democritus presented enigmas to make people learn.

The disquisition continues into realms we have explored already; namely, how priests in league with unnatural forces tied their unnaturally produced dyes to the worship of daimons, while the secrets of the naturally produced dyes were fully hidden from the eyes of those whose sound character deserved them.

One might see a certain contradiction here in that the treatise opened with what looked like a defense of strict controls and secrecy with regard to tincture manufacture, only for him then to associate sacerdotal secrecy with blackest spiritual corruption. Perhaps Zosimos's stress is on the fact that the art was held to be of great value and at least, until perverted, the old controls kept standards high and poor or perverted practice down. In other words, the art flourished, whereas when the true secrets were hidden, the art sank. He may have been making a case that the destiny of the realm depended on the attitude toward the art. If the art flourished under benign, if strict, control, then so, too, would the state in all its dimensions.

He is, of course, building up to his identification of the perverted unnatural, pseudo-secret tinctures with the "false prophet" who is misleading Theosebeia: "Even so, O woman, they [the daimons] want to gain you to their cause, through the intermediary of their false prophet [Neilos?]; they flatter you; being hungry, (they covet) not only sacrifices, but also your soul."[20]

Zosimos follows this dire warning with some spiritual advice that rings as true today as it did 1,700 years ago.

> Do not let yourself be deceived, O woman, as I explained to you in
> the book on Action. Do not delude yourself in seeking God, but
> sit at your home, and God will come to you, who is everywhere;

he is not confined to the lowest place, like the demons. Rest your body, calm your passions, resist desire, pleasure, anger, grief, and the twelve fatalities of death. In directing yourself thus, you will call to yourself the divine being, and the divine being will come to you, who is everywhere and nowhere. Without being called, offer sacrifices: not those (sacrifices) advantageous to these men, and destined to nourish them and to their delight; but (sacrifices) that distance them and destroy them, such as those advocated by Membres [?], addressing Solomon, King of Jerusalem, and chiefly such as those described by Solomon himself, according to his own wisdom. By doing so, you will obtain suitable, authentic, and natural dyes. Do these things until you become perfect in your soul. But when you recognize that you have arrived at perfection, then dread (the intervention) of the natural elements of matter: and hastening toward Poimenandres [*sic*] and receiving baptism in the mixing bowl [*krater*, see *Corpus Hermeticum* 4.4], hasten up toward your own race.[21]

Now this is not only good advice, and brings together very neatly indeed Zosimos's polemic with the core of the Hermetic philosophical corpus's evangel, but it also reveals the plain process of what I called earlier, rather facetiously, "alchemical yoga," or really, yoga simply. *Yoga* means "union," and the union most to be desired is union with God, or what Hindu sages have called "samadhi." The recommendation to sit at home, rest the *body* (so its endless fidgets cease), and systematically calm the passions, until the divine being comes, conforms precisely to Aleister Crowley's amusing "concise compendium of initiated instruction" as regards yoga, namely:

SIT DOWN
SHUT UP
STOP THINKING
GET OUT

ᴀ

Magus Crowley had been impressed by a method emanating from an
Indian gnostic in late Victorian times who had studied Sufism and
other religious traditions and come up with a sort of synthesis of
"jnana" or *knowledge* yoga. It involved the usual discipline for sitting
still, and stilling the mind, and directed the yogi to enter as *spirit*
of Brahman through the crown chakra (meaning "wheel") at the top
of the head, descending through the supposed energy centers of the
body (including forehead, throat, heart, solar plexus, stomach, and
fundament), and, as it were, cleansing or spiritualizing each before
shooting back up from "kundalee" at the base of the spine back to the
crown, spiritually renewed (details are in my book *Aleister Crowley in
India*). Crowley obtained "knowledge and conversation of his Holy
Guardian Angel" in an analogous manner; his divine being came to
him in 1906. We may also reflect on the seven traditional chakras, or
wheels, and their relation to the seven classical planets through which
Zosimos has to rise in his vision, and in the first Hermetic tractate,
through which the pupil of Poimandres must rise.

> [24] "You have taught me all things well, O mind, just as I wanted.
> But tell me again (about) the way up; tell me how it happens."
> To this Poimandres said: "First, in releasing the material body
> you give the body itself over to alteration, and the form that you
> used to have vanishes. To the demon you give over your tempera-
> ment, now inactive. The body's senses rise up and flow back to
> their particular sources, becoming separate parts and mingling
> again with the energies. And feeling and longing go on toward
> irrational nature. [25] Thence the human being rushes up through
> the cosmic framework, at the first zone surrendering the energy
> of increase and decrease; at the second evil machination, a device
> now inactive; at the third the illusion of longing, now inactive; at
> the fourth the ruler's arrogance, now freed of excess; at the fifth

unholy presumption and daring recklessness; at the sixth the evil impulses that come from wealth, now inactive; and at the seventh zone the deceit that lies in ambush. [26] And then, stripped of the effects of the cosmic framework, the human enters the region of the Ogdoad; he has his own proper power, and along with the blessed he hymns the father. Those present there rejoice together in his presence, and, having become like his companions, he also hears certain powers that exist beyond the Ogdoadic region and hymn god with sweet voice. They rise up to the father in order and surrender themselves to the powers, and, having become powers, they enter into god. This is the final good for those who have received knowledge: to be made god.

"Why do you still delay? Having learned all this, should you not become guide to the worthy so that through you the human race might be saved by god?"

[27] As he was saying this to me, Poimandres joined with the powers. Then he sent me forth, empowered and instructed on the nature of the universe and on the supreme vision, after I had given thanks to the father of all and praised him. And I began proclaiming to mankind the beauty of reverence and knowledge: "People, earthborn men, you who have surrendered yourselves to drunkenness and sleep and ignorance of god, make yourselves sober and end your drunken sickness, for you are bewitched in unreasoning sleep."[22]

The parallel is remarkably consistent. As Hermes directs himself to guiding the human race, so Zosimos in section 9 of his treatise promises to come to the aid of Theosebeia's "inadequacy."

Coming gently down to earth, Zosimos returns to the subject of dyes with a summary.

These dyes have a clean nature. They result from the decomposition of products, sometimes numerous, sometimes in small numbers; they are manufactured in small furnaces, with glass vases, or in large and small crucibles: we thus operate in different appliances, by means of fires variously regulated. The test shows the goodness of the products obtained by following these various improvements. Here you have the demonstrations of the fires in the letter Ω, as well as those of all the things sought. This shall be my beginning, O woman in the purple robe.[23]

And with this, our fragment of Zosimos's *Final Quittance* ends.

SEVEN

What Did the First Alchemists Do?

WHEN WE TRY TO FOCUS on what our first alchemists actually did with their knowledge, scholarship has mostly speculated that practitioners owed primary attachment to the Egyptian temple system. However, there are serious shortcomings in that notion which prevent us from assuming such was the case. The Egyptian temple system had already slipped, and was slipping further into a long decline in Zosimos's time, with Egyptian Christian opposition rising in the fourth century, as temples limped along, sometimes neglected and suffering from disrepair as pagan sacrifices were intermittently forbidden by imperial law. Christianity eventually triumphed over paganism, with express state support, in the sixth century, especially under Byzantine emperor

Fig. 7.1. A curious tubular alembic (*Codex Parisinus Graecus* 2327, fol. 289v)

Justinian. Temple rites of any kind had apparently faded from most of Egypt by the beginning of the seventh century.

There has been much discussion about metallurgical skills fostered under what was called the House of Life, with senior priests ordering work undertaken by artisan-priests, with tinctural knowledge guarded by "prophets" high in the temple hierarchy, who kept dye secrets in dark and obscure places. It has proved tempting to place Zosimos within or in close proximity to the supposed system, such as being a teacher to those outside it.[1]

However, as far as Zosimos's own writings inform us—not to mention the somewhat anachronistic tendency to picture temple functions based on records of pre-Roman rule—Zosimos wanted nothing to do with the old system; Democritus and Mary were his chief written authorities. Zosimos wrote expressly against worship of statues, a practice condemned in Jewish and Christian accusations of idolatry. Zosimos accused priests of bamboozling people with the idea that statues exercised magical and spiritual powers. Daimons, he believed, were ultimately responsible for holding the uninformed in thrall to them. Priests were accused of encouraging people to believe the images were animated by powerful, magical spells from knowledge beyond the laity's reach: powers essential to a successful passage through death. In this sense, Zosimos was an intellectual iconoclast of the old temple system.

Zosimos makes it vividly clear that whereas in the past, tinctural knowledge had served the priestly system—and done so "wickedly" after that science was corrupted by priests in thrall to daimons (responding to empty temples)—and while some contemporary practitioners, such as Neilos, were still attached to the magical thinking behind those functions, Zosimos believed himself involved in applied, and profitable, natural science, producing effects for objects to be purchased for private use as inspiring ornaments or for civic display.

I reiterate my main point here. The most probable setting for Zosimos's work was independent industry devoted to high-end orna-

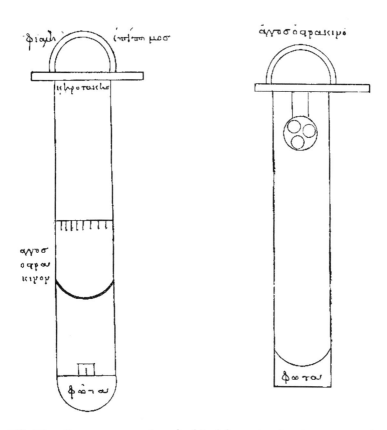

Fig. 7.2. Digestion apparatus in cylindrical form, in clay (*angos ostrakinon*; top right), placed on fire (*phōta*) (*Codex Marcianus*, folio 196v). Berthelot notes that the cylindrical apparatus was only employed by the most ancient alchemists; cylindrical objects are depicted only in *Codex Marcianus* and its derivatives (but not in Paris Mss. 2325, 2275, or 2327).

mental and textile commerce. When he described Theosebeia affectionately as "purple-robed," one might reasonably speculate that making purple dyes for textile industry was, given what we suspect, likely the lady's income source.

Evidence for these conclusions is enhanced by Syriac extracts from Zosimos's writings not found in the Byzantine corpus, translated into French by Rubens Duval in association with Marcellin Berthelot and published in 1893. Book 6 of the Syriac Zosimos extracts is titled

*Beginning of the book on the work of copper, letter vav.** It gives us a good idea of one of Zosimos's practical techniques, while being interspersed with his fascinating views on temple statues and germane philosophy.

> 1. The vav letter contains the doctrine on the cooking of copper, which is used in the operations of dyes. The first dyes are applied to silver and copper. Priests used these methods for their preparations, such as doubling and multiplying the metals. In the case of a gold dye, they were using it for the doubling of gold. If it was a silver dye, for the doubling of silver; if it was a copper dye, for the doubling of copper.
>
> Likewise, in proportion, for the multiplication of gold or silver; for the softening and rolling of metals.[2]

In section 2 we learn that techniques to render metals black can be applied to "images" (Duval notes the Syriac word could also mean "idols"), for statues, whether of birds, trees, fish, or animals, or indeed anything else required.

> 2. Manufacture of black metal blades, or Corinthian alloy.—One uses it for the work of images, or statues that one wants to make black. One operates equally on statues, or trees, or birds, or fish, or animals, or on any objects you'd like.
>
> Copper of Cyprus, a mine [or wealth]; silver, eight drachmas— that is to say—an ounce, gold, eight drachmas. Melt, and after melting, sprinkle with sulfur, twelve drachmas; untreated ammonia salt, twelve drachmas. Take and put in a cleaned vase, placing below the

---

*I am somewhat mystified by Duval's note to the "letter title" of the extract. He uses the Hebrew word *vav* for the letter in question (the Syriac equivalent being *waw,* sixth letter of the Syriac alphabet), and then shows the Syriac letter *kap* (equivalent of the Greek *kappa*). One would presume Zosimos would have used a Greek letter (as in the omega text), but it's unclear what that letter might have been given the appearance of Duval and Berthelot's vav.

ammonia salt. Then sprinkle with ammonia salt what was thrown. Allow to cool. Then take, heat, and immerse this preparation in vinegar, two half-heminas [*hēmina,* a measure of half a sextary; sextary = approximately an English pint]; lively black vitriol, eight drachmas: all for a copper mine [or wealth of copper]. If you want to operate on more or less, take the preparation in proportion, and let it cool in the ingredient.

Take, roll the metal, but do not roll it to the length of more than two fingers. Then heat, and every time you heat, plunge into the ingredient and remove the filth, so that it gives a radiance.

This copper will retain its blackness when it is ground and reduced to powder; when it is melted, it will also remain saturated with its black color.

3. Other preparation: with iron slag, black vitriol, sulfur, arsenic, aphronitron [aphrodite-nitron = washing soda], black of pitch smoke, bitumen, &c.

4. It is necessary to know how the treatment of coatings and enameling was done, according to the first book on the alterations of silver, its softening or blackening. This essential recipe was the main one for the elders [old authorities], and it was kept hidden. Not only was secrecy obligatory, but it was also prescribed by all the oaths that sanctioned its mystery.³

Pliny the Elder, who died in the famous eruption of Mount Vesuvius in 79 CE, remarked in his *Natural History* (33.46) on Egyptians blackening their works of silver. He opined it was a way of showing devotion to the god of the dead, Anubis (normally depicted with a black jackal's head). Pliny found it amazing that not only had the practice extended to Roman triumphal arches but also that bright silver afterward made black was valued more highly than glittering silver!

Picking up on the theme of the old secrecy surrounding the technique, Zosimos cannot help making his own position on priestly reserve plain, as well as a similar attitude adopted by anyone outside the priesthood possessing such technical knowledge. Zosimos doesn't justify such secrecy as being necessary for trade protection (trade secrets) but condemns it simply as mean vanity of self-inflation: considering oneself an elite, contrary to the Hermetic viewpoint that such passionate attachment to the pleasures of the body inhibited the spirit from rising to the divine realm.

> As we have said, the various symbols of the priests have been explained by the ancient masters and the various prophets, whose names became famous, and who prevailed with all the power of science. For myself, I have seen how much one suffers difficulty in obtaining these descriptions from envious people, because of the hope of vanity based on them, and the enjoyment they derive from it. But in this pleasure is also some torment, and this torment begets foolishness. The series of all wickednesses begins with envy: I speak of wickedness as they cannot be described in detail. Having thus seen the degree of their foolishness and their poverty of spirit, I have turned my face away from all these writings, and I have decided not to take them in hand and to no longer be concerned with oaths, jealousies, and excessive wickedness; I gave up interpreting them, without any jealousy on my part, because they are the product of passion.[4]

As far as seems plain, Zosimos does not share the Jewish objections enshrined in the second commandment against making graven images of living creatures of earth or heaven. While the Hebrew word for "image" usually has the connotation "idol," the emphasis against image-making in contemporary Jewish life was rooted in the fact that in the ancient world, images were made for worship or to depict deities, to humanize, materialize, or anthropomorphize them. The Jewish God is spiritual and beyond form. In Greek and Roman civilization, images were more often made to amuse or stimulate, or to celebrate, but that, too, fell under the ire of Jewish ethics connected to the body, worship of human beings, and sexual impurity. Jews were scandalized by pagan indifference to nudity. While Zosimos makes clear his own attitude to idolatry, he apparently sees nothing wrong with making images of ordinary men and women or good beings; for him, perhaps, a celebration of the wonder of creation and pleasure in creative life, pointing to the source of spiritual beauty reflected in the qualities of nature. Were he against color, as so many puritan zealots have been, he would hardly have stomached the very trade he was in: coloring and covering raw nature with human ingenuity. He appears to be well proud when a person sees the work and takes it for reality; imitating people or celebrating good principles with images is all right.

8. *To make an image of man, giving him colors.*—Operate by [Forming (?), the word is erased] a Phrygian figure [Greek *phantasia,* "appearance, from imagination"; "a fantasy"], significant to the eyes of those who will see it and who believe it is a living being. If you want to make it the color of a copper cauldron, mix with a part of Cyprus copper, having first melted the copper several times, until it becomes purple-colored. After you've filed it [or ground it], put it in with these quantities (of ingredients) that have been indicated to you.

9. *For the image of women.*—Gold, one part; silver, four parts. The mixture has the appearance of women's skin; it shines like a flash. Such it will be, when finished. Black images are also made with gold, silver, copper, and other mixtures. These are the mixtures and preparations about which we have told you, &c.[5]

As Zosimos continues his notes on dyes involving copper, note how he makes an exception of priestly use of secrets to make idols; this he is expressly against. He also castigates priests blaming outsiders for using the recipes, though Zosimos himself doesn't approve of persons bragging about secrets and causing envy. Besides, he says, everyone knows the secrets are in the books of Hermes and are, he implies, more or less available to those who seek them; he plainly holds these views in tension with a conviction that really, only the spiritually worthy should practice the art.

10. *Another preparation.*—Cyprus copper, magnesia, iron, acacia juice.

11. *Another:* Molten copper, iron, black vitriol, Judaean bitumen, arsenic, Indian or Scythian ink, sulfur without odor. The dye is called *pinosimos*. The tincture is intended for the surface; it includes all kinds of colors and metal types. White dye is one that penetrates, by means of an ingredient, into the depth of the body.

19. It's said that the book of this preparation was found by Tertullus, who was from Mesouloutyou[?]; following others, by Mepanris [?], &c. Many others want to give their name to the recipes; no one prevents them. But they are blamed by the priests, by those who have the books. The priests have a copy of them read in the shrines of the temples. Everyone knows that these books are by Hermes and other Egyptian authors. Some say that one finds there the black dye and the excellent white dye of copper. This use should not become an object of envy, because it is also blamed by the priests. Moreover, we know that this copper is used for the [manufacture?, word erased] of idols. Lehdou, son of Dionysos, son of Moumdos of Apidos (Abydos?), son of Thormathidos, made with it (the statue) called Minerva.

It is necessary to know the mixture of white copper, used to reproduce silver, in objects that imitate this metal.

20. *To bleach the cast of the weathered Indian (copper).*—"Egyptian copper, one part; purify it well and project silver on it. Others take forty-eight parts; lead, twenty drachmas; lamellar alum, fifteen drachmas. Grind all these bodies together and put them to melting, shaking with a carefully heated iron rod, in a way that they mingle and merge together. Then take and pour from a single flow, while the product is hot; let it cool. It can receive brightness, be heated

and chiseled. This is one of the mixtures of our art; for all these processes fit into our art.[6]

After another copper-based recipe for producing a gold appearance ("*Mixture of yellow.*—Milky white copper, ocher, scraped rust, celandine; oil paste, with resin and vinegar; crushed calcite [carbonate mineral]") there appears a note in the margin, whether by Zosimos is unclear: "*Let all passers-by admire the idol and be proud of the sculpted object, as Pabapnidos, son of Sitos the imposter, made it.*" Pabapnidos must have been quite a sculptor, with chemical skills as well; pity we know nothing more about him. At this point Zosimos allows himself a certain aesthetic pride in what knowledge of the art can generate in the onlooker.

> In the same way you will be amazed, operating as it was said. The color will be stable, the one discussed about the white above. How moved is one when one admires the invention of the arts; how beautiful the view is! Thus it has been said that this invention belongs to Pabapnidos, son of Sitos, this master of statues; it was he who constituted this color. How much he must be admired for his inventions! The color will turn blue by adding the seed of solanum nigrum (Greek *alichachazon*, "black nightshade"), willow juice and white laurel, &c."[7]

Zosimos goes on to mention other impressive uses of the art. In addition to statues, the dyes can be combined into decorative images of many kinds, as well as those images that delude and abuse their victims.

> The philosophers who carried out a preparation said how it should be intended. One makes figures, statues, images of snakes and animals; the statue of the Good Angel (Agathodaimon), that of Good Fortune, that of Chance, that of the Earth, and that of Destiny (?), that of the Nile, which is the Gihon [a river flowing from Eden Genesis says encircled "Cush," that made Ethiopians identify Gihon

with the Blue Nile], that of fruits, heads of grain, and the image of those things that lend themselves to the error and to the illusion of the abused individuals. I despise the disciples of Neilos who admired things unworthy of admiration; they were indeed ignorant, and one applies to them the saying: "Know you yourself." This very saying, they did not admire.

Such are the things relative to the dyeing of copper and its alloys, O woman![8]

Zosimos is soon back with his anti-Neilos polemic, with the added implication that if people really understood the art of making images of gods, it would not be the gods or the priests' powers they would find awesome, but the science of the artificers. Indeed, those who knew the truth had in former times been afraid to speak and could only voice their knowledge in hiding. Now he, Zosimos, is happy to convey to Theosebeia knowledge that even the elders in their day were too jealous over their superior knowledge to publish.

I think that the elders, by reason of their spirit of jealousy, did not write these things; but they made them known in secret to the priests alone. Men were seized with fear at the sight of the images; they thought they were animated and that they held their colors by living nature; to such an extent that they dared not look them in the face, for fear of the living nature of the limbs and the figure of the fashioned object. Few were those who thought that they were made by the composition and artifice of men; whereas this was only said in secret and in hiding.[9]

Making Talismans?

Book number 12 of the Zosimos Syriac texts translated by Duval is intro-duced by the following rubric: "*Book on electrum, which is a special metal. Every precious gift and every present comes from above and is given to those*

who are worthy of it." What follows is varied and curious. Buried within
it is a fragment suggesting Zosimos had knowledge of how to make something like an electrum mirror as a "talisman"; that is, an object to attract
a good result, or a shield to ward off a threatening phenomenon with a
spiritual cause. The implication seems to be that since a talisman has, in
Zosimos's telling, an anti-daimonic function it does not fall under the
usual Zosimian condemnation for propitiating daimons. In this context,
the treatise's first section opens with a rather difficult statement: "Like
the old books, O woman! Because of the dissimulation of daimons,
deceiving those who are not enlightened about them, it is necessary to
investigate whether (electrum), just as it is close to gold by its properties,
must also be any closer for its use and for its work."[10] The parallel with
daimonic deception is not very clear, unless he's saying daimonic presence
has influenced knowledge of electrum and its use, especially as it's close to
gold and therefore, possibly, a source of temptation and corruption.

The general approach seems to be that recipes referred to in the
treatise are not those that used naturally occurring electrum (alloy predominantly of gold and silver) but those intended to create an electrum
artificially by fusion. While harder than gold, electrum is not as hard as
bronze, and so its uses seem to have been primarily decorative or cere-
monial. However, Zosimos in his long narrative about electrum conveys
a mythology of its bearing magical and spiritual powers, especially when
ground as a reflective mirror, and these properties occupy Zosimos's
mind the most, for they relate to a world beyond superficial reasoning and transient consciousness: a key theme of the treatise. In modern
terms, an electrum mirror could activate what we call the unconscious,
or subconscious, whose scope Zosimos would associate with noetic and
divine characteristics.

> *The Philosopher indeed says:* Make the metal white (silver), by means
> of cinnabar, salt, and alum; then make it red (gold), by means of
> vitriol, sericon [a red tincture of unknown composition], copperas
> ["flower of copper": green crystals of hydrated ferrous sulfate]. and

unburned sulfur, or as you will hear. Project on the silver and it will be gold and so on. These recipes were kept secret and were only passed on with an oath not to be revealed to the public.

2. *Other recipes for electrum.*—One reads there the words croticados, sougnatis, pouqaidos, &c., as ingredients entering into the composition of electrum.

3. Also learn how silver mirrors are made (loura): know that you will find traditional demonstrations in the letter delta [treatise]. You should polish (silver), as for a mirror. You must also understand all the work done using the following mixture: burnt copper, one part; Cyprus copper filings, Indian iron (sahoum), each part, &c.

Following. The author recommends operating the fusion in the spontaneous draft apparatus (*automatareion*). Failing this apparatus, use the glass furnace.

Following. One projected croticados [unknown ingredient], which were reduced to filings, with mercury; they were cooked with sulfur. When the product was dry, it was digested in a jar, then the liquid poured over here and there. Those who did not project it cooked with the Phrygian stone [stone used in dyeing, thought to be like pumice, drying and astringent], or with the one called apitou (pyriform?). The book says that this was a secret recipe.

Ancient history records that Alexander the Macedonian was the inventor, as follows. Lightning fell constantly on the earth and ravaged every year the fruits of the earth and the race of humans, to the point of leaving only a few.

Alexander, having had knowledge of these facts and being afflicted, invented this alloy, formed by gold (siwan) and silver (loura): this is why the alloy has been called electrum; that is to say, interlaced, because it is a mixture of these two shiny metals. [From Greek *electron,* "amber"; like amber when rubbed with dry cloth, it attracts other substances as it becomes *electrically charged.*]

It reports the visible results obtained by their alloy.—That is why it is said that if an individual in that time was (exposed to being) struck by lightning, he prepared with the shiny metals a brilliant electrum, and (by virtue of this body) he was not overwhelmed by the plague, just as Alexander was not.

It was at this time that Alexander prepared some kind of engraved coins, made of gold and silver, and scattered them into that earth on which lightning fell; he harrowed it and abandoned it to itself, and lightning did not fall there anymore. He had in his house a kind of mirror, which, he said, was a protection against all evils; and his word is true, for it no longer happened that he was exposed to evils and fights such as those that he had endured.

The kings, his successors, inferior to him, believed him, and they acquired this mirror, (which they put) in their house as a talisman. This mirror, when a man looks at himself in it, suggests the idea of examining himself and purifying himself, from head to fingertips.

The mirror was then brought to the priests in the temple called the Seven Gates. These mirrors were made to the size of men and showed them that they had to purify themselves. All this was exposed in the form of a mystery, as I made known (to you, woman!) in the book which is called *Circle of Priests*.

The mirror was not set up for this purpose, that a man should contemplate himself materially; for as soon as he left the mirror, he immediately lost the memory of his own image [the memory enters the subconscious]. What was that mirror, therefore? Listen.

The mirror represents the divine spirit; when the soul looks at it, it sees the shames that are in it, and it rejects them; it makes its stains disappear and rests blameless. When she [the soul] is purified, she imitates and takes the Holy Spirit as her model; she herself becomes spirit; she possesses calm and constantly refers to that higher state, where one knows him (God) and where one is known by him. Then having become spotless (without shadow [here implying chemical refinement?]), she gets rid of her own bonds and her own chains and those which she shares with her body, and she (rises) toward the Omnipotent. What indeed does the philosophic word say? Know you yourself. She indicates by the spiritual and noetic mirror. What, therefore, is this mirror if not the divine and primordial spirit (of the Father)?

Unless it is said that this is the principle of principles, the son of God, the Word, the one whose thoughts and feelings also flow from the Holy Spirit. Such, O woman! is the explanation of the mirror.[11]

Not content with that, Zosimos continues to say that when a man looks there and sees himself, he turns away from all those things people call gods and daimons and attaches himself to the Holy Spirit; becoming a perfect man, "he sees God who is in him, by the intermediary of that Holy Spirit." The mirror is placed above the "Seven portals," near to the west, so the one who looks at it sees the east, where shines the noetic light, which is above the veil. It is placed also in the south, above all the portals that meet the Seven heavens, above the Twelve houses (zodiac) and the Pleiades, which are the "world of the thirteen." Above them exists that "Eye of the invisible senses, that Eye of the spirit," which is present there "and in all places. One sees there this perfect spirit, in whose power everything finds itself, from now and until death. We have reported this, because we have been led there by means of the electrum mirror; that is, the mirror of the spirit."[12]

There is an eye that sees everything. This is not only the legendary "All-seeing Eye" familiar from *The Thief of Baghdad* but also the eye of the unconscious, whose power of imagination links us to divine spiritual eternity. It is fitting then that this peroration leads Zosimos to challenging the wisdom of Aristotle on the grounds that its scope (that of terrestrial, sense-dominated reason) does not go beyond the aforementioned portals, being closed to what those doors lead to.

Impart this (woman [Theosebeia]) to those philosophers who are worthy of it, and teach them the things of the spirit; turn away from the old (doctrines), and acknowledge that all this exposition contains the type of the invisible things.

4. *Here are the impressions of Aristotle.*—He did not promise to explain . . . ; because while a philosopher of things visible, he has not well distinguished the existence of invisible things; that is to say, that of intelligences or spiritual substances. The angels who inspired him with science did not know them and therefore could not communicate what they did not possess. He himself didn't know what he had not received from his masters, for there was no one who possessed tradition. He was not the Holy Spirit either; but a mortal man, a mortal intelligence, and a mortal body. He was the most brilliant of the non-luminous beings, contrasted with the incorporeal beings. . . . As he was mortal, he could not ascend to the celestial sphere nor could he make himself worthy of it. That is why his science and deeds remained in the lower region of this sphere.[13]

Undaunted by supposed limitations in the Greek philosopher of terrestrial forms (rather than eternal ideas), Zosimos is keen to tell what *he* knows about using electrum in anti-daimonic talismans attributed to King Solomon, an account loaded with fascinating lore.

5. Among the Egyptians there is a book called the *Seven heavens,* attributed to Solomon, against daimons; but it is not true that it is from Solomon, because these talismans were brought to our priests another time; this is what the language used to designate them already suggests, for the expression *talismans of Solomon* is a Hebraic expression. At all times the high priests of Jerusalem drew them, in the simple sense, from the lower abyss of Jerusalem [*Gehenna*? wonders the translator].

After these writings had been spread everywhere, being still incomplete, they were corrupted. It was he who had invented them, as I said earlier. But Solomon wrote only one work on the seven talismans, while commentaries were made, at different times, to explain the things that this work contained; and in these commentaries there was fraud. All, or almost all, agree on the work of talismans directed against daimons. These talismans act as prayer, and the nine letters written by Solomon the daimons cannot resist.

But let's go into more detail about what we have in mind. The seven bottles (talismans), in which Solomon held the daimons, were made of electrum. In this regard, the Jewish writings on daimons should be read with faith. The altered book, which we possess and which is titled the *Seven heavens,* contains, in summary, the following: The angel ordered Solomon to make these talismans (bottles). He adds: Solomon made the seven talismans (bottles), according to the number of the seven planets, conforming to the divine prescriptions on the work of the stone (philosophical) [the philosopher's stone does not actually appear before the seventh century, so this word is probably an anachronistic guess by French translator Rubens Duval], for the mixture of silver, gold, and copper of Cyprus, with the body called oricalcum [legendary Atlantean metal in Plato's *Critias*] and copper of Marrah [mountains in western Sudan]. We take a part of the metal provided with its shadow, we put it in the presence of all the sulfurous stones: The best of them all begets shadow-deprived metal. There are nine of them in all. It is through them that all is accomplished, as you know.

The wise Solomon also knows how to evoke daimons—he gives a formula of conjuration, and he indicates electrum; that is to say the electrum bottles, on whose surface he inscribes this formula.

You will find the mixture, weight, and treatment of each of the bodies and gems in the Jewish writings, and mainly in Apilis, son of Gagios [otherwise unknown]. If you discover the meaning of these scriptures, you will discover with sincerity what you are pursuing. If not, seek your refuge with the crocitidos, especially the one in the manual [*encheiridion*] where we produce gold (siwan) with iron (sahoum) dyed red. There is (in the manual) the complete indication of the nine necessary things.

If you do not want to use this means, know that the following bodies are necessary for preparation of electrum: gold (siwan) burned, silver (loura) said of the ant (*murmikos*), copper (saroch) bleached, iron (sahoum) tender and softened, lead (tou?), silver (moon) purified. You will find their treatment everywhere, &c.[14]

It may be presumed Zosimos's ethics of usage regarding alchemical products were not observed by all practitioners, though Zosimos tried to assure Theosebeia that chances of technical success relied on an ethically sound, spiritually cleansed mind, and a respect for proven authority. The noetic mind is the best defense against possible abuse of a craft operating in a world below the source of *nous*.

Needless to say, one thing our first alchemists were not doing was trying to transmute base metals such as lead into familiar mineral gold. Besides, it is worth bearing in mind Pliny's view of the value of gold: "We must not forget to mention that gold, for which all mankind has so mad a passion, comes scarcely tenth in the list of valuables, while silver, with which we purchase gold, is almost as low as twentieth" (*Natural History* 37.204).

Since surviving records do not enter into issues of theory—anymore than car manufacturers require advanced degrees in geology to handle steel—there is little ground for a still widely repeated view that alchemy was based on a principle that there existed a kind of proto-metal or substrate common to all metals that, if acted upon, enabled protean transformation from one to another if one added the right secret ingredient to a metal first reduced to a supposed neutral state. No recipe for creating such a product exists in the record, nor is there any suggestion that any practitioner thought such a neutral base existed or was desirable. No, *gold* meant mineral gold as an ingredient, golden or yellow color, or an alloy with gold in it. The unity common to all metals was the dynamic unity practitioners observed in all nature, visible and invisible; namely, that of the four elements that provided creative interaction: air, earth, fire, and water.

This conception of the elements should definitely *not* be confused with the way we see air, earth, fire, or water. The word *element* meant that everything that existed could be seen in some respect in terms of these categories or in their interaction and interdependence. The elements were not to be strictly identified with specific substances or component substances. There was something like, or analogous to, or suggestive of the idea of each element in everything, more or less, in terms of airiness, liquidity, fieriness, earthiness, or dryness, wetness, heat and coldness, or other qualities, such as volatility, mutability, softness, color, flexibility, ability to flow, or rise, or darken, or congeal, or melt, and so on. Elemental air could mean vapor or spirit or lightness, or any combination, including other elements. The visible universe expressed and corresponded to incorporeal powers at all levels of creation, while the higher incorporeals transcended the whole while remaining necessary to the life of the whole. The first alchemists' universe was thoroughly dynamic, and their work provided daily proof of that, and their work was, in Zosimos's view at least, legitimated by their intentions and the degree to which nature responded to sympathy with nature's regular ways. Nature was not capricious and did not need to be bribed, though processes naturally *encouraged* changes, through natural sympathy, attraction, and repulsion, some of which changes were startling to the eye (sand into glass, for example) and suggestive to the soul. While doubtless some practitioners saw the art as being intrinsically bound up with a magical universe of daimonic causation, Zosimos did all he could to keep the practice on the right side of the good angels and in tune with the highest mind (*nous*).

Successful operations surely generated gold in abundance—that is to say, money—so much, in fact, that according to seventh-century chronicler John of Antioch, the reign of Zosimos's contemporary, Emperor Diocletian (284–305 CE), witnessed not only the last great persecution of Christians amid state promotion of pagan sacrifices but also Diocletian's order to destroy all chemical books en masse because the emperor perceived profits obtained from the art were funding rebelliousness in Egypt. This account was later misunderstood to mean that alchemists were producing bullion by their art. Had they been doing so, the emperor would have detained the practitioners to labor for him at the imperial mint! Alchemical processes certainly turned lead, along with iron, tin, copper, silver, and all the other ingredients, into greater wealth than the raw minerals generated by themselves.

As ever, art fostered wealth; only materialists persistently fail to grasp this fact. But you don't get something for nothing.

EIGHT

How Did They Do It?

THERE SEEMS LITTLE DOUBT that the greatest spurs to the growth of independent alchemical practice in Egypt took place toward the end of the second half of the first century BCE. The three primary factors were the direct governance of Egypt within the Roman Empire after 30 BCE (reducing the power of the priesthood), the invention of glassblowing (leading to an expansion of suitable receptacles and tubes, as well as a vast new market for decorated objects), and the development of furnaces capable of heat-adjustable melting of principal metals over 1000°C. Copper melts at 1085°C; gold at 1063°C; silver at 961°C; tin at 232°C; iron at 1536°C; while mercury melts at 38.86°C and boils at 357°C. Glass had properties of chemical neutrality (mercury did not corrode glass as it did other container materials) as well as endurance under high temperatures. Other aspects of the art were already in place, such as gem fabrication and coloring. The Stockholm Papyrus mentions several of pseudo-Democritus's recipes for manufacturing gems, such as how to soften and dye rock crystal to make "emerald." If you wanted to fabricate pearls, the papyrus recommends the "mirror stone" (*lapis specularis*); that is "mica," which is pearly with some of the characteristics of glass.

Take and grind an easily pulverised stone such as window mica.
Take gum tragacanth and let it soften for ten days in cow's milk.

When it has become soft, dissolve it until it becomes as thick as glue. Melt Tyrian wax; add to this, in addition, the white of egg. The mercury should amount to 2 parts and the stone 3 parts, but all remaining substances 1 part apiece. Mix the ground mica and the molten wax and knead the mixture with mercury. Soften the paste in the gum solution and the contents of the hen's egg. Mix all of the liquids in this way with the paste. Then make the pearl that you intend to, according to a pattern. The paste very shortly turns to stone. Make deep round impressions and bore through it while it is moist. Let the pearl thus solidify and polish it highly. If managed properly it will exceed the natural.[1]

The importance of glass can be seen in a dialogue between "Synesius and Dioscorus," a commentary on pseudo-Democritus and attributed to a late (in our context) figure, Neoplatonic Christian philosopher Synesius (ca. 370–413).

S: Sharpen your mind, Dioscorus, and pay attention to the expressions employed.
D: How does he express it?
S: If therefore you handle (the substance) as you should, you extract the nature. It involves earth of Chios [Aegean island], asterite, white cadmia [oxide of zinc], &c. This is what he said, Dioscorus: mix the bodies [metals] with the mercury, file them finely and add any other mercury: in fact the mercury draws all things to itself. Let this ripen for three or four days and put it in a botarion [specialized flask or digestion vase, or cucurbit] and place in a bath of hot ash that isn't heated by an ardent flame but is heated gently; that is to say, on a kērotakis bath [bain-marie]. While the fire heats, a glass instrument having a breast-shaped protuberance, adapted to its superior part [possibly a retort], with a lid [alembic cap?] is slotted into the botarion; catch the escaping water at the tip of the channel

Fig. 8.1. A small alembic on a pot serving a bain-marie, held on a tripod (taken from Ms. 2327, fol. 33v); it appears in the work of Synesius and corresponds to his text (fourth century)—an apparatus still used in 1888 for distillation in two stages.

Fig. 8.2. Elementary drawing of the alembic in figure 8.1 (*Codex Parisinus Graecus* 2325)

(neck) and keep it for the fermentation: this is called divine water (or sulfur water).

It produces the transformation; that is to say, the operation that extracts the hidden nature, that which one calls the dissolution of the bodies. By this distillation you extract the nature hidden inside. This is called dissolution of the (metallic) bodies.

When this (preparation) has been fermented, it takes the name vinegar, Aminaios [province of Italy] wine, and analogous names.[2]

Sulfur Water; Divine Water

Matteo Martelli has devoted much scholarship to understanding better the many references in early alchemical texts to that crucial liquid that may often be read as either "divine water" or "sulfur water." The ambiguity stems from the Greek word for sulfur, *theion,* which in its genitive, *theou,* can mean both "of sulfur" and "divine," or "of god" (*theos*). The ambiguity intrigued early alchemists, mostly due to the critical nature of a liquid whose ingredients could be many and various (though pure sulfur and lime seem predominant) but whose usage was consistent; that is, used chemically to affect the substance in which it came into contact, mainly by corrosion. Martelli observed one simple recipe for its making in the Leiden Papyrus (10.87).

> The discovery of sulfur water: mix one drachma of lime [asbestos] and the same quantity of sulfur that has been crumbled in a vessel containing strong vinegar or the urine of a virgin boy. The liquid is then burnt by applying fire below so as to make it like blood; filter to remove sediment and employ it neat.[3]

The recipe produces a solution of polysulfides of calcium able to attack and change the color of metal surfaces. The same papyrus gives an idea of how the liquid could be applied to act upon an alloy of four parts silver and one part gold in a complex dyeing process (recipe no. 88). A similar solution of sulfur, lime, and alum dissolved in vinegar is found in Leiden recipes 40 and 68 to perform a "stypsis" on crystal as a first step in coloring stones. The process weakens the surface, making it more receptive to dyes. The water might also have ingredients of a color matching that of an intended dye and could pass by numerous names, many attached to the words *urine, milk, juice, wine, beer,* or *vinegar.* There is no consistent information on the content of any given divine water, but while pseudo-Democritus left only one reference to divine water,[4] sulfur dominates, its importance in processes most likely established by pseudo-Democritus, a significance underlined in the following recipe for a compound in his *Physika and Mystika.*

Take white sulfur; you shall whiten it, dissolving with urine in the sun or alum and salt brine: it will shine having become totally white. Dissolve it with realgar or heifer's urine for six days, until the pharmakon [the medicine] nearly approaches the likeness of marble; when it becomes so, great is the mystery for it whitens copper, softens iron, takes away the creaking of tin, makes lead not fusible and makes substances unbreakable and dyes permanent. For sulfur mixed with sulfur makes substances divine [note the pun], since they (sulfurs) have a close kinship with each other. Natures rejoice with natures.[5]

That the various kinds of sulfur (including "pure" or "untouched" [*athikton*], "made with lime,"[6] and "unburnt" sulfur) were ubiquitous in treating silver and other metals is hardly surprising since crystalline and powdered sulfur are bright yellow, and that color made it a corresponding substance to gold, meaning that something *elemental* in them related the substances to one another (the colors yellow and white were related to air; the Latin for gold—*aurum*—shares a root with the Greek for "breath" or "wind": *aura*).

Apparatus

Matteo Martelli has noted how Egyptian papyrus references and codex evidence suggests that alchemists (or *technai*), whether expert in gold, silver, fabrics, or precious stones, made use of existing equipment, such as glassblowers' and potters' furnaces, and possibly worked in fabric dyers' shops, one of which was discovered by archaeologist Flinders Petrie at Athribis. His findings, published in 1908, described three vats in the "bench of the north" and beyond a cistern a vat room with sixteen vats in the raised bench at the sides, all of them stained with cement of "black blue with indigo" or red.[7] Dyers' workshops also employed lead pots and earthenware casks.[8] Martelli shares the general view that Graeco-Egyptian alchemists were responsible for increasing specification for specialized equipment, such that they probably found it necessary to appropriate exclusive spaces to accommodate their sometimes dangerous work.[9] We have already seen how Zosimos respected Maria's descriptions of various kinds of kērotakis, and stills, with alembics (the still head called a *chalkeion*), the tribikos (a "receiver" attributed to Mary; see page 82), various copper vessels, pipes (*sōlēnes*), glass flasks (vials), and seals.

Practitioners were ready to exploit the speedy volatilization of some minerals; mercury's low boiling point helped them to extract the metal from cinnabar, one process for which was recorded by Pliny in his *Natural History* (33.123), where he describes cinnabar being put in an iron shell in flat earthenware pans before being "covered with a convex lid smeared with clay," whereafter "a fire is lit under the pans and kept constantly burning by means of bellows, and so the surface moisture (with the color of silver and fluidity of water) which forms on the lid is wiped off it. This moisture is also easily divided into drops and rains down freely with slippery fluidity." We shall look at Martelli's re-creation of the process at the end of this chapter. The process would have required two vessels, a lower one (the *lōpas*) and an upper *ambix* (Arabic *al-anbiq;* our "alembic") that was widest at the middle with the upper part tapered like a cone to a narrower aperture, from which condensed mercury could be collected. It was possibly Maria who first separated the two vessels with a pipe and added another tube attached to a digestion vessel to the alembic. Martelli thinks her equipment was more suited to distilling liquids than sublimating ores like cinnabar,[10] a view possibly confirmed by references in the work of a later writer on alchemy, Neoplatonist Stephanus of Alexandria (ca. 580–640), who lectured in Constantinople, and distinguished between a "humid vapor" extracted by *phanoi* ("lamps" but could also mean a glass vial) with a "breast-shaped vessel" (alembic), and the "dry vapor" extracted by means of vessel and copper cover, as described above by Pliny. The "dry vapor" Stephanus compared to white vapor of cinnabar, and his "phanoi" probably indicates the lower container in the apparatus. Nevertheless, Martelli concludes that Mary's system was probably also used for dry ingredients like cinnabar.[11]

Pliny's description indicates the heating of solid cinnabar, whereas pseudo-Democritus preferred to grind the cinnabar ore and mix it with nitron oil prior to distillation.

Maria's distilling techniques were well suited to making divine water, as Zosimos recorded.

> Mary takes care of it, describing the treatments of the small object: "The divine water will be lost for those who do not understand what has been written, namely that the (useful) product is returned up by the matras [lōpados] and the tube [sōlēnos]. But it is customary to designate by this water the steam of sulfur [theon athikton] and arsenic sulphides [orpiment and sandarac]. Because of this you have mocked me, because in one and the same speech I have exposed to you such a great mystery."[12]

Mercury could also be obtained less subtly by the "cold method" of taking a copper or bronze pestle and pounding cinnabar with vinegar, as indicated by Pliny (*Natural History* 33.123). The first alchemists applied the distillation method to other substances, such as in the treatise *Isis to her son Horus,* where orpiment (arsenic sulfide mineral) and realgar are treated.

> 17. Here is how to raise the sublimated steam: take arsenic [orpiment], boil it in water, and put it in a mortar, pile-up with stachys [ear of corn] and a little oil; put it in a flask and close its mouth with a vial; put it on charcoal until vapor rises up. Arrange the appliance until the steam is gone. Treat the sandarac [realgar; red sulfide of arsenic] in the same way.[13]

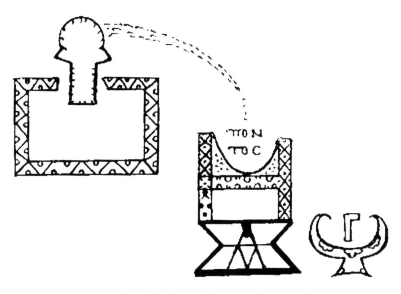

Fig. 8.3. Apparently a distillation furnace, from *Codex Marcianus,*
between first and second lesson of Stephanus. The distilled liquids fall
into a hemispheric basin called "pontos" (the sea).

Fig. 8.4. Apparently the chapiter of
a similar apparatus (to figure 8.3): a
sketch in red ink (*Codex Marcianus,*
fol. 106v).

Martelli notes that if alchemists wished to extract arsenic from
the orpiment (or realgar), a simple sublimation of it is ineffec-
tive because arsenic oxidizes quickly in the air, whereas liquid substances could protect the sublimate. Use of liquids thus appears
in both Greek and Syriac pseudo-Democritan recipes; for example, a Syriac text for obtaining "arsenic elixir" recommends taking a pound of ground orpiment and mixing it with aristolochia
rotunda (smearwort plant), grinding into a powder, and triturating

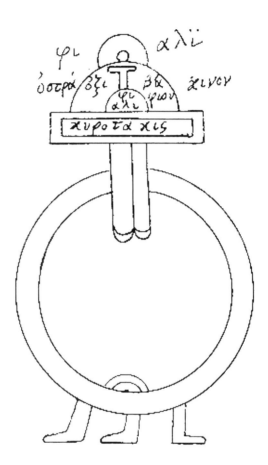

Fig. 8.5. Vase to kerotakis: showing variants and details of apparatus (figures 3.11 and 3.12) (*Codex Marcianus*, fol. 112, in margin); a different disposition of the spherical digestion apparatus. Possibly for a retrograde operation: the material fallen to the bottom by melting re-ascends by volatilization to the superior part. Berthelot (1888) thought it probably concerns the sublimation of mercury, or arsenic, destined to whiten the copper, in alliance with it. The Greek text probably comes from the sixteenth century. Figure 8.5 was not in the original *Codex Marcianus* but was added toward the sixteenth century from another, now lost, manuscript.

the blend with vinegar for seven days, after which they were to be dried and triturated again before putting them in a pot sealed with clay. A fire was to be lit, the pot heated, then the blend was to be ground and triturated once more, and the vapor distilled seven times.

It would be helpful if we knew more the kinds of furnaces that were used, especially as success depended on the degree of roasting of substances over prescribed periods. However, despite Zosimos knowing of a work called *Kaminographia* (On Furnaces), it has not survived. It is likely that furnaces for melting metallic bodies were not necessarily the same devices as used for processing substances.[14] Likewise, none of the early evidence gives us any certainty as to where specifically practical alchemy took place; that is to say, whether there was ever in the period some kind of laboratory, later understood as an integral aspect to the practice. It should be borne in mind that while Zosimos, for example, spends more time referring Theosebeia to written texts rather than practical exercises, such work as was undertaken was most likely to have been practical and commercial rather than what we should understand by experimental, and the commercial issue may have dictated where work was undertaken.

Putting the First Alchemists to the Test

Very recently an exciting interdisciplinary project was undertaken in Italy under the auspices of Matteo Martelli and Lucia Raggetti of Bologna University's Department of Philosophy and Communication Studies, along with Marianna Marchini, Massimo Gandolfi, and Lucia Maini of Bologna's Chemistry Department. The idea was to bring together chemists and historians of science to investigate the element of mercury in the context of ancient Greek, Syriac, and Latin sources and to see if replicated recipes proved feasible and viable.

This was considered the best way to "anchor such ancient texts to the chemical reality that they were intended to encapsulate."[15] While it proved unworkable to guess exactly what equipment was used and try to reconstruct it, modern labware was safely adapted to the recipes. The work centered on the hot and cold extraction of mercury from cinnabar. Remarkably, following ancient procedures led to identifying reactions unknown to modern chemistry labs and literature.

Cold extraction of mercury was first recorded in fourth-century BCE Theophrastus of Lesbos's *On stones* wherein mercury was obtained by grinding cinnabar with vinegar in a copper mortar. The team followed in the footsteps of chemist Kenneth C. Bailey, who ground cinnabar with copper turnings in a mortar with vinegar in the 1920s. While the cinnabar went black, indicating copper sulfide, the copper turnings became coated with a copper-mercury amalgam. The Bologna team found similar results. Copper is today recognized as a key reagent, though it was chemist L. Takacs who in 2000 asserted Theophrastus's recipe the first witness to a mechanochemical reaction.

Zosimos had attributed the method to Maria and Chymēs with lead and tin pestles and mortars as additional variants, and he was aware of copper's reagent status when he recorded *adding* copper turnings to a grinding in vinegar preparation. According to the Bologna team's report:

We initially tested this reaction by manually grinding synthetic cinnabar (HgS) and copper (Cu in powder) together with some drops of glacial acetic acid. The powder slowly turned black and after one hour of grinding, droplets of mercury (Hg), never recorded in any previous experimental report, were clearly visible.[16]

Ball milling cinnabar with copper and drops of glacial acetic acid produced a complete reaction in six hours, comprised of HgS + $_2$Cu→

Cu_2S + Hg, an unexpected result compared to recent study reports. Other researchers had limited the number of different possible sulfides to "probably CuS." The team's work demonstrated that Chalconite-Q (Cu_2S) was the reaction product, not, as had been reported, Covellite (CuS), proving that in existing literature the reaction had not been reproduced, only cited. This indicated how incorrect citing from one scientific paper to another generates inaccuracies and incorrect assumptions.

Glacial acetic acid, like vinegar, had 6 percent acetic acid and was obviously catalytic, perhaps removing a protective oxide layer on the cinnabar. Replications proved Zosimos was right about lead, as lead could reduce mercury. Using lead, the X-ray powder defraction pattern indicated lead sulfide but no mercury droplets, owing to a powdery HgPb amalgam. Using tin in the reaction, an amalgam (HgSn) is easily obtained, but tin's oxidation to produce a probable tin sulfide hardly showed in the defraction pattern. The amalgam, a soft silvery paste, was probably taken by ancient alchemists as a form of quicksilver; they were aware of different mercuries being produced depending on the metals employed for extraction.

Ancient sources describe three types of hot extraction of mercury from cinnabar: simple heating of cinnabar; heating it in a sealed vessel with iron; heating it with nitron oil. This latter method had gone unnoticed by historians who only referred to cinnabar's reaction to oxygen at high temperatures ($HgS + O_2 > SO_2$ [sulfur dioxide]). In the first century BCE, Roman architect Vitruvius referred to moist clods of cinnabar being put at the base of ovens, whereafter mercury condensed, collecting on the oven bottom and on the clods. The ancients were aware of mercury's toxicity, so the procedure most referred to was in closed vessels. Whether this was less efficient, the Bologna team put to the test by putting cinnabar in an alumina crucible with a lid on it.

Inside, the cinnabar reacted with atmospheric oxygen, with the lid yielding condensed mercury, though the reaction was not complete due to lack of oxygen. Residual cinnabar and black metacinnabar were always observed, including when heated. The team then followed a first-century CE procedure of Dioscorides's in which cinnabar in an iron shell was put in an earthenware casserole, enclosed in a convex top sealed with clay. A charcoal fire heated the casserole (see page 167). Vapor condensed on the lid: quicksilver. The operation was replicated with the cinnabar on an iron plate in an alumina crucible, covered with a lid. When heated, cinnabar reacts with iron thus: $Hg + Fe > FeS + Hg$. The reaction is not long in coming, leaving residual powder containing iron sulfide. Iron had played the reagent role, something absent from modern studies of ancient extraction methods.

Pseudo-Democritus provided the third method: grinding cinnabar with nitron oil, the resultant placed in a "double vessel" to capture the vapor. There is uncertainty as to what nitron oil consisted of. The general view is that it was from sodium carbonate decahydrate, that is, "natron," which was mined in Egypt from the nearly dry lake, Wadi el-Natrun. The "oil" suggests introducing it into a solvent, with liquids providing faster reactions to solids. A Byzantine alchemist considered nitron oil "vinegar of nitron," so it's reasonable to think sodium carbonate was dissolved in water, vinegar, or castor or linseed oil.[17] Historically, when natron was blended with oil, it served as soap, and had preservative qualities useful for food and wounds. Absorbing water, it served as a drying agent in mummification. Added to castor oil, it made a smokeless fuel.

The Bologna team found that sodium carbonate was crucial to closed-vessel extraction. When cinnabar was heated at 300°C for forty-eight hours *with* the sodium carbonate, it was fully converted into mercury; without it, reaction was poor. Confirmation of the role of sodium carbonate was obtained by performing the extraction in a vacuum so no atmospheric oxygen would react with the cinnabar. This produced in addition to extracted mercury, sodium sulfate

(Na_2SO_4). Scientific studies previously only reported this once, with the residual powder described as a mixture of Na_2SO_4 and sodium sulfide (Na_2S). In the team's experiments, the latter never appeared under analysis.

Having confirmed the importance of the sodium carbonate, the next task was to ascertain the nature of nitron oil; solutions in water and vinegar were tested to resemble the viscosity of oil. It's long been known that sodium carbonate reacts with vinegar to produce sodium acetate and bubbles of CO_2. Both water and vinegar solutions were tested; water evaporated, producing mercury and sodium sulfate. There was no improvement on tests in dry conditions. Sodium carbonate with vegetable oil was particularly poor, with the oil burning easily and its decomposition preventing extraction. It's as useless even if heat is reduced to stop burning. According to the team: "To summarise, like iron in the second method described, nitron serves as a reducing agent in the reaction when carried out within a closed apparatus. The use of such equipment, always emphasised in ancient alchemical texts, contrasts with the common assumption that mercury was produced by simply roasting cinnabar in the presence of oxygen."[18]

The overall conclusion showed that details in ancient recipes were highly significant. For example, the use of an iron shell was not simply a handy material for containment but was determinative in chemical results; likewise copper in cold extraction (initially just the pestle's metal). Nitron oil aided extraction yield. Furthermore, the choice of nitron itself may have been as cultural a stimulus as a technical one. Nitron had usage in sacred settings, such as nitron balls used to clean mummies, and of course its association with purity in embalming the dead and as a health aid. Investigating *what* alchemists did became for the team an analytical exercise into how and why they did it.[19]

Martelli and his colleagues are nowadays not alone in their interest of turning ancient texts into practical chemical demonstrations. In

February 2014, the Smithsonian Institute's magazine published an article by naturalist Richard Conniff under the headline "Alchemy May Not Have Been the Pseudoscience We All Thought It Was." Conniff focused on the work of historian of science Lawrence Principe of Johns Hopkins University, Baltimore. Having read seventeenth-century alchemical recipes about growing a Philosopher's Tree from a seed of gold, Principe concocted an amalgam of prepared mercury and gold and placed it in a sealed flask, buried in specially heated sand. According to Conniff: "One morning, Principe came into the lab to discover to his 'utter disbelief' that the flask was filled with 'a glittering and fully formed tree' of gold. The mixture of metals had grown upward into a structure resembling coral or the branching canopy of a tree minus the leaves."[20] In April 2014, Principe's Philosopher's Tree experiment was exhibited at Düsseldorf's Kunstpalast museum for a show of important alchemy-influenced artworks.

In the article, Principe was asked if the realization that scientists like Robert Boyle, Isaac Newton, and Antoine-Laurent Lavoisier had built on their reading of alchemical texts somehow lessened their greatness, Principe answered that people like the idea that something they've done is really new, whereas in fact scientific ideas "tend to develop out of older ones by a slow process of evolution and refinement." As Conniff suggests, this may mean the scientific revolution so dear to historians of science for many years may not have been as revolutionary as people have been taught, but was rather a transmutation of focus. The article highlighted that since the 1980s, "revisionist" scholars have been less wary than used to be the case in boldly arguing for the practical importance of alchemy to science, and that the image of transmutation obsessives was unworthy propaganda. Alchemists were not lunatics. As we have seen, much of the misunderstanding may have come from lack of knowledge of what the first alchemists were actually doing, leading to their work being fundamentally misinterpreted centuries later. What they were doing was applied science capable of repeated demonstration under controlled conditions. To say that their science was rudimentary is rather like accusing Wilbur and Orville Wright of not having fashioned Concorde in 1903.

NINE

Where Did They Do It?

WE'VE ALREADY HAD CAUSE to mention the existence of guilds in late antique Egypt, though evidence is not all we should like it to be.[1] A guild is generally understood to be a sodality gathered about a common interest in a particular trade, offering advancement and security to chosen members. Guilds serve trade. There are also religious guilds or confraternities where persons who are not themselves priests may occupy service roles just outside of the ordained religious community. While historian of alchemy Shannon Grimes has interpreted Zosimos's texts to place him within a temple community and in particular the Egyptian House of Life, with traditional interest in sciences of astronomy, geometry, philosophy, and the like, directing artisan-priests and having privileged access to written records, she has also written eloquently concerning guilds being a setting where Zosimos may have exercised an alchemical role.

Fig. 9.1. Four geometrical images from Ms. 2325 (fol. 111); also in Ms. 2327 (fol. 106r) and others

One can of course imagine those overseeing temple artisans also having an interest in obtaining additional support from laypersons dedicated to the local religious cult, though Zosimos's own testimony is antithetical, if not openly hostile, to such a placement. According to Grimes: "Most Egyptian priests served only part-time, on a rotation basis, so it is likely that Zosimus and his colleagues were also affiliated with professional guilds outside of the temple environment."[2] I should think the evidence insufficient to support this leap. As Grimes notes, some of them apparently supported a local deity, caring for votive objects and the like. Again, Zosimos excludes himself from such activities on grounds of conscience and knowledge of history regarding "unnatural tinctures" (see pages 96–100). If movement through such a guild was by secret initiation, this also is something Zosimos found inimical to practice of the sacred art, joking to Theosebeia that were mysteries *so* necessary, then *everyone* should have a book of chēmeia.[3]

While Grimes speculates that Zosimos may have obtained knowledge of Hebrew chemical techniques through meeting Jews in guilds, it is worth considering the possibility that it was *Theosebeia* who was part of a Jewish guild, especially when we recall that her name means "God-fearer," a title for non-Jews who adopted the Jewish faith. Over seventy years ago, Mark Wischnitzer wrote a paper outlining a history of Jewish guilds, noting how Jewish philosopher Philo observed four Jewish occupational groups in Alexandria: artisans, farmers, shippers, and merchants, with artisans organized in guilds for goldsmiths, silversmiths, weavers, coppersmiths, and blacksmiths (*In Flaccum* 8; first century CE). In the second century CE, tanna rabbi Judah, visiting the city, noted the five guilds occupying their own seats in the synagogue basilica (*Tosephta Sukkah* 4.6). Other than training apprentices, the guilds provided social services for members, including help for families in adversity. According to Wischnitzer: "Just what their economic functions and policies were is not known, nor do we know very much about their legal status and constitution."[4] Jewish artisans in Egypt did join general trade corporations but did not participate in pagan religious ceremonies. When Zosimos castigated Theosebeia for insisting that her trainees take oaths along with secrets, these people could have been apprentices rather than students.

In her paper "Divine Images: Zosimos of Panopolis's Spiritual Approach to Alchemy," Grimes presents a picture of Zosimos advising metallurgists within temple economies and in guilds (rising, it appears, as temple economies declined), while getting annoyed with "greedy teachers" and, as Grimes puts it, insisting "even to metallurgists who aren't in the priesthood—that spiritual purification and self-knowledge is necessary for the proper execution of metallurgical procedures."[5] While spiritual integrity was vital to Zosimos's thought and practice, I think the cardinal error here lies in locating the spiritual purification advocated by Zosimos as being a privilege of priestly training and temple service. There are other considerably better options, and in Zosimos's case, one need only attend to the sources he most employs when advocating his spiritual convictions. Those convictions are undoubtedly a blend of Jewish scripture and apocrypha, Graeco-Egyptian gnostic lore, and, predominantly, the spiritual-philosophical tracts attributed to Hermes Trismegistos. As to the latter, most commentators believe them chiefly products of the second and third centuries CE, rising, it would appear, in arguably the same wave of enthusiasm as Graeco-Egyptian alchemy itself. We may discuss in due course whether they also arose in the same *setting*. Conflating Zosimos's spiritual ideas with temple cults is, I think, the flaw in Grimes's setting. Zosimos's ideas of spiritual integrity were not drawn from contemporary pagan belief and practice in Egypt, except as a critique of them. If one wishes to argue that the Hermetic tracts themselves were pagan, insofar as they were (arguably) neither Jewish nor Christian, one must recognize first that the images evoked of Egyptian temple practice within the Hermetic writings were primarily idealistic, even romantic, throwbacks to imagined, fanciful beginnings of Egyptian worship (indeed to its deified progenitors), with very little knowledge of conditions four thousand years and more before the last of the Ptolemies. While the tracts refer to (still) popular figures in Egyptian custom and tradition such as Agathodaimon and, much more rarely, to Isis and Horus, the overwhelming impression of the tracts is a cosmogony dominated by supreme being (Mind) infusing a cosmos that is "One," with materialist vision (love of the body) as the great sin, allied to a henotheist tolerance of traditional sacredness below the Ogdoad. Friedrich Schelling coined the term *henotheism* to speak of people who adhered to one god while admitting the existence or possibility of lower deities. In other words, the tracts exemplify philosophical syncretism aiming at a universalism suitable for the new world imperial setting to which post-Cleopatran Egypt was adapting, with the bonus for Egyptians that Hermes's claims glorified Egypt as the ultimate source of spiritual authenticity in a manner Greeks and Romans could grasp.

Despite what I consider flaws perceptible in Shannon Grimes's assessment of Zosimos's *sitz im leben,* the thrust of the conclusion to her paper "Secrets of the God Makers: Re-thinking the Origins of Greco-Egyptian Alchemy" is sound: "Rather than looking to Greek philosophy to explain the origins of alchemy, scholars should look more closely at the cultural and professional context of ancient metallurgists—how they lived and worked—and especially at the economic changes brought about by trade guilds, which provide a more plausible explanation for the appearance of alchemical texts in the Roman period."[6]

So, then, if Zosimos was practicing within or in association with some kind of guild or community context (other than, or allied to, a manufacturing base), one should expect it to have been one devoted to literary Hermetic and gnostic beliefs and concerns. In this regard we may note how Zosimos advises Theosebeia to alienate priest Neilos and hasten to the home of her "race," a word taken from Hermes Trismegistos's distinction between those who've undergone spiritual "rebirth" and those who have not. In *Corpus Hermeticum* 13,

Hermes's son Tat realizes through rebirth that he is born "of the paternal race."

A Hermetic "Lodge"?

According to Dutch scholar Roelof van den Broek, we may seriously entertain the idea of the existence in Egypt in late antiquity of something he calls a Hermetic "lodge." The word *lodge* is in quotes lest it otherwise be interpreted anachronistically as a precursor to lodges of Freemasons attested in some form from fourteenth-century England and Scotland. The idea inherent in the word *lodge* is of a kind of club or society that has a spiritual philosophy uniting its members but is not necessarily centered on religious practices and enjoys a social imperative, uniting members in a bond without priestly sacerdotal dominance and providing an occasional and temporary rest or relief from the usual pace of life and business. Van den Broek bases his idea principally on two documents that came to light among the Nag Hammadi codices discovered in the Thebaid in 1945. These documents appear in Codex VI of the collection and are titled a *Prayer of Thanksgiving* and a *Discourse on the Eighth and Ninth* (or *on the Ogdoad and the Ennead*).

The principal Hermetic writings are teaching pieces about man's place in the cosmos and his relationship to God. However, references made to prayers, hymns, meals, and initiations into mysteries make van den Broek ask the question: "Does all this point to the existence of Hermetic groups in which the 'way of Hermes' was taught and celebrated in a more or less structured way? Or are we only concerned here with a literary device, without any basis in real life?"[7] While previous scholarship had dismissed the idea that the tracts presupposed any exclusive organization, since there were no references to things like priests, processions, incense, and ceremony, it could be argued equally that the gospels give no information about Christian churches, while the early assemblies of Christians were simple meetings, often in secret, without priests, processions, or ceremony customary to state-sanctioned religion.

It is arguable that early Christian assemblies in Egypt created a model, and the same could be said of gatherings of Essenes and Therapeutae, as described by Philo of Alexandria in Judea. Early pioneer of Hermetic studies A. J. Festugière was convinced the Hermetic writings represented a kind of mystery of literature only, taking the idea that because Hermes was not their author, then likewise the details were purely imaginative. Van den Broek has challenged this assumption.

For example, *on the Ogdoad and the Ennead* insists that the praise uttered by those who follow Hermes's instruction mirrors that of the *plerōma,* or fullness of God's heaven, and this singing can be heard when the soul rises to the eighth sphere, where the angels sing their praises silently. For van den Broek this is a telling, as well as symbolic, detail. One has to be in the "mind" of Hermes, not in the world. A Hermetic "lodge" might be considered "time off from the world" and might add to the idea's attraction, especially for persons dedicated to high arts. The thirteenth Hermetic tract (v.16) has Hermes and followers joining in prayer and sharing a meal, with reference to an evening prayer to be said in the open air facing the south and a morning prayer facing the east. Perhaps such prayers were also said in the mind, silently as far as the world was concerned, but heard in heaven. One might say them while at work. Philo's treatise *de vita contemplativa* describes similar practices among "Therapeutae" meeting near Alexandria.

On the Ogdoad and the Ennead also mentions a loving kiss after a prayer before a mystery is revealed. This was a practice universal to early Christians. Van den Broek concludes this was also a practice among "Hermetists."[8] The kiss in the Nag Hammadi text *on the Eighth and Ninth* immediately precedes the descent of light from above and is intended to indicate rejoicing that this will occur and preparation of the soul for its arrival. One is reminded of Zosimos's advice to Theosebeia that she sit quietly, her body stilled, and God will come to her (see pages 138–40).

The Nag Hammadi *Prayer of Thanksgiving* refers to a sacred meal: "When they had said these things in prayer, they embraced each other and they went to eat their holy food, which has no blood in it" (Nag Hammadi Codex VI, 65.3–7). Van den Broek sees such a meal as a natural conclusion to an initiation. In Christian churches, the meal followed baptism, according to Justin Martyr (ca. 150 CE; 1 *Apology* 65.3). Sacred meals were of course a feature of the mystery religions that proliferated in the empire and also provided models for independent gatherings. Actual initiation in van den Broek's proposed Hermetic "lodge" would be something like the content of the ascent to the eighth and ninth spheres itself. Was there a guided "trip"? Or could initiates have been given instructions to make such an ascent independently? Van den Broek reckons it could have occurred not at death but in terms of a meeting, with times set aside from other matters. Such is not impossible, especially if we consider the very great analogy between the Hermetic ascent and the possibilities of a yoga system in which the cosmic ascent is internalized, with the individual as microcosm and the whole experienced imaginatively once a separation had occurred between mind and body. The Hermetic philosophical *libelli* 4 and 13 have no doubt that the successful ascent to the realm of *nous* is a "rebirth," a spiritual rebirth and means thereby to join a specific "race" of those who had likewise attained. The rebirth enabled the individual to see the entire cosmos, and human society, and oneself, from a completely new perspective: one had identified with God (no self). If we think of this in terms of individual experience, it would make sense for there to be an opportunity to meet others from time to time who shared the experience, for the concerns of the world tend to make us forget, and to doubt (as in Jesus's famous parable of the seed choked by the world before fruition). As Platonists held, all knowledge is *being reminded*.

It is difficult to imagine one such as Zosimos not being heart-warmed by the cosmic experience at the end of Secret Hymn No. 4 (*Corpus Hermeticum* 13.20), for in this we are reminded of the four elements that make alchemy possible.

O spirit-bearer, O craftsman, You are God! Your man shouts this through fire, through air, through earth, through water, through spirit, through your creatures!

In *on the Ogdoad and the Ennead,* after the prayer and kiss, and the "power which is light" coming down upon them, one present (probably the initiate or pupil) exclaims: "I see, yes, I see indescribable depths!" (57.31–32). St. Paul in 1 Corinthians 2:10 speaks of the Spirit exploring "everything, even the depths of God's own nature." Valentinian Gnostics, according their opponent bishop Irenaeus (ca. 180 CE), called God "Bythos"—that is, "the Depth" (as in unfathomable ocean)—adding that Valentinians said God in his essence was "Depth and Silence" (*Adversus Haereses* 1.1.1). Valentinus, not surprisingly, was Egyptian. Silence is appropriate, for as the pupil exclaims in the *Discourse on the Eighth and Ninth,* language is unable to reveal what he has seen in the "light."

Language such as this suggests to van den Broek a real experience, perhaps something heard in real life, or once uttered, never forgotten. Literary people rarely confess themselves unable to describe something! So while we may say the angels sing their silent hymns, it may not only be because angels were privy to a special, holy language but also that perhaps silence of a kind is the most profound language, suitable for the depth that has no limit. The one who has risen sees the *All.* And *seeing the All* is the root of Mary's alchemy, as it is of Mary's—to her unknown—pupil, the principle which Zosimos attempted to impart to a potentially or actually wayward Theosebeia. *Know thyself,* he constantly urges. The sacred art mirrors the creative mind, and to grasp its depth, one must rise to the heights.

According to van den Broek: "The new Hermetic texts from Nag Hammadi, and the *Discourse on the Ogdoad and the Ennead* in particular, show clear evidence of the existence of Hermetic groups, communities or lodges, or whatever one would like to call them, in the ancient world. The view that they merely existed in the minds of writers who wanted to promote a special brand of religious philosophy has to be abandoned."[9]

It is arguable that Roelof van den Broek may be rather too incautious to assert that we have "clear evidence of the existence of Hermetic groups." I should say that there is reason to believe such may have been the case, and even that such a sodality was likely, but not certain, in the absence of direct independent testimony to a Hermetic "lodge's" existence.* As I stated in the introduction, evidence for this period leaves massive, untold, and incalculable amounts of doubtless vital information unknown; we have but the ashes and residues of a once living fire. We do not know where Zosimos was able to share his syncretic amalgam of Hermetic, Jewish, and Christian Gnostic thought—and *chēmeia*—but he must have got his sources from *somewhere,* and been able to share them somewhere, and we may speculate quite reasonably that the milieu was likely some kind of group of like-minded persons.

There is certainly evidence for numerous independent, spiritually oriented assemblies in Egypt; Gnostic groups apparently proliferated there in the second, third, and fourth centuries. Encratite bishop of Salamis, Epiphanius, for example, wrote scathingly of a close encounter, when aged about twenty, with a seductive Barbelite Gnostic group in Egypt in 330 CE in his anti-heretical *Panarion* Book 1, section 2, series 26 ("Against Gnostics, or Borborites"), 17, 4–9. He alerted a local bishop, which led to some *eighty* persons being ejected from the unnamed Egyptian city concerned. The Nag Hammadi codices themselves testify to an intensity of Gnostic and Hermetic interest among Christians in the Thebaid, as well as in the north, in Alexandria, throughout the period. In 367 CE the bishop

---

*Christian H. Bull cites an interesting case from the early fourth-century CE papyri of Theophanes, who carried letters from Hermopolis, two from Anatolius "Chief-Prophet of Hermes Trismegistus": one to a friendly Greek philosopher, Ambrosius, and one to a "Sarapion" wherein Anatolius excuses himself due to devotions to Thoth (processions, festivals). Such a person may have been interested in a philosophical Hermetic "lodge."[10]

of Alexandria, Athanasios, wrote a festal letter ordering destruction of all uncanonical works in upper Egypt (and these were held among supposedly orthodox church people). However, when Zosimos was writing—possibly less than a century before Athanasios's letter—Christian doctrine had not secured imperial support, as it would in 325 CE, so what orthodox bishops regarded as heresy had flourished independently, and sometimes within, orthodox churches.

While we cannot indiscriminately lump Christian Gnostic groups in with any supposed Hermetic sodality, the atmosphere was ripe in third-century Egypt for such bodies to take root. As stated earlier, it is perfectly possible that Zosimos and Theosebeia had been, or were still, members of a group where views like his were celebrated and encouraged. It may be legitimately speculated that something like such a group may actually have been associated, directly or indirectly, with Zosimos's trade in metallic, mineral, and textile dyes and constituted some kind of guild, with a peculiarly, if not exclusively, Hermetic outlook and prayer discipline. Panopolis would have been a most suitable urban center for such a body (though certainly not the only one), and we may only have tiny fragments of what was once, to inhabitants, an obvious, living fact. As to this, Christian H. Bull refers to the late third- and fourth-century CE archive of Ammon Scholasticus in Panopolis. His family held high priestly rank in Panopolis's titulary deity Min's temples, and members were knowledgeable in Greek letters. Astrology and fate play a significant role in his decision-making, with Agathodaimon a deity of good fortune. As Bull admits, this is no evidence for Hermetists in Panopolis but suggests an arguably sympathetic milieu. Bull writes:

> Zosimus of Panopolis was probably writing around the turn of the fourth century, and was thus roughly contemporary with Ammon and his family. Recently Shannon Grimes has argued, on the basis of those writings of Zosimus that are only preserved in Syriac, that Zosimus must have been connected to the House of Life, the

Egyptian temple scriptorium, and since he refers to other alchemists as prophets, he might be one himself. In that case he might have been personally acquainted with some of the priests in Ammon's family, namely his father Petearbeschinis, his half-brother Horion I, or the latter's son, Horion II. *However, it is not certain that Zosimus was a priest.* [my italics][11]

Bull goes on to elucidate his doubt that Zosimos was a priest on the same lines as we've explored earlier. He makes a fascinating observation in this regard as to how Zosimos appears to have turned around the story in the Hermetic *Asclepius* where the attraction of divine powers into temple statues was regarded as an achievement, by making the infusion into statues a daimonic trick to obtain worship. Furthermore, Zosimos even takes as already fulfilled the famous prophecy in *Asclepius* of a coming time when it will have seemed Egyptians had served the deities in vain, when the temples would be empty and the gods flown, leaving only wicked angels and a country full of tombs: "Zosimus had read the prediction of Hermes, and perceived it to have been fulfilled by the crisis of the third century, when indeed the Egyptian temples were in decline, the country was briefly under the control of the Palmyrene empire, and the Thebaid was invaded by Blemmyes [desert people] from the south." Bull concludes: "It is plausible and even probable that Zosimus was part of a Hermetic ritual community."[12] And further:

Even though far from all the names, mythemes, or practices described in the Thebes-cache [magical papyri of which some, Bull believes, were likely written by persons educated in the House of Life] have any parallel in the philosophical Hermetica, the substantial overlap makes the continued existence of a Hermetic community in early fourth century Thebes not only possible but even probable. Thebes is furthermore mentioned in the Discourse on the Eighth and the Ninth, where Hermes instructs his son to inscribe the treatise on a hieroglyphic stele in his temple in Diospolis, probably referring to Diospolis Magna, one of the names for Thebes (NHC VI 61.19).[13]

Notwithstanding, by the end of the fourth century, church and state had joined forces at particular times to extirpate where possible all knowledge of unorthodox belief. It is likely we should have known nothing of Zosimos had it not been that his writings were preserved by persons with specific interest in the art and science he promoted. Had he been known as a religious writer, he may have been to history just one name, otherwise unknown, in lists of episcopally condemned persons. Who knows? One day we may yet uncover the archive of such a hypothetical guild. That would give scholars something to chew over.

A Guild for Theosebeia?

Olivier Dufault, in his *Early Greek Alchemy, Patronage and Innovation in Late Antiquity*, draws attention to a Syriac translation of an otherwise lost work by Zosimos indicating that Theosebeia instructed persons (possibly employees) on practicing *chēmeia*.

The philosopher (i.e., Democritus) claims: "they hid the writings on the natural substances under the multiplicity of matter." Perhaps they wanted to exercise our souls. Now, if they exercise the souls, well, philosopher, why to deny it? But you know how to exercise either the body or the soul, and it always leads you to achieve the perfection. In fact a wise saying reads: "studying is everything." And also Isidoros says: "studying increases your work." I know, this is not beyond your understanding (my lady), but you know it well, since you are one of those who would have liked to hide the art, if it had not been put in writing. For this reason you formed an assembly and administered the oath to each other. But you (my lady) moved away from the various topics (of this book); you presented them in a shorter form and you taught them openly. But you claim that this book cannot be possessed unless in secret. Now, even though secrets are necessary, it is quite fair that anyone has a book of alchemy, since it is not kept secret for them.[14]

It would seem from this that Theosebeia had set up her own scenario for instruction, but, from Zosimos's point of view, she had deviated from his own approach to instructing. According to the *Suda* (*zeta* [ζ], 168), Theosebeia was Zosimos's "sister" (*adelphē*) so, as we've suggested, they may have enjoyed a prior fraternity in a group or have been still party to such. However, the instructing with binding oaths suggests she may have been establishing a guild, possibly to bind employees, if she was in business, to the concern. Zosimos's quotation that "studying increases your work" might be a jocular reference to achieving more success in business through deeper attention to time-honored recipes. Or, as suggested earlier, Theosebeia was simply adding instructions to apprentices within a preexisting guild or additional body to such a guild.

Olivier Dufault has argued that Zosimos was "a client scholar, i.e., a person who was informally hired by a patron to teach or expand upon Greek or Latin literature and/or to produce new works."[15] However, while it is one possible scenario for their relationship, it rather takes it as read that Theosebeia was in a position to patronize, and that Zosimos required patronage. Furthermore, the idea of Zosimos being a "scholar"—that is, of a school—rather removes him both from practical artistry and commercial profit-making, with which he and his skills are evidently and preeminently concerned. Too much I think is made of Zosimos's reference to "noble lady" and Theosebeia's being "purple-robed" (see page 145). Such compliments could just as well be cheeky, amused familiarities or gracious, even ironic, flattery. Again, the idea that Zosimos was competing for a patron's attention with Neilos or Paphnutia is more assumption based on presupposition than fact.

Dufault's presentation of Theosebeia leading a group of alchemical students does not make much sense if "students" suggests persons
pursuing academic discipline. Training artisans is an essential part of
craft business, what we today call "learning on the job." Zosimos might
have dreamed of his art being included explicitly in a gentleman's liberal
education, but such was a most unlikely prospect. It has been argued
by Alexandre M. Roberts ("Framing a Middle Byzantine Alchemical
Codex," Dumbarton Oaks Papers 73 [2019]: 81, 101–2) that the elevation of alchemy to such a status was the intention of codices like the
Codex Marcianus 299,—namely, to add alchemy to the quadrivium "as
a culmination of higher education"—but if that was the intention, it
was largely unsuccessful in the wider sense, even some six centuries after
Zosimos.

Michèle Mertens's translation from Zosimos's *On the Vaporization
of the Divine Water that Fixes Mercury* describing Zosimos's trip to
Theosebeia's "house" to "instruct" her—presented somewhat imaginatively by Dufault as the invitation to a "client scholar" to attend
a "banquet by an aristocratic friend"[16]—is, when one examines the
text, tied closely to Zosimos's astonishment at the cooking practice (boiling a chicken with a sieve) of someone Theosebeia called
a *strouktōr;* that is, a slave who cooked; a "chef" (Latin, *structor*).
While Zosimos draws a lesson applicable to the tinctural art from
the novel experience, the immediate context is a kitchen. Zosimos
says nothing about an invitation to a banquet but simply that he was
staying at her house to instruct her. Giving guidance as to best use
of apparatus could have been a straightforward business kindness
and does not mean Zosimos was paid or patronized for it, or that
the visit was not also a sociable one with professional assistance for
her perhaps incipient business plans. Indeed, the reference to house
could equally mean place of business, company, shared apartments,
or atelier. It's also worth mentioning that Zosimos's many references to Maria the Jewess may have been to encourage Theosebeia
in business, which to me is the most likely and logical setting, along

perhaps with the formation of a guild related to business, for their mutual interaction. An inference one could reasonably draw without too much fantasizing is that Zosimos and Theosebeia were more or less operating in the same, or closely related, game, with Zosimos enjoying a considerable head start in his knowledge of it. Dare I speculate? They may even have joined forces in such business (hence "sister") or indeed fallen out over differences that his admonitions to her clearly show irked him.

Laboratories?

Our word *laboratory* as a reserved space for chemical experiment goes back at least to the early seventeenth century, being derived from the Latin *laborare,* meaning "to labor." Presumably, its cognate noun *workshop* did not suit gentlemen who began devoting themselves to "chymistry" in that period and who regarded themselves above both trade (shop) and work (manual labor). This class consciousness has had a baleful effect on how the ancient alchemist was conceived of in those times and subsequently. It never seems to have occurred to any Renaissance or late Renaissance alchemist that their practical predecessors could have been primarily engaged in ornamental and textile commerce, and the prejudice against sullying one's hands with trade has stuck fast.

In 1598, German alchemist Heinrich Khunrath's marvelously illustrated tome *Amphitheatrum Sapientiae Aeternae* (which identified the philosopher's stone with Christ) included a visual pun on the word *laboratorium* by dividing up this non-classical "Latin" word into two. The book contained a superb engraving by Hans Vredeman de Vries (died 1604) depicting the well-equipped alchemist's environment. On the right, carved in stone above a large, ornately canopied furnace fireplace, is the word *LABORATORIUM,* while on the left, the gentleman alchemist himself is on his knees, arms outstretched, eyes gazing heavenward before a round tabernacle, an oriental-type tentlike struc-

Fig. 9.2. Alchemical "Labor-oratory" in Heinrich Khunrath's
Amphitheatrum Sapientiae Aeternae, Solius, Verae (Hamburg, 1595)

ture, around whose crucifix-bearing dome is embroidered the word
ORATORIUM, below which an altar supports an open Bible and
book of astrological alchemy as incense rises into the chamber. *Labor*
is combined here with *Oratorium;* that is, a place of prayer, with the
assumption that this is the true meaning of the word *laboratorium.*
The "work," or opus, positively transcends ordinary labor. This is how
Zosimos's sacred view of the art appears somewhat peculiarly some
1,300 years after his telling Theosebeia that study would create more
work! It's amusing, and suggestive, too.

Alembicus ſeu ga-
lea dicitur,aut pileus,horum etiam

Fig. 9.3. An alembic, in Andreas Libavius, *Praxis alchymiae,* 1604

Matteo Martelli has noted how when learned alchemist and elixir-seeking medical doctor Andreas Libavius (1555–1616) wrote about the alchemical laboratory in 1606 he had to create the word *chumeion* for such an environment because there was no word handed down from late antiquity for "laboratory," the presumed setting for the ancient alchemist. Libavius's *Praxis alchymiae,* published in 1604, includes neat engravings of laboratory equipment, most of which Zosimos would have recognized. Libavius's neologism was taken from the newly rediscovered Greek *chumeia* (probably from the Byzantine *Suda* compendium).[17] He may have thought it more authentic than Khunrath's alchemical laboratorium, a word that had been gaining currency. Anyway, the chumeion, quasi-authentic or not, did not catch on.

That no work of early alchemy designates a specific work environment must suggest that the art was conducted according to the ready facilities, trade base, and access to furnaces and apparatus of any given operator. We have plenty of evidence for goldsmith and metallurgical shops being attached to temples in Egypt, of course, and naturally elsewhere, and even today we speak of an engineer's workshop without expecting purchasers and sellers. The Wadi Natrun region has yielded

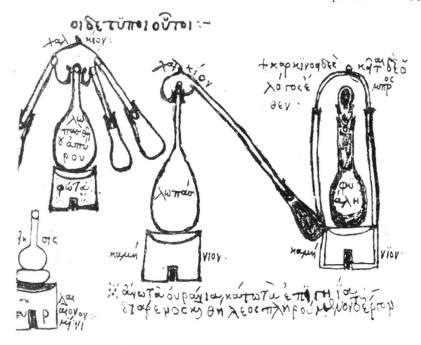

Fig. 9.4. Two alembics and two digestive vases, from *Codex Parisinus Graecus* 2327, folio 81v, grossly inferior to *Codex Marcianus;* an alembic with three recipients (tribicos of figure 3.8), plus an alembic of one recipient and some digestion vases. Though cut off in the past, the Greek words can be found complete in figure 3.9 (*palai stiaion kaminon*).

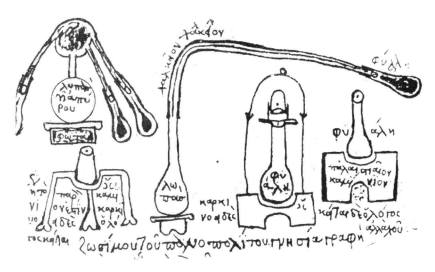

Fig. 9.5. Variants of figure 9.4, Ms. 2327, fol. 221v

several Roman glass workshops with what Martelli calls "basic furnaces" between Cairo and Alexandria (first century BCE to first century CE), and around Lake Mariout (also rich in nitron). The Greek suffix *-eion* was attached to the substance name of the craft to describe a particular craftsman's workplace, while the word *ergastērion* (with the Greek *ergon* meaning the same as the Latin for "labor") was a general word for a craft workshop.

An engraving in Daniel Mögling's (a.k.a. Theophilus Schweighardt's) "Mirror of the Rosicrucian Wisdom" (1618) plays on this word *ergon,* with the idea of the "work" transmuted into the intense spiritual praying at the oratory (no manual labor there), with the "parergon" (by-product) of the work being chymical success through manipulating apparatus—that is to say, the *real* work of alchemy, for Khunrath, was spiritual: the transformation of the operator, an inner-Christ realization, after which apparently miraculous discoveries might follow.

Fig. 9.6. "Ergon" and "Parergon" in Daniel Mögling's "Mirror of the Rosicrucian Wisdom" (Theophilus Schweighardt, *Speculum Sophicum Rhodo-Stauroticum,* 1618)

In the ancient world, work meant work, and as Martelli observes, the word *ergastērion* was "much connected with mining and metallurgy,"[18] though interestingly, it occurs once in the magical papyri in connection with the making of a "Typhonian ink" for a magical spell: "*To do well at the workshop* [ergastērion]: On the egg of a male bird write and then bury the egg near the threshold where you live." The prayer concerning the egg went thus:

> Great God, give favor, business to me and to this place where the egg lies, in the house I do my business . . . and / Good Daimon, send to this place every business and good daily profit. You are my work. You are the great Ammon, who dwells in heaven. Come, help me.[19]

This certainly suggested a workshop associated with fervent prayer, but not in the way Khunrath imagined it!

TEN

The Myth of Transmutation

WHENEVER THEORIES OF ALCHEMICAL TRANSMUTATION have been discussed in the past, there has usually been some discussion about how Greek philosophies of matter provided rationale for the belief that one metal could be transformed into another metal. Such disquisitions usually stress the so-called Aristotelian four-element theory (earth, air, fire, water), of which everything is said to be composed. This is often tacked on to a notion that all metals were believed to have a universal, protean substratum (or primary matter common to all), which, if acted upon appropriately, would manifest distinctions peculiar to a particular metal—while Nature herself had already effected that action to give us familiar metals and alloys; that is to say, external causes can affect the form (or governing potential of the substance, according to Aristotle). Applied to alchemy, this would suggest that the form, or body (metal),

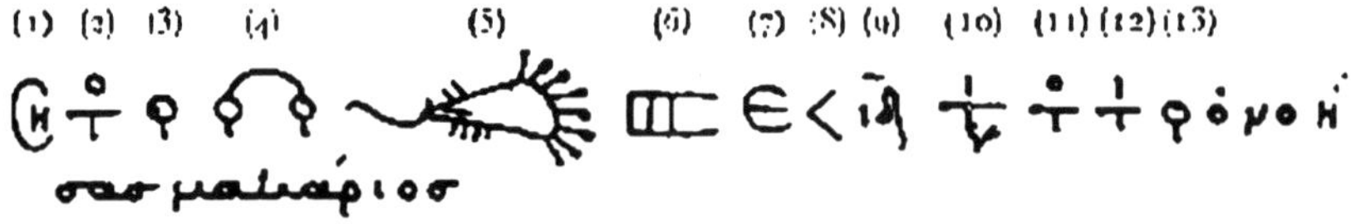

Fig. 10.1. Mysterious formula of the crayfish (cancer) or scorpion, which seems to summarize a transmutation (also fol. 83 of Paris Ms. 2325). It's found at the end of the memoirs of Zosimos (*Codex Marcianus*, fol. 193). Its interpretation is given on the cover page of that codex in a fourteenth-century hand.

may act as a kind of solvent for volatilities (called "spirits" by Mary the Prophetess) that would cause it to suffer change of identity. Early alchemists, according to these suppositions, allegedly believed that holding to the principle "All is One" compelled them to accept that universal interchange of determining qualities or substances was possible through sympathy and antipathy. Hence, transiting from a "lower" to a "higher" metal might not only be desirable but also theoretically conceivable.

However, proponents of this theory of early alchemy don't seem to recognize that were the theory to be universally applied, it would make sense to claim an ability to transform a leather sandal into a giraffe, or an aqueduct into a fingernail; that is to say, acts of miracle or magic could be performed naturally once one had located a common substrate to different forms. While many uninformed people doubtless took the labors of alchemists for magic, the best of the practitioners knew that they did not need magical rites to achieve real goals, only an understanding of nature: the reflection and extension—as Egyptian cosmology had it—of divine, spiritual principles above. We have no reason to think our late antique forebears were any more stupid than ourselves. They did not lack common sense, though there will have been exceptions, though perhaps less common than today. Another significant factor is that while all metals had definite distinguishing properties, gold was rather out on its own as a substance, insofar as it possessed a single, unique property, so unique in fact that the metal symbolized incorruptibility in a corruptible world, because it did not rust or darken or diminish with time; such a quality could hardly grow from the corruptible; it corresponded to the sun, radiant giver of life.

Philosophical Background

Shannon Grimes has come to regard Greek philosophy's claim to be a defining feature of alchemy as "problematic because it reinforces Western biases toward science and rationalism and tends to obscure the Egyptian contributions."[1] As we've seen, the Egyptian contributions

Grimes most recognizes are those of sacerdotal learning and temple practice. However, we have observed that the thinking background to our earliest alchemical texts may be described as remarkably syncretic. There's a Persian element represented by the name Ostanes, a Greek element represented by the name Democritus, a Jewish element represented by the names Mary and Moses, and an Egyptian element represented by the names Cleopatra, Pebichius, and, of course, Hermes Trismegistos. Zosimos stands, arguably, at the delta where all these tributaries meet and mix. There are grounds for thinking a Christian Gnostic element may also have been present, or may have been introduced by Zosimos.

Nevertheless, beyond all this, we must maintain that our first alchemists were, above all, practical people who learned from successful practice, not theory. Recipes were not speculative tracts. Business provided empirical imperatives to find empirical solutions to what *worked*. This was, after all, a Graeco-Egyptian culture with a dose of Roman realism suffusing it. The spiritual-physical universe in which late antique alchemists in Egypt operated was already a syncretic amalgam of Egyptian divine immanentism competing with Jewish spirituality, Platonist idealism, Stoic pneumaticism, pre-Socratic *nous* speculation, gnosis (Christian and otherwise), Aristotelian praise for logical mathematics, Euclidean physics, and a hierarchical, crystalline, and spherical cosmology that would find definitive, mathematical form in Claudius Ptolemy's works amid the fervid atmosphere of second-century Alexandria.

Investigating Zosimos's *Book on electrum* we noted that Zosimos considered Aristotle a stranger to greater cosmic verities of spiritual intelligences, but though relegated as a mortal man confined to the body of things, Zosimos nonetheless called Aristotle "the most brilliant of the non-luminous beings" (see page 157), which is a bit of a backhander since it's hard to be brilliant without luminosity! Zosimos may have taken something from Book 3 of the *Meterologica,* which if not by Aristotle himself is certainly of his school, as regards differences between metals and other mineral bodies.

Aristotle deviated from Plato's theory of origin of material substances (that they derived from formal ideas expressed as three-dimensional, geometric figures) by considering observations made on earth using the four-element theory. For Aristotle, form was not an idea with a home in eternity, so to speak (like beauty, for example, with many *things* below sharing this ideal), but was inseparable from sense-perceived things on earth. According to the *Meteorologica,* metals and fossils, formed in the earth, are products of "exhalations" caused by the sun's heat (or *fire*—note the reliance on four-element theory). Two kinds of exhalations are considered. First, a vaporous quality (containing *water*) exists in the *air* around bodies; the second exhalation comes from the *earth* and is very *flammable,* and smoky and dry (thanks to the *earth*). The dry, earthy exhalation produces fossils and stones that cannot be melted or fused, such as realgar, ocher, ruddle (red ocherous iron ore), sulfur, and so on. Fusible and ductile metals such as iron, copper, and gold are produced when vaporous exhalation encloses stones whose dryness compresses the vaporousness and solidifies it; that is to say, the metals' melting-potential suggests *water* or fluidity, with the wateriness being, after solidification, a hidden or invisible potential. A like-action to the sun—namely *fire*—could theoretically realize (or release) the potential within. Now, it may be that this latter Aristotelian notion of melting as a freeing of a potential nature within the solid body informs Zosimos's and Mary's ideas, or it may not. The same may be said regarding distillation, where potential for vaporization or evaporation may also be seen as freeing a "nature"; that is, a "male" or "female" substance.

On the other hand, such a freeing of potential solar product may be a notion later brought to bear on early alchemical texts to generate a common idea of transmutation as being the *philosophical work* of the alchemist. Thus in "Synesius and Dioscorus," a commentary on pseudo-Democritus attributed to Neoplatonic Christian philosopher Synesius, Dioscorus asks Synesius: "What transformation [literally "turning inside out"] is he [Democritus] talking about?" Synesius replies: "That of the bodies [metals]." Dioscorus inquires further: "And

202 ᗰ The Myth of Transmutation

how to accomplish it, how to transport nature out [or "turn the nature inside out"]?" Synesius tells him to listen more carefully and grasp what had been said earlier; that is: "Transform their nature, for nature has been hidden within."[2] The Greek verb "to transform" ([ek-]strephō) means more literally to "turn inside out" in the sense of bringing out what was hidden. It doesn't take much imagination to draw a parallel with this idea and that of an esoteric notion of *going within* to find a secret, spiritual, and transformative principle, located in a "body."*

While to us, the idea of a transformation suggests a new arrival, here the sense is on a *return* to something: a potential, already present, but hidden. Drawn forth from hiding and thereby *turning out* what was once inside necessarily causes visible form to change in appearance.

It seems whoever wrote the dialogue between Dioscorus and Synesius misunderstood pseudo-Democritus's *Physika kai mystika*. Where Democritus was writing about "doubling" gold by adding gold, and metals in value up to gold (*diplōsis*), the text was interpreted to mean that by feeding metals progressively higher in value, it was possible to transmute what one began with through exposing a formerly hidden potential. Misunderstanding may have come through applying Aristotle's theory, which suggested that gold and other metals were made in the earth thanks to the vaporous exhalation of the sun, and that *that* potential— the potential to make gold—could be drawn forth from the body as a volatile. Such a theory might also explain post-Zosimian fascination with divine water, if the water element of the sulfurous volatile were seen as manifesting an *original* solar, vaporous, and humid exhalation.

---

*Naturally, one cannot once more avoid thinking of the famous quote from the Gospel of Thomas in the Nag Hammadi library (logion 70): "If you bring forth what is within you, what you bring forth will save you. If you do not bring forth what is within you, what you do not bring forth will destroy you." The crucial nature of this hidden potential seems to have been a preoccupation of Egyptian mystics in the second century— when the gospel is thought to have been composed. The fascinating question of whether alchemy affected or effected a distinctive religious gnosis, or vice versa, we shall explore in due course. Western esoteric traditions would eventually synthesize alchemy and gnosis.

However, as far as the evidence of the first alchemists goes, they did not, in fact, set out to accomplish such a transmutation, being content with achieving profitable appearances—though Zosimos's dream narratives suggest he experienced a personally authentic freeing and rising of the spirit in contemplating the processes themselves; that is, identifying with them inwardly and consciously. For him, the processes constituted an initiated analogue to the spiritual cosmos described by Hermes and a means of imaginative and spiritual entry to the same: a sacramentalizing of nature. Furthermore, for Zosimos, transmutation (*ekstrophē*) occurs when incorporeals have taken a body by the effect of the art; that is to say, when a metal's dyeing is complete. In a difficult passage in *On the Body of Magnesia and its Treatment,* attributed to Zosimos, he elucidates this theme, a paragraph before stating Pebichius's view that divine water was better than fire at breaking down the bodies (metals) until they became incorporeal.

> Thus, to convert and transmute in these authors means to give a body to the incorporeals; that is to say to the fleeting matter . . . when the fleeting [or disappearing] materials have taken on a body, the conversion takes place for all the bodies, by their dye in white or yellow. Indeed this conversion is called transmutation, after the incorporeals have taken a body, by the effect of art.[3]

The remainder of the paragraph gives us another means for breaking down the body; that is, by fire. Fire can break down "strongly diluted materials" whereby they're rendered fleeting again and in a state of becoming incorporeal. At this moment they are reduced to "the last degree of division." This last degree of division is when the fleeting materials become vapor. Zosimos concludes: "Sublimated steam, the first of the incorporeal materials, thus leads to supreme art."[4] The steam, I conjecture, may perhaps have been brought to bear on a metal direct, or been distilled to a potent dye, or dye ingredient. Anyhow, transmutation is the effect on the metal of an effective dye, a complete union of body and spirit where spirit has transformed body. The spiritual analogy is obvious.

While the four-element theory, if taken literally—as Aristotle seems to do to some extent in *Meteorologica*—can suggest that differences among materials are solely down to proportions of the four elements within them, so that theoretically, any kind of transformation would be possible by manipulating such proportions, it's clear that until Zosimos at least, such philosophy did not decide the work of the alchemist. Aristotle's theory would *never* have given the Greek philosopher the means to turn a dull pot into a glittering work to command a high price among discerning buyers. The four-element theory was essentially descriptive, not quantitative. It was philosophy—that is, a means to find the world intelligible or rationally thinkable—not an instruction to the artisan. Indeed, Aristotle's philosophy was partly based on general observations of craft practices, while the idea of a "demiourgos" or "creator," properly means an *artisan*.* This cross-

---

*The concept of artisan-creator god was taken literally, indeed mischievously, from Plato's *Timaeus* by radical second-century Gnostics who reimagined the craftsman as the figure Ialdabaoth, or "jealous god" (of the Old Testament). Having copied imperfectly, and spiritlessly, the *ideas* of the true but unknown Father above, the imposter-god, knowing nothing higher than himself, then imprisoned hapless Man within his oppressive lower creation, from which only awareness of pneuma might release the captive being and effect restoration (*apocatastasis*) to the divine world beyond the Ogdoad. An image of a counterfeiting demiurge explained for such radicals the mortality, pain, insecurity, and alienation of this world. One can see clearly how redemption from such a world by hidden pneuma could easily cross-refer to hidden, incorruptible "gold," or spiritual potential, where achievement of ultimate transmutation could be seen as emblematic of release from the leaden character of terrestrial life. The stone becomes symbol of *a-cosmic* transcendence. But note also the *psychological value* of the myth of the Gnostic demiurge. If the demiurge is seen as the ungoverned ego of the universe, the "Big I AM," we see also a clue to understanding how it is that Man's self-will, self-obsession, self-reflection, self-armoring narcissism, and so forth prevent the soul from encountering the divine, higher man (what Zosimos calls *Phōs*) above. Hermetists called such a state "love of the body"; that is, to be blinded by matter and the superficial reflection of self wrapped up in its own *image* in sense perception, from which only higher spiritual awakening and action can redeem it. Thus, in Renaissance alchemical writings, the stone as *divine tincture* is identified with Christ, the whole, the true Man (Light) in his divine and penetrating, mercurial aspect.

over between craft wisdom and philosophy would later be used by Byzantine authors to attempt to dignify the alchemist as philosopher (with no taint of trade!), leading to such terms as the stone of the philosophers, or philosopher's stone. Zosimos might have said, had he guessed what was coming, either that his perception of nature was *superior* to much philosophy (including Aristotle's) or was a *higher* philosophy, being a revelation of *nous* with respect to the interior and exterior of cosmic creation.

What seems to have occurred is that after Zosimos's time, and possibly as a result of suppression of alchemical knowledge by Roman authority, the study of surviving texts seems to have fallen largely into the hands of writers who wished the works to gain the respect accorded to Alexandrian Neoplatonic philosophers, such as Synesius (late third/early fourth centuries), Olympiodorus (late fifth/sixth centuries), and Stephanus of Alexandria (late sixth/early seventh centuries). Alchemical works attributed to Synesius and Olympiodorus are most probably not the work of the two philosophers of those names. Stephanus of Alexandria, however, is almost certainly the author of *On the Great and Sacred Art of Making Gold,* a commentary on earlier texts. His works occupy a large part of the *Codex Marcianus.* After the triumph of Christianity in the empire, a process of Neoplatonizing the mystical potential of the tradition, combined with Christian and Aristotelian philosophical interpretation of the texts, and an overriding interest in theory, seems to have been most responsible for the generation of, and fixation on, the "philosopher's stone to transform lead into gold" idea, dependent on divine grace; that is to say, the idea of transformation mutated into transmutation as we have been taught to understand it. I hope this book contributes to correcting a vast historical error; namely, that alchemy may be defined as the practice of transmuting base metals into gold.

It appears to me that the textual tradition, as far as evidence permits one to say, lost contact with the practical industry of dyeing. This would naturally create a mystery of itself, into which theory and speculation could be poured. A most analogous scenario undoubtedly occurred when Freemasonry was sundered in England from the art and trade of master freestone masons after the year 1716, which generated any number of variants and mysteries of "Freemasonry" on the European continent, much, remarkably, intertwined with a revival of alchemy in Germany, France, and Italy in the eighteenth century but severed from the particularity of the original integrated practices of tradecraft traditions.

The Stone

As for the origin of the stone as transmutational agent, numerous possibilities present themselves, though it should first be understood that the term *philosopher's stone* does not appear in alchemical texts until the seventh century CE, and then only as an ambiguous title gloss where *stones* appear in the main text, during what may be called the Byzantine period of alchemical development, when, during the reign of emperor Heraclius (610–641 CE), collections were made of Graeco-Egyptian alchemical texts. However, these collections have not themselves survived except in tenth-century and considerably later copies. References to the philosopher's stone or "philosophical stone" are largely from Renaissance and post–Renaissance era copies. For example, a treatise containing extracts from Zosimos, Mary, and later alchemical writers titled "On the Philosophical Stone"[5] is only

Fig. 10.2. A mystical design taken from *Codex Parisinus Graecus* 2327, folio 47v and representative of a chemical operation (Berthelot compares them to "atomic equations"). Found toward the end of the third lesson of Stephanus's words: "It's the summer stone, the polychrome support (of the tinctures?)." There follows a mystical disquisition on the philosophical stone.

known in Paris ms. 2327 (1478), in an undated Vatican-held collection (according to Berthelot[6]), and seventeenth-century alchemical collections (Paris mss. 2251, 2252), when the term was already well known from medieval elaboration on Byzantine and Arabic material. The text "On the Philosophical Stone" was obviously suggestive, appearing to go back to the earliest authors. It opens with statements from Mary about "black lead" as being unlike ordinary lead, for it has been made black (possibly referring to molybdochalkos). Metals must be deprived of their metal before being reconstituted as metal. Fire must send sublimated steam upward.

2. The philosophers shared all the operations of the stone in four phases: 1 blackening; 2 bleaching; 3 yellowing, and 4 purple dyeing. Between blackening, bleaching, and yellowing, there is levitation or maceration and washing of the species. However, it is impossible for these things to be done otherwise than by the treatment operated by means of the channel apparatus and the union of the parties.

4. The alabastron is the whitest stone, the brain stone, the one that is like a burning glitter. Take it, pulverize it, and macerate it in vinegar; put it in a cloth, and bury it all in horse dung, or in bird dung, for 20 days, as the divine Zosimos says. . . .

11. Mary says: "If all the metallic bodies are not attenuated by the action of fire, and if the sublimated vapor reduced in spirit does not ascend, nothing will be completed."

The molybdochalkos is the summer stone. In all the operation, the preparation is black to begin with. . . .

13. Mary says: "Join the male and the female and you will find what is sought." And Mary said elsewhere, "Do not touch with your hands, for it is an igneous preparation." . . .

22. Zosimos said: "Do not be afraid to heat strongly; deplete the liquid element of the bodies. There are a thousand (modes of) heating copper; they make copper more suitable for dyeing. Bring out nature

without, and you shall find that which is sought; for nature is hidden within. Now, the nature being extracted, the white is no longer seen; but after the expulsion of the mercury indicated above, the yellow appears, by the announced yellowing of the ios. Where are those who declare it impossible to change nature? Now nature is changed; it becomes fixed and takes the quality of gold, returning to the dark. Indeed, if the moisture from the expulsion of mercury, circulating in the terrestrial (nature) of the solid body of the dry powder, will not dissolve and expel the liquidity, in accordance with the essential property of this expulsion of mercury, then nothing will happen of what is expected. If the liquid element is not dissolved and exhausted by heating, nothing will take place of what is expected. If the product is not dissolved and heated and then cooled, nothing will take place that is expected. But if all things are done in their place and by order, you can hope to achieve the result, with the help of Divine Providence." . . .

24. This is the summer stone. Sweeten the dry powder (of projection) and dry. Fix and refine the dry powder, taking: couperose, three parts; magnesia, one part; refined copper, one part; dry powder, one part. Wash together, watering in the sun with white vinegar, for seven days; then cook for two or three days. By removing (the product), you will find the gold dyed red blood color. This is the cinnabar of philosophers and the golden man. The powder of projection condenses itself (at the expense) of liqueurs. If the fire is excessive, it becomes yellow; but (then) it is not useful.[7]

It will be noted that here, as elsewhere in commentaries apparently collected from texts dating from between the late fifth century, the tenth, and later, quotations from early Graeco-Egyptian texts do not contain references to the philosophical stone. The idea of the philosopher's stone then seems to have come from ruminating on various inherited passages, such as those above, and finding recurring references to certain indeterminate stones intriguing, especially in the absence of their original context; that is to say, dyeing. The word *philosopher* whether referring to a singular or plural identity came about through reading multiple references to "the philosopher" (the often unnamed Democritus), or to the elevation of alchemists to that status during the Byzantine period, as natural philosophers in the line of physicists like Democritus of Abdera. The stone has many names, and none. The treatise *On the Philosophical Egg* opens with these words:

> Here's what the ancients say on the egg:
>
> 1. Some (call it) copper stone, ["others, the stone of Armenia," in Paris Ms. 2327, 1478]; others, the brain stone; others, the summer stone; others, the stone which is not a stone; others, the stone of Egypt; others, the image of the world. [In the margin to the tenth-century *Codex Marcianus* copy: "this must be heard in a mystic not a physical sense."] . . .
>
> 4. The liquid parts of the egg are called: the separate parts, the ios and ios of copper, the green water of copper, the water of native sulfur, the liquor of copper, the preparation of copper with the appearance of honey, the sublimated steam, the bodies reduced into spirits, the universal seed. (These liquid parts) are still receiving many other designations. . . .
>
> 13. There are two compositions made by the metallic bodies and by the divine waters and plants; they transmute matter, that which you will find in pursuit of the thing you seek. If two do not become one, and three one, and the whole composition one, the goal sought will not be achieved.
>
> END OF THE EGG[8]

A variant treatise on the "Nomenclature of the Egg: it's the mystery of the art" gives us a clue to the egg's identity: "It has been said that the egg is composed of four elements, because it is the image of the world and contains the four elements in itself. It has also been called the 'stone that turns the moon,' a stone that is not a stone, an eagle stone and alabaster brain." Berthelot notes that according to the tenth-century alchemical *Lexicon,* "alabaster" is lime drawn from eggshells; the shell encloses the egg like the cranium the brain.[9]

One last example of where the expression "the philosophical stone" has become a title for a treatise that does not actually use the term begins with supposed quotations from Zosimos:

> 1. I'm going to explain comaris.* Comaris, by its addition, brings the pearls to perfection. Under this name one designates the stone that draws out the spirit, by the power of the powder of projection. None of the prophets dared to expound this mystery in their discourses; but they knew that this was the way to fix this precious feminine power; for it is the venerable whiteness, according to the interpretation of all the prophets. We obtain this power of the pearl by cooking it in oil.
>
> 2. Taking the Attic pearl, cook it in oil, in an uncovered vase, for 3 hours in the middle of the fire. Rub the pearl with a wool cloth, to rid of oil and keep it for use in dyes. Because it is with the help of oil that we bring the pearl to perfection.[10]

A variant quotation attributed to Zosimos, but without the "Philosophical Stone" title, occurs in the treatise *On Lime.* Berthelot reckoned the early part of its "obscure recipes on fabricating the philosophical stone" came from Zosimos, but later on reference to Stephanus of Alexandria, who lived some three hundred years later, reveals at least this part of the text as a later concoction. It does not read as something coming from Zosimos at all, and I should suggest that any authentic core has been greatly elaborated upon.

Comaris has been described as something "difficult to find, which the Persians and Egyptians call talac, and others talc" (CAAG, vol. 2, 5.7, 334–35); in *Alchemical Lexicon,* "Aphroselinon (Silver foam)—This is the comaris, the coupholith" (light-stone); talcum (clay mineral) or selenite, according to Berthelot. Also in *Lexicon:* "It's arsenic."

This is the mystery not communicated, which none of the prophets dared to divide by the word; but they revealed it only to the initiates. They have taken it from the brain stone in their symbolic writings, the non-stone stone, the unknown thing that is known to all, the despised thing that is very precious, the given and unspoken thing of God. For me, I will salute it with the name of (stone) not given and given from God: it is the only one, in our work, that dominates matter. This is the preparation that possesses the power, the Mithraic mystery.

2. The spirit of fire unites with stone and becomes a spirit of a united kind. Now I will explain to you the works of stone. Mixed with comaris, it produces the pearls, and this is what has been called chrysolite. The spirit operates all things by power of the dry powder. And I will explain the word comaris, something that no one dared to divulge; but these (the ancients) passed it on to intelligent people. She holds the feminine power, that which one must prefer; for whitening has become an object of veneration for every prophet.[11]

Fig. 10.3. A symbol in the form of an inverted heart, containing the sign of gold, mercury, etc. (*Codex Marcianus*, fol. 5); occurs in a Zosimos treatise: the "last debris of an ancient symbolism" (CAAG, vol. 1, 155), anterior to the alchemical writings we possess, representing the most ancient mode of transmission of the science, requiring oral tradition for explication.

Fig. 10.4. Mystical design from third lesson of Stephanus, Ms. 2327, fol. 46v, taken from Ms. 2325. A singular design, it seems to be a variant of the symbol of figure 10.3.

Close inspection of terms reveals this was a recipe for fabricating pearls using talcum or selenite and, as one might by now expect, has nothing to do with any alleged goal of alchemists of transmuting lead into gold.

Gold fever takes many forms.

The Tome of Images

In his discussion paper "Nature Rejoicing in Nature: On the Origin of the Philosophical Stone," student of Egyptology Daniel Burnham accepts that the term "philosopher's stone" or "philosophical stone" post-dates Zosimos of Panopolis but is nonetheless compelled to hypothesize that what came to be called by that name nonetheless derives from a specific recipe dear to Zosimos.[12] The recipe's origin, purpose, and chemical composition Burnham seeks to establish with the aid of a tenth-century* Arabic work purporting to be Zosimos's authentic thought on the subject. The *Muṣḥaf aṣ-ṣuwar* (*Tome of Images*) is a long (more than 400 pages in translation[13]) illustrated work framed as a question-and-answer session between Zosimos and Theosebeia. Its construction indicates that it is really a commentary on Zosimos, drawing on some passages in his work we may recognize, with the lady playing an unconvincing role as eager student trying to get her revered tutor to let her in on the secrets she believes he is obscuring. Nevertheless, Burnham considers the work "one of the most important alchemical texts to have survived into the modern era," because it contains detailed explanations of alchemical operations and their symbology. In Burnham's view, to take the textual evidence at face value and consider Zosimos's recipes as being primarily concerned with dyeing metals is an approach both too literal and too superficial. The *Tome of Images,* he argues, supports the idea that the

---

*The actual manuscript was produced in Egypt in 1270 CE.

creation of the "stone that is not a stone" is of the essence of Zosimos's true intentions.

Because the Arabic work conforms to the scholarly consensus view that the "philosopher's stone" idea is late and was thrust back onto considerably earlier texts, Burnham's hypothesis would not impinge upon our attention but for the fact that Burnham believes the Arabic author understands Zosimos better than we do and may have had access to additional works by Zosimos not included in the Greek or Syriac corpus, understanding of which is vital, in Burnham's view, for understanding the real Zosimos. For that reason, we must examine the hypothesis.

Burnham feels that only by understanding the symbolism within the *Muṣḥaf aṣ-ṣuwar* can we acquire what he calls "alchemical consciousness," a means of discriminating between true and erroneous interpretations of familiar words given to ingredients. Burnham's paper hints that its author has acquired something of this consciousness. In his view, the issue hangs on whether we take the names given to ingredients literally or as indices of qualities only related by association to those words (for instance, the word *copper* may be used when it is only the softness of that metal that is intended). The problem of this approach is obvious. Nevertheless, we know that in numerous recipes, words are indeed often used in nonliteral ways (*divine water* being an obvious example among many), and this has been a familiar factor aggravating to students of the subject for nigh on two millennia. Indeed, in the Arabic text, Theosebeia herself is irritated and baffled by the obscurity engendered by polyvalent language.

Having examined the Arabic text, specialist in the reception of Zosimos in the Arabic world Bink C. Hallum found it contains some material attributed to Zosimos.

The Tome of Images includes a number of excerpts from other Arabic works attributed to Zosimos, at least three of which survive, allowing the texts to be compared. The first of these is the *Third Epistle of Zosimos* [addressed to Theosebeia], one of a collection of seven epistles known only in Arabic, but certainly translated from the Greek and attributable to Zosimos. Almost the entire text of the *Third Epistle* is reproduced in the *Tome of Images* (end of book 1 and majority of book 2) and nearly verbatim, but with a number of details (e.g., names of people and places) often missing or badly disfigured.[14]

Compiler of a facsimile publication of the *Tome of Images,* Theodor Abt noticed use of an Arabic text attributed to Zosimos—namely, the *Book of Keys* (*Kitāb al-mafātīḥ*)—while a section from an Arabic work titled *The Sulfurs,* known only in two Greek fragments, also appears.* That parts of the works were translated from Greek does not automatically qualify them as authentic Zosimos as numerous "Zosimian" works in Greek are of doubtful provenance. Theosebeia does *not* appear in *Sulfurs;* the *Tome* includes her for reasons of its own. The relationship of *The Sulfurs* to known texts of Zosimos, Hallum expresses as follows:

> To begin with, no mention of Theosebeia is found in *The Sulfurs* [unlike the *Tome*], which is a sort of chemical encyclopaedia in six books, further divided into short chapters, each dealing with a substance or technique, in which Zosimos addresses himself to an anonymous (masculine plural) readership. The two Greek fragments confirm that *The Sulfurs* is neither a dialogue nor an epistle and is not addressed to Theosebeia, and the versions of these fragments in *The Sulfurs* shows that the Arabic follows the Greek text closely and for the most part faithfully. The section of *The Sulfurs,* Book I/II,

---

*The fragments we know as *On Quicklime* (in *Les alchimistes grecs,* book 4, part. 1, *Zosime de Panopolis: Mémoires authentiques,* edited and translated by Michèle Mertens, XIII [Paris: Les Belles Lettres, 1995])—corresponding to *Sulfurs,* books 1 and 2 (first two books undifferentiated in the *Tome of Images*), chapters 15, 16, and the first part of 17; *Explanation Concerning Fires* (CAAG, vol. 2, text 3.55)—corresponding to *Sulfurs,* book 4, chapter 3. For a description of *The Sulfurs,* see Stapleton and Azo, "An Alchemical Compilation of the Thirteenth Century A.D.," 65–68; more recently and with a comparison of the two Greek fragments and the corresponding sections of *The Sulfurs,* see Hallum, "Zosimus Arabus," 132–92 and appendices 1A and 1B.

chapter 15 (Rampur, Raza Library MS *kīmiyā'* 12, fols 60b, l.18 [to] 61a, l.12), which is in turn a translation of ll.1–27 of the Greek fragment of Zosimos known as *On Quicklime* (*Mém. Auth.* [Mertens] XIII), appears in the *Tome of Images* (fols. 220a, l.6 [to] 220b, l.16) in a heavily adapted and, of course, dramatized form. During the process of inclusion in the *Tome of Images,* the integrity of the text of this fragment suffered much more at the hands of the compiler than did either the text of the *Third Epistle* or the passages from the *Book of Keys*. Much material has been both excised from and added to the text as found in *The Sulfurs* or the Greek fragments, upon which the version in the *Tome of Images* is only very loosely based.[15]

Burnham omits to mention Hallum's observations that not only are there plainly post-Hejira references in the *Tome* but also that the *Third Epistle* has been reworked in the *Tome* to make it fit a question-and-answer scenario, whereas its source was written in epistolary form, making the *Tome* version "less sound."[16] It is also notable that Burnham also omits Hallum's overall criticism of Theodor Abt's publication of the *Tome*. According to Hallum, Abt's Jungian agenda makes his comments on the text more pertinent to the psychologist than the historian, the latter requiring establishment of context; Abt's approach then, from the historical point of view, is methodologically unsound.[17] Hallum also shows failures of logic regarding Abt's views of the *Book of Keys* and demonstrates that Abt's contention that the *Tome* was originally a Greek work is utterly unsustainable. Hallum shows the *Tome* as an original Arabic composition employing some Greek elements reworked, of which only some are attributable to Zosimos.[18] Therefore, Burnham's statement that "it is clear that the author of the *Muṣḥaf aṣ-ṣuwar* had access to a significant cross-section of the authentic writings of Zosimos,"[19] requires greater qualification, to say the least.

Most illuminating as to the distance between our earliest relevant Zosimos text and the use of it in *Tome of Images* is Hallum's comparison of Greek lines attributable to Zosimos, followed by a translation into the Arabic *Sulfurs,* thence reworked for the *Tome of Images.* The comparison speaks for itself. First, Michèle Mertens's translation from Zosimos's treatise *On Lime* (*Mémoires authentiques* 13.2):

> Zosimos said concerning quicklime: I [will] make things clear to you. Know that the alabaster-like stone is called "the brain" because it is that which restrains every fugacious dye.

Next, the Arabic *Sulfurs* (frag. 1, 2.2–3):

> I am making clear to you the matter of quicklime, for it is from the feminine power. I would like you to know, O sages, that the stone that is called *alābaṣṭrūn,* they have called a brain, because it restrains every dye which does [sense uncertain] remain.

And lastly, the *Tome of Images* (fol. 220a, 6–11):

> She [Theosebeia] said: / Explain to me your discourse concerning the *al-naṣṭrīṭis.* He [Zosimos] said: It is quicklime when it becomes the stone that we call / *naṣṭrīṭis,* and we only call it *naṣṭrīṭis* due to the brilliance [literally, "strength"] of its whiteness. As for / [why we call it] quicklime, this is due to fire being concealed within it just as fire is concealed within common quicklime. / As for [why we call it] "the brain," the dye is concealed inside it and it [the brain] hides it [The dye] in its subtleness just as / the brain contains the idea, and people can see the brain while they cannot see the idea within it. Likewise, / the colour white is seen within the stone while the dye concealed within it is not seen.[20]

Hallum concludes: "So, an alternative to Abt's hypothesis of the origin of the *Tome of Images* is as follows: it is not a translation from the Greek, and therefore does not originate with Zosimos or his circle, but is an important compilation of Arabic versions of authentic Greek texts."[21] Hallum believes that while Abt's publication may stimulate welcome interest in Arabic alchemy, its comments on history and sources are more likely to confuse than clarify serious study of the field. Let us now hear what Daniel Burnham has made of this source in his attempt to show Zosimos really was interested in the "stone that is not a stone" as transmutational agent, bearing in mind that he appears to have used Hallum's review of Abt's publication in a manner advantageous to his argument, and omitted Hallum's serious objections, which compromise it. We are also compelled to regard the accepted canon of Zosimos's work as primary source and not elements of it that appeared some six centuries or more later in Arabic works. So we had best begin with the accepted source for the key text, since Burnham generously regards Zosimos's *On Lime* as "the makings of a real, graspable chemical composition."[22]

As Berthelot puts it, *On Lime* (or "Quicklime"; 3.1) "consists of a series of obscure recipes for making the philosopher's stone. The last ones are posterior to Zosimos, as indicated by the centuries-later quotation of Stephanus from section 2b (missing in eleventh-century Byzantine ms. *Marcianus graecus* 299, but taken from Paris mss. 2327, dated 1478); with the exception of the final sentence of §3, which expresses very clearly the formation of copper sub-salts, or copper* flowers."[23]

ZOSIMOS SPEAKS ABOUT LIME

1. I will make (things) clear to you. One knows that the stone alabastron [according to the tenth-century Byzantine alchemical *Lexicon*: "It is the lime from egg shells, the salt from the efflorescences, ammonia salt, common salt"] is called brain [according to Berthelot: "the philosophical egg"; see Zosimos's treatise on the

---

*As for the copper, Zosimos says about it: "Altered by most waters, because of the humidity of the air and the heat, it increases in volume and is covered with flowers, which are much softer; it fructifies by the productive action of nature."[24]

Egg, page 209, because it is the binding agent of any volatile dye. Taking then the alabastron stone, cook it one night and one day; have lime, take vinegar very strong, and boil: you will be amazed; for you will make a divine manufacture, a product that whitens to the highest degree the surface (of metals). Leave to place, then add very strong vinegar, working in a vase without a lid, to remove the sublimated steam, as it forms above. Taking more strong vinegar, raise this vapor for seven days, and thus work until the vapor does not rise any more. Leave the product for forty days (exposed) to the sun and dew, at the fixed time; then soften with rainwater. Dry it in the sun and conserve.

This is the uncommunicated mystery, which none of the prophets dared to reveal by word; but they revealed it only to the initiates. They called it the encephalal ["brain"] stone in their symbolic writings, the not-stone stone [*Lexicon:* "It is lime and sublimated steam, diluted with vinegar"], the unknown thing that is known to all, the despised thing that is very precious, the thing given and not given by God. For myself, I will greet her with the name of (stone) not given and given by God; it is the only one in our work that dominates matter. This is the preparation that possesses the power, the Mithraic* mystery.[25]

The next paragraph attributed to Zosimos we have already seen (page 211), being that beginning: "The spirit of fire unites with the stone and becomes a spirit of a unique kind," whereafter readers are promised an explanation of the "works of the stone," whose determinant is the "spirit" working by power of "dry powder." As noted earlier, these passages and that following are actually describing a recipe for fabricating pearls not one for producing the philosopher's stone.

---

*Originally Mithra was the Indo-Aryan god of light and of the sun. As "Mithras," the figure became a Roman cult and was considered to have been born from a rock, which is suggestive, alchemically.

I will also explain to you the power of the pearl. It fulfills its works, put in decoction in oil. It represents female power. Taking the pearl, you will put it in decoction with oil, in an unplugged vase, without lid, for 3 hours, on a moderate fire. Taking a chiffon of wool, rub it against the pearl, in order to remove the oil and here you are, (the available pearl) for the needs of dyes; for the accomplishment of the material (transformation) takes place by means of the pearl.[26]

Nevertheless, according to Burnham, the chemical reaction alluded to in the first section of the treatise is to produce the "stone and not a stone" and has elements of "what some modern alchemists refer to as the 'acetate path,'"[27] meaning production of acetate salts to be distilled to produce chemical compounds. Mertens is cited as thinking *alabastron* may mean "alabaster" (limestone) but could be code for the "egg." We've seen an interpretation of alabastron as eggshells above. Limestone and eggshells both consist of calcium carbonate ($CaCO_3$), with eggshells also containing calcium phosphate, magnesium carbonate, and proteins. Quicklime (calcium oxide) is produced when calcium carbonate is heated sufficiently to release a carbon dioxide molecule. The quicklime is poured into a pot of vinegar, producing a reaction between quicklime and perhaps some calcium carbonate and the acetic acid of the vinegar. Calcium oxide reacts with acetic acid to produce calcium acetate and water. Similarly, calcium carbonate reacts with acetic acid to produce calcium acetate, carbon dioxide, and water. From this, Burnham concludes:

Certainly this is one of the earliest prototypes for the concept of the "philosophical stone." However, in this case we have a clear chemical identity for this stone. The reaction when completed and dried will produce (among other trace constituents) whitish crystals of calcium acetate. It is a stone and not a stone, a brittle crystal.[28]

It is difficult to make proper sense of this statement, especially the use of the word *certainly*. "Earliest prototype for the concept" begs all kind of questions. What concept? It is established that the concept of the philosopher's stone was created long after Zosimos, and its use as headings for fragments of his work represents a later projection backward in time, presumably, given the evidence at our disposal, because the texts concerned refer to a stone of unusual value to the dyer. If the desired stone is not a stone, we may conclude that it could not possibly be a philosopher's stone because that, as far as nomenclature goes, *is* a stone, albeit a special one. Now it's perfectly possible that certain epithets could have been lifted up and applied to the picture of a philosophical stone later, and then, as though by a trick, it would look, from the similarity of epithet, that the same *thing* was being described in the past. However, the point is that if you had never heard of the philosopher's stone you would not conclude from the text above that *that* was what was being referred to: the concept must come first, and it does not come from the text, only from later elaboration on it. The conclusion from a study of the text alone would naturally be that the operation described produces a remarkable ability to whiten a surface. Base metals and gold are not even mentioned.

Burnham then brings in copious quotations from the *Tome of Images*. Additional processes are described that are not in the original work, such as the manufacture of a "poison" that becomes very red in color. Such additional material only demonstrates that the thinking of the author of that text was different from the original, which is what we should expect, given the great number of intervening years and the determination of Arabic-speaking alchemists to take the alchemical operation to greater heights if they could.

Going back to Zosimos, we find that the spirit of the fire reacts with the "stone" to produce a unique spirit—that is, an active ingredient—but the text does not tell us whether this spirit needs to be extracted, only that the stone mixed with comaris produces pearls called "chrysolite," a word usually applied to numerous green and yellow-green gemstones, though in the context the meaning may be "like chrysolite." Some idea of chrysolite in Zosimos's mind might be found in a late alleged quotation from Zosimos in the Greek work attributed to early alchemist *Pelagius the Philosopher on the Sacred and Divine Art* (section 8).

> Zosimos says, "Natural gold, being changed into spirit by means of chrysolite [Berthelot asks: "Is this the dissolution of gold by metallic sulphide?"], dyed according to its nature; silver, if we dissolve it by means of divine water and if we change it into spirit by means of chrysolite, dyes copper into white." He also said this in other terms: "Indeed, the two dyes do not differ in any way from each other, except by colour, that is to say, they have a single mode of treatment, according to which (the bodies are) first dissolved by divine water and later the solid powder is changed into spirit by means of the chrysolite." Now they differ in colour. Each of them dyes according to its own nature: gold dyes gold, and silver dyes silver. Do you not hear the old writer saying, "He who sows wheat begets and harvests wheat; gold also begets gold; likewise silver begets silver" [the quote is from *Isis to her son Horus*].[29]

Whatever was intended, Burnham speculates by assuming "an unspoken operation."[30] Sublimation (change of state by heat absorption) of calcium acetate produces acetone plus some acetate essential oils of strong acidic quality. Calcium acetate distilled produces calcium oxide, carbon dioxide, and acetone. Burnham notes the "giving back" of calcium oxide suggests an ouroboros-like cycle. Burnham presumes allegedly unknown "acetone" is the product whose uses appear in *On Lime* (section 2). While accepting that acetone-based products are today used in dyes, Burnham quotes from the *Tome* that his imagined product dyes pearls and whitens copper toward a gold color (whereas the original says the stone plus comaris produces pearls, and the pearls have great properties). He then questions whether the *Tome* reference to copper may be symbolic, while the word *whiten* would incline copper to a silveriness rather than gold, so perhaps *whiten* means "brighten." One is fast getting into confusion, but Burnham proceeds. He sees now an "implication" that we are starting with oxidized (darker) copper and an intention to lighten it. Acetone, we are told, restores oxidized copper and "would help to incline its color toward the color of gold."[31] So, acetone could be for Zosimos "a water with the spirit of fire." Burnham next points to a possible by-product of the operation.

Calcium acetate sublimation, in addition to acetone, produces complex chemicals or acetate oils, including a bright red oil, capable of turning litmus paper cinnabar-red. Burnham wonders if *this* was prized by alchemists, more than acetone, the latter a clear liquid that possesses a comparably weak acidic potency. Burnham concludes that the "stone of the sages" may be identified as calcium acetate "with a fair degree of certainty."[32] Despite this claim, which is not without interest but is without certainty, he admits that the text only points to a possible formative operation of the acetate salt and doesn't conclusively prove that that was the use of the salt. After that, he looks into the *Tome* to see if its involved use and serious elaboration of Zosimos's translated text was hiding something by deliberate obscurity, and we are at once reminded of the classic *obscurum per obscurius* argument frequently leveled at alchemy in general. In any case, this book is not the place to explore a development of Graeco-Egyptian alchemy undertaken by Arabic-speaking alchemists many centuries later.

If it really was Daniel Burnham's intention to make the philosopher's stone the true central interest of Graeco-Egyptian alchemy, I should say his speculation on acetates rather confirms the view that dyeing was its central interest, adding strength to the idea of the ingenuity of practitioners of the art in late antiquity. It is also possible that his identification of calcium acetate with the brain stone, if not the philosopher's stone, might prove of lasting value, though its scope would be limited to the credible and the creditable and does not, from its stated properties, seem quite to satisfy Zosimos's declaration in *On Lime* (section 2) that the stone *he* is referring to deserves greeting "with the name of (stone) not given and given by God; it is the only one in our work that dominates matter."

Dominates matter . . . Many years ago I asked album designer Jean-Luke Epstein to design a cover for a projected sequel to my book *The Gnostics*. His response was intuitive. He drew a large-headed man in a dark overcoat. In the center of his forehead was a sphere that seemed to represent something in his head. I can't help wondering now if there was at least a pun going on with the idea of the brain stone. Without necessarily laboring the point with the Hindu doctrine that the divine Brahman, or spirit, enters the human system through the crown of the head, could it not be that the "stone which is not a stone" is in one sense at least, the *mind;* that is, the *nous,* or "higher reason," the mind-over-matter without whose direct and penetrating application the alchemist is, according to Zosimos, at the mercy of fate? Zosimos was of course familiar with the text of *Corpus Hermeticum* 4 wherein the people of the earth are summoned by a herald to baptism, or dipping, in a *kratēr*—a large vase for mixing wine with water—which has been filled with *nous,* offering access to divine vision: the mind of God. Those who heed the summons are saved from the downward pull of fateful matter: the rest march on, incomplete, at the behest of merciless fate. The use of the mixing bowl (kratēr) apparatus is at least suggestive of alchemical preparation (compare, "He who trips on that stone shall be broken; but he on whom the stone falls shall be winnowed," Luke 20:18).

Myth and Reality

It was encouraging to see that our findings as regards a myth of transmutation in early alchemical texts are consistent with those of Olivier Dufault's extensive paper, "Transmutation Theory in the Greek Alchemical Corpus" (2015). Dufault's introduction reads like a conclusion: "A closer look at the texts reveals that the apparent uniformity of ancient Greek alchemical doctrine implied in most modern discussions is not supported by the evidence."[33]

Dufault, too, traced the assumption that Greek philosophy held structural keys to early alchemy. He found the assumption wanting. For example, it has become almost a cliché in accounts of alchemy to state the first process involved a blackening, as if the alchemists were trying to reproduce in the furnace or crucible Aristotle's prime matter (*prōtē hylē*) at the start of the universe.[34] We see this is a result of the classic "selective texts" syndrome. You find a text and build a theory on it, oblivious to the weight of alternative evidence. In disentangling early alchemy from assumptions about Greek philosophy and physics, Dufault proceeds to delineate three groups of theories by which historians have attempted to produce a single transmutational theory.

The first of these is the "Natural Sympathy Theory": something we've explored already in relation to pseudo-Democritus's importation of Persian wisdom on how nature interacts with itself in mutual sympathy and corresponding antipathy: "nature delights in nature, nature conquers nature, nature masters nature" (see page 37). The problem for the theorists is that pseudo-Democritus had no transmutational theory to offer based on Ostanes's observation of a mutually dynamic natural order. Pseudo-Democritus did not imagine a substance that had no qualification, a kind of neutrum, or as Dufault calls it: "an unqualified substrate,"[35] something on which mutation could act, or a substance that could be made to mutate. Besides, it would not be a mutation if there was nothing effectively to mutate from. Different metals reacted differently with, thankfully for the artist, different materials, generating different results.

The second theory Dufault calls the "Maturation Theory," which means either metals grew in the earth, and could grow from lesser to higher metals over long periods (with "gold" as final stage of growth), or that metals and non-fusibles resulted from humid or dry exhalations (which idea we've also investigated). While as analogies, alchemists

might have found common ground with these ideas, they had no obvious or operational notion of metals growing in a strict order of superiority. Non-fusibles were equally vital. If they were silvering an object, they wouldn't want gold, or try to "stop gold from happening" if the process went too far! There was no periodic table of mineral ascendancy.*
There were associations of what people valued most for particular objects, but you would not put in gold eyes where the client longed for lapis lazuli! And the same goes for crystals and gemstones and all the other ingredients. Lead, "low" as it might be, could make all the difference between glittering triumph and muddy failure. The interest was always on the effect, not the theory. Besides, again, gold was not the most valued mineral in the world to all people. Rarity was what counted, and what was done artistically with the material was what counted most. Anyhow, there's no evidence that Aristotle thought that all the metals were just stages in gold's temporal maturity; it sounds like an old wives' tale.

The mutation Zosimos does discuss and picture analogically is that of the spiritual growth *of the man,* not the metal, from "man of copper" to "man of gold," but everyone knew what happened when you buried a man in the earth without appropriate embalming. He didn't grow into anything. As for Zosimos, he knew very well that if you wanted to double your gold you had to have *gold.* I'm sure he'd have nodded affirmatively on hearing our old English saying, "You can't make a silk purse out of a sow's ear."

The third theory Dufault notes is what he calls the "Form-Transfer Theory." This is based on the idea aforementioned whereby prime matter was an unqualified substrate from which anything might be mutated. Dufault shows that Aristotle's view of elements has been

---

*There was, as we have seen, a hierarchical ascendancy of planetary correspondences with metals, and while this was primarily symbolic, it might affect, say, Zosimos's analogy of spiritual ascent, or rising through the spheres, but it would hardly make a practical crossover into operational conditions, however rich the analogies, for there are no corresponding spheres for cinnabar, zinc oxide, magnesia, arsenic, sulfur, or sulfides, etc.

taken too simply and doubts if the philosopher ever thought such a neutral substance could exist in a world whose nature's obvious elemental characteristics were varieties of contrarieties; a neutral substance contradicts the natural sympathy theory. If prime matter lacked form, it lacked existence also.

Anyhow, there's no evidence in the recipes that reducing substance to such a somewhat inconceivable condition was ever recommended, or even envisaged. One could imagine perhaps Zosimos being indignant at the notion that the highest powers could provide such a fruitless material! "Nothing comes from nothing." For him, the creation was not a tabula rasa but a living spiritual reality of endless abundance. Dufault shows that writers who have followed the theory of form transfer have used quoted texts in such a way as to reveal the theorizers have confused dyeing and transmutation, the very error that entered alchemical tradition in the Byzantine period, whose cause was most likely a lack of knowledge of the true setting and a surfeit of philosophy and mysticism.

Dufault expresses his response to the idea of Greek philosophy providing transmutational theory thus:

> In what kind of ancient intellectual environment could these multiple theories have coexisted? It seems to make little sense to continue assuming that alchemical writers operated on philosophical grounds, especially if the result is to conclude that they were bad philosophers. Greek philosophy is not the single interpretive key of the Greek alchemical corpus; rather, philosophy was only one of the systems of reference within which alchemical writers described dyeing and metallurgical practices.[36]

Having now established that the first alchemists did *not* operate with the end in mind of fabricating a philosophical stone or philosopher's stone to transmute base metals into gold, we have a slight inherited problem: *How do we define* alchemy?

So, like any fool, I Google the word *alchemy* in search of a definition, only to find it described as

> the medieval forerunner of chemistry, concerned with the transmutation of matter, in particular with attempts to convert base metals into gold or find a universal elixir.

Now perhaps we can see why it's often better to buy a book than rely on the internet. Haven't we all been caught?

ELEVEN

Forbidden Knowledge

MANY'S A POPULAR NARRATIVE based on the idea of forbidden knowledge. One only has to think of Mary Shelley's Victor Frankenstein getting into a fatal mess over his desire to reanimate the dead by Promethean science and Galvani's conception of electric charges to get the idea. Then there's that science-fiction regular: the mad scientist (often sited in what resembles an alchemist's lab) who, though the world dismisses him as mad, considers himself the pioneer genius, admired by advanced intelligence. Arch-villain Blofeld in the Bond story *On Her Majesty's Secret Service* has devised the means to introduce mass infertility into the food chain and wipe out whole species of food and livestock forever worldwide and is not the least bit defensive about his achievement. Asserting superior rights, S.P.E.C.T.R.E. supremo says something like "the methods of advanced thinkers have often baffled conventional minds." There has been disquiet over the misanthropic potential of so-called pure science since ancient times. Third-century BCE Syracusian genius Archimedes, inventor of the heat ray, Archimedean screw, and much else, was killed by an irate Roman soldier when the distracted inventor refused to abandon his diagrams (so the story goes), to the consternation of invading general Marcellus, who saw Archimedes as a great asset, with his unlimited imagination and proven ability with war machines. The knowledge may have come from hell, but, hell,

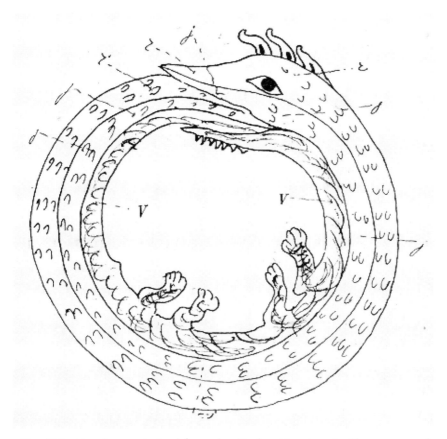

Fig. 11.1. Ouroboros derived from the *Codex Marcianus's Chrysopoea of Cleopatra* (formed from three concentric circles)
(Paris Ms. 2327, fol. 196)

knowledge doesn't half give the invader an advantage! Rightly says Ecclesiastes (1:18): "For in much wisdom is much grief: and he that increaseth knowledge increaseth sorrow." Even rulers who prefer to keep populations in the state of innocence suggested by Qoheleth in Ecclesiastes cannot resist patronizing science, mostly for power and bullying dominion. The only large institution that hasn't done this, interestingly, is the Roman Catholic Church, which, while repressing science for centuries, did not use it to build itself an advanced arsenal, preferring to manipulate the already irrepressible tendencies of greedy leaders. Behind every mad dictator you will find obedient scientists. Werner von Braun managed to switch from serving Hitler to U.S. secret projects without too much heartache. Without him, Neil Armstrong and Buzz Aldrin could not have "come in peace for all mankind" to the moon in 1969. Today we fear with justifiable alarm the gathering number of bellicose minds who have at their disposal weapons and information that could never have come to them but for the allegedly disinterested pursuit of knowledge we dignify with the word *science.*

So where did all this science come from? Well, as we know, according to Zosimos it came from rogue angels (or *daimōnes*) who brought it to earth from heavenly realms with ill intent and who, though dispersed in various regions, still use their powers to extract worship from idolaters while reaping satisfaction from mayhem and destruction wrought by the tainted toys of warriors. The story of the Watchers in the Book of Enoch clearly satisfied Zosimos's preferred version of history where the secrets of dyeing were concerned.

The most detailed use of Enoch by Zosimos, with the emphasis on forbidden knowledge, is found in Syriac treatise *On Tin* (Letter Eta).

The Holy Scriptures, O woman! say that there are some daimons who trade with and manage women. Hermes also mentions this in his book on natural (sciences) [*Physika,* according to the Synkellos paraphrase; see page 45]; and his entire book offers a meaning that is at once manifest and hidden. He mentions it in these terms: The ancient and divine books say that some angels were taken with passion for women. They came down to the earth and taught them all the operations of nature. It is about them that our Book (the Bible) said that filled with pride these were they who'd been driven out of heaven, because they'd taught men all the bad things, which do not serve the soul. It is they who composed the works (chemical), and of them comes the first tradition on these arts. One calls their book Chema (*koumou*), and it's from there chemistry (*koumia*) got its name. The Book consists of twenty-four sections; each of these has its proper name, or letter, or treatise . . . One of them is called Imos; another, Imout . . . One section is called key . . . In this book we find the arts publicised in thousands of words.[1]*

According to Erik W. Larson, when Zosimos's city of Panopolis was excavated by Urbain Bouriant in the late 1800s, a grave in a cemetery near the site yielded a parchment manuscript containing parts of the apocryphal Gospel of Peter, the Apocalypse of Peter, and . . . the first thirty-two chapters, in Greek, of 1 Enoch: most of that section called the Book of the Watchers.[2] Known as the *Codex Panopolitanus,* this version of 1 Enoch has a different arrangement to the Ethiopic and Aramaic texts, suggesting the copyist has attempted a more biographical sequence than the Ge'ez or Dead Sea Scrolls versions.† Anyhow, a Greek version of 1 Enoch is likely what suggested to Zosimos the Greek name for daimons in his *Final Account,* the ones who used unnatural dyes to get offerings: *ephoroi,* which means "guardians," "overseers," and "watchers." The word gives Zosimos an interchangeable description both for manipulative priests, and daimons who governed those aspects of life subject to fate (the stars).

---

*It's odd that Zosimos tells Theosebeia that the daimonic work ("koumou") has twenty-four sections, each named after a letter, with one called *Imout,* when Synkellos reports that *Zosimos* wrote a work called *Imouth* (his "ninth") with twenty-four sections named after a letter. Synkellos may have read carelessly, or followed a secondary source on the passage. Notwithstanding, one suspects there is an elaborate joke of Zosimos's in all this, evident perhaps in the tonal leap from the address at the heading of the Syriac version (above) "To Theosebeia, the queen, greetings!" to the next line where she is addressed: "O woman!"

†See Elena Dugan, "Enochic Biography and the Manuscript History of 1 Enoch: The Codex Panopolitanus Book of the Watchers," *Journal of Biblical Literature* 140, no. 1 (2021): 113–38.

At the end of *Final Account,* Zosimos, with some irony, suggests to Theosebeia that there are indeed "sacrifices" that *may* be offered to ruinous daimonic entities: those sacrifices known to King Solomon and shown to him, Zosimos believed, by an Egyptian magician.

The story behind this allusion exists in several forms. It's come down to Western Magic today as the "Key of Solomon," or the book of the "Goetia," having gone through numerous variations. In the Greek *Testament of Solomon,* which Zosimos probably knew, the king was given a magic ring with a pentagram on it, enabling him to summon daimons from their small places and command them to assist with building the temple (a reference to a magic ring and an ourobouros exists in the Leiden Papyrus V; see page 22). In the version familiar to Zosimos, the daimons give Solomon knowledge of which angels can thwart their wicked designs, and he obtains power to entrap the daimons in his will. What Zosimos is saying is that if Theosebeia can banish the daimons from her tincture-making, she'll find the true tinctures and times, meaning propitious times in the *natural* order of things (including ordinary astrological fate), rather than seeking daimonic help to intercede vainly in the order of nature to attempt to alter it unnaturally for private gain at the unenviable price of thralldom to their deceits.

In some versions of the story, Solomon's work is undone by the wiles of a woman who persuades him to make sacrifices to other gods; the king should have sacrificed any such perceived advantage and conquered his lust, Zosimos would doubtless have thought—and Theosebeia ("O woman!") should have acted likewise.

We have seen how in Zosimos's Syriac treatise *On electrum,* an angel instructs Solomon on constructing seven electrum bottles to trap daimons (electrum mirrors reveal sin; in other versions daimons are confined to bronze jars).[3] Whichever way the story is told, knowledge comes at a high price, and Zosimos was particularly aware of how easily knowledge of dyeing could be abused. Theosebeia might

have argued that it was for that very reason that she bound her trainees with oaths, something Zosimos disapproved of. Zosimos, however, sees no harm in the knowledge itself, so long as it is pursued in
tune with God's will expressed in orderly nature; the harm lies in the
mind and will of the user, which should oppose daimonic inflation
and aim for the highest, whence the knowledge derived. We witness
today where chemistry can lead in its concern with the elements and
its worldly rationales operating in alleged "scientific states," and might
wish Zosimos's advice had become for all concerned an unavoidable
imperative. The barbarians now have the keys—*And what lies behind
them?* Zosimos might well ask. And he might answer: look more
deeply into this and you will find God alone is master of nature and
none can usurp him.

Given Zosimos's evident high-mindedness, it is arguably surprising
that Zosimos so closely embraces the account of the fallen Watchers
familiar to 1 Enoch, since the text describing the wickedness wrought
by the seducer angels (possibly based on Genesis 6) refers so explicitly
to his favored, noble, and holy art of tincturing and presumably could
have been used against Zosimos himself by unscrupulous and twisted
persons given to twisting things to net the innocent. This surprise
has motivated Kyle Fraser to pen a paper on the subject: "Zosimos of
Panopolis and the Book of Enoch: Alchemy as Forbidden Knowledge"
(2004).[4] While Fraser considers Zosimos's embrace of the fallen angels
story consistent with the anti-daimonic stance expressed in *The Final
Account* (or *Quittance*), and *On the Letter Omega,* he describes it as a
stance "rooted in Gnosticism,"[5] for Fraser identifies Zosimos's daimons
lurking about earthly confines as ministers of planetary rulers; that is
to say, of the *archōnes* (rulers) of Gnostic myth: dark angels who serve
a jealously imprisoning demiurge. The problem here is that *Zosimos*
does not conceive of the demiurge in the radical manner of, say, the
Apocryphon of John, where the greedy monster Ialdabaoth and dark
subordinate hench-angels conspire to keep the mystery in Man to

themselves by dungeoning the hapless human, while comprehending not the mystery of which they're so jealous. Zosimos's daimons in low places are about as evil as the cosmos gets, and they can be avoided. That is not the case for the radical Gnostic, whose whole cosmos is counterfeit.

According to Fraser: "The goal of alchemy, for Zosimos, is liberation of the spiritual part of the human from the bonds of matter and Fate—from the clutches of the archons and their daimons."[6] One can only say to that: *Well, it is, and it isn't.* Certainly I think we can skip the reference to the archons; it's not a term familiar to Zosimos's discourse—though his term "overseers" bears some analogy if not pushed too far—but the conclusion assumes too much. Second, we have adequate reason to imagine Zosimos enjoyed his earthly vocation of tincturing and was in no great hurry to evaporate up the heavenly tube to condense upon the divine ambix. He had faith in life, in which he found much to amuse himself and others, even, and perhaps especially, among his opponents. One feels Fraser has not fully understood the fact that we're discussing an artist or artisan, if you will; a man making a living, not a full-time theologian! The goal of alchemy for Zosimos is to make superb works of dyed metal, stones, and fabrics, with—O, bonus parergon!—a path to becoming a more evolved person spiritually, with greater insight into the wonders, not the evil, of the cosmos and its subsistence on heavenly, loving, and creative intelligence to which Zosimos would be happy to surrender when the proper time came. Still, Fraser foams up his tack, as one fresh from the airy pages of Carl Jung: "alchemy works directly with material substances, and seeks salvation through a spiritual regeneration of matter. Alchemy works through the world—a world ruled by hostile daimonic powers."[7]

I think this kind of thing would require much unpacking with little in the way of gift at the end of it. *Alchemy works through the world* . . . I'm sure I don't know what this could possibly mean.

Perhaps I should work through the world to find the answer. "Zosimos joins Enoch in condemning profane alchemy . . ."[8] When does Enoch condemn profane alchemy? According to 1 Enoch, tincturing was brought from heaven by Azazel and his accomplices. Enoch is instructed to condemn Azazel and the Watchers, not profane alchemy, whatever that might mean. Perhaps "profane alchemy" refers to passing knowledge to unworthy people who put it to ill use; if so, "profane" should apply to profane usage, not to the knowledge itself.

Fraser sees a deep problem for Zosimos in that while he seems content with the Book of the Watchers' account of the arrival of the knowledge of tincturing, he must yet face the idea that according to his own strictures, liberation from the daimonic is vital for salvation, and vital, too, for proper exercise of the tincturing knowledge. I must say that I fail to see any great problem here for Zosimos. The issue, if it is one, seems to stem from an error of proportion. Zosimos *chose* to recount to Theosebeia the story of the lustful Watchers deliberately, not out of any great theological motive nor, I suspect, through any great belief in the story as determinative history, but primarily because the story wittily encapsulated or wrapped up for him the lessons he wanted Theosebeia to recognize, which were:

1. The daimons seduced *women* with promises of knowledge, including vanity-soaked ranges of cosmetics and decorative arts—while simultaneously letting loose instruments to ensure the storms of war and confusion upon humanity. The women, Zosimos implies, were willing to be seduced by these upwardly (and downwardly) mobile beings, aspiring to what they offered, consumers of novelty blind to the consequences of daimons controlling their lives and consciences (he's nudging at Theosebeia of course); that is to say, Theosebeia should investigate very carefully whence she obtained her information, for the one thing daimons had certainly done was to twist knowledge to

their own advantage and against that of their willing dupes (women like Theosebeia).

2. Those daimons or fallen angels were still to be found around temples and statues and priests, looking for ways to entice gullible persons into their power. Such beings did not care whether their goods were sound. Zosimos counseled that the goods had been perverted by unnecessary magical entreaties and spells for conditions both unnatural and unnecessary. The true tinctures had in fact now been liberated from their control and should stay that way. The art did not require supplications to daimons. Coming from heaven originally, the art could be safely pursued so long as one stayed clean of mind, of good intent, without vanity, and remained properly attentive.

3. The world that God created was still very much intact, and God's wisdom could be discerned by following the natural paths he ordained. Fate, Zosimos believed, was part of the way nature worked, but the noetic person need not fear falling foul of it, or under it, for fate acted on the lower nature, not the spiritual. Therefore, shun the lower nature and its false teachings and teachers and . . . stick with Zosimos who had seen through the sham magic of the priests and the temples and the manifold deceptions of daimons and those they motivated.

I suppose here in these points is the answer to the mad scientist and our fear of science gone wrong. Dedicate our knowledge to the service of the highest conceivable being, and forever keep a close watch on our temptation to slip, and be alive always to the call of conscience. Seems Zosimos has a message. Well, he certainly had a message for Theosebeia, and one might argue that he used a sledgehammer to crack a nut as he basically accused her of making the most fundamental mistakes possible to one who believed in a terrestrial world governed in the way he thought it was governed. However, it's worth remembering that the likelihood is that if there was one person who took pains to preserve Zosimos's strictures it was Theosebeia, so we may presume that she did not dismiss his advice, at least not entirely, and wished it to be passed on safely. One can speculate further about their relationship, but it was clearly a close and concerned one, and the degree of self-justification in the surviving texts suggests Zosimos's opponents tried very hard to ridicule and undermine a man who quite possibly went against the whole grain of the trade at the time, one who dismissed so much of the magic and obfuscation that accrues to a process that at the time was very much experimental and was seen perhaps by very different alchemical exponents to be one that trod on territory requiring daimonic assistance and supplication. If truth will out, and folly be forgotten, as is often the case, we might think that Zosimos went very much against the interest of other practitioners and perhaps was ridiculed and even persecuted by factions who felt threatened by his forthrightness and commitment to disciplined technique and precise knowledge.

One thing Zosimos could have argued, but did not, was that though man's first knowledge of tincturing came about, as he wrote, by a disgraceful slippage in the cosmic scheme, human beings might have come to understand this knowledge anyway in the course of observing nature over time but been in a better stage of development to deal with it. Indeed, his aliveness to technical improvements suggests very much to my mind that he did not feel he owed *his* knowledge of the art to daimons, for he had found out through practice and attention to the ordinary courses of nature and had no interest in asking for daimonic guidance. He relied on himself and on the inherent wisdom of nature and sound, elevated mind. He advises Theosebeia to be a vessel open to truly divine inspiration, which comes freely to the willing port: if you wish to receive divine messages, make of yourself a clean, spotless piece of papyrus that the radiant word might become visible. In that sense, Zosimos presages a kind of new age of scientific exploration, a development of the art under divine inspiration, freed from overbearing hierarchies of the past, reliant on the wisdom, learning, and good sense of the professional practitioner. This rather makes Zosimos something of a synthesis of the Renaissance and the modern type of person, one with a foot in both worlds, and all the more stable for it. Arguably, Zosimos's rightful future has not yet come.

TWELVE

A Strange Relation

Alchemy and Gnosis

As has been obvious throughout our investigation into the origins of alchemy, it's frequently impossible to avoid awareness of a curious interplay at work between the symbolic language and practical processes of the sacred art—especially in the case of Zosimos—and the symbolic language and myths of gnostic writers, supposedly writing about purely spiritual things. Sometimes the allusiveness is almost direct, sometimes it hovers about peripheral vision in somewhat ghostly fashion. Sayings numbered 22 and 23 of the Gospel of Thomas spring to mind.

> Jesus said to them, "When you make the two one, and when you make the inside like the outside and the outside like the inside, and the above like the below, and when you make the male and the female one and the same, so that the male not be male nor the female; and when you fashion eyes in the place of an eye, and a hand in place of a hand, and a foot in place of a foot, and a likeness in place of a likeness; then will you enter the kingdom." Jesus said, "I shall choose you one out of a thousand, and two out of ten thousand, and they stand as a single one."[1]

Devotee of the "One" and the "All," Mary the Prophetess is, we recall, quoted by Zosimos to assert that while bodies (metals) don't evaporate in the fire, when a body is mixed with an incorporeal, the bodies become incorporeal ("fleeting" substances) and the incorporeals become body. Mary declares: "If two don't become one—that is to say—if the volatile (materials) don't combine with the fixed materials, nothing will happen of what is expected."[2]

That the bodies become incorporeal by becoming one with the incorporeals is for Mary a practical necessity for distillation. According to Mary, "reduced in spirit," the incorporeals then rise as sublimated vapor, becoming bodies again.[3] Mary likened the body and the incorporeal materials to male and female, with the imperative "Join the male with the female and you will find what is sought": a union effected by fire, suggestive of passion.* "Do not touch with your hands, for it is an igneous preparation," Mary counsels.[4] The presence and importance of winnowing fire is discernible in logion 10 of the Gospel of Thomas: "Jesus said, I have cast fire upon the world, and see. I am guarding it until it blazes."[5] The world must yield the spirit: effected by fire. It might also be noted that it has been thought the "male" and "female" of the Gospel of Thomas distinguish those who are pneumatic (male) from secondary psychics (female), which perhaps bears some analogy to the bodies and incorporeals of Mary's God-given distillation process.

Now, we know that Mary, despite talking in what seems at first sight a paradoxical way, is nonetheless referring to an industrial process. Nevertheless, one can discern a symbiosis—difficult to put one's finger on—between the practical sphere of operation and the blue-sky gnostic message.

---

*Compare with *Asclepius* 21–29 (Codex VI, 8, in the Nag Hammadi library): "For the knowledge of the things that are ordained is truly the *healing of the passions of matter*" (my italics); translation by James Brashler, Peter A. Dirkse, and Douglas M. Parrott, *The Nag Hammadi Library in English*, 301.

We may recall references to "making the inside like the outside" as the literal meaning of *transmutation* in the treatise "Synesius and Dioscorus," where Dioscorus asks Synesius: "What transformation [literally 'turning inside out'] is he [Democritus] talking about?" (see page 201). Synesius replies that Democritus speaks of the bodies— that is, metals—and in answer to a subsequent question about how to "turn the nature inside out," Synesius says it's necessary to "transform their nature, for nature has been hidden within."[6] The Greek verb translated as "transform" ([*ek-*]*strephō*) means to "turn inside out," exposing something formerly within by getting inside matter. The sense in this passage is of a *return* to a former, if secreted, state. There is of course an analogy here with gaining access to the "low self," or subconscious, to crystallize higher knowledge to consciousness, and Carl Jung did not miss it, believing as he did that the "Gnostics knew already"* what he'd taken a lifetime trying to understand about the mysteries of the psyche.

The Gospel of Thomas contains numerous indices of the principle of two becoming one. In that unity, "they" not only "stand as one" but that very state also encompasses "the All" (*Pan*). In logion 77 of the sayings, collection, or "gospel" of Thomas the Twin, the "All" is identified with Jesus: "It is I who am the light which is above them all. It is I who am the all. From me did the all come forth, and unto me did the all extend. Split a piece of wood, and I am there. Lift up the stone, and you will find me there."[7] Fragmentary treatise *Authentic Memoirs on Divine Water,* sometime attributed to Zosimos, is also, as we have seen, eloquent on an analogous conception of the All as great, mercurial mystery.

---

*These words were reported by Prof. Gilles Quispel during the making of the British Channel 4 TV series *Gnostics* (1987) when he (Quispel) recalled presenting Jung with the Valentinian work from Nag Hammadi, the Gospel of Truth, in Switzerland in the 1950s. Quispel told me the same story on tape when I first interviewed him for the TV series at Bilthoven, Holland, January 1986.

1. This is the divine and great mystery, the object we seek. This is the All. From him (comes) the All, and through him (exists) the All. Two natures, one sole essence; for one attracts one; and one dominates one. This is silver water, the hermaphrodite, which always flees, which is attracted to its own elements. It is the divine water, which everyone has ignored, whose nature is difficult to contemplate; for it is neither a metal, nor water always in motion, nor a (metallic) body; it is not dominated.

2. It is the All in all things; it has life and spirit and is destructive. He who understands this possesses gold and silver. The power has been hidden, but it is recovered [drawn back?] in erotylos [*erotylos* is a gemstone, sometimes called "love-stone," see page 121].[8]

It is the All in all things; it has life and spirit and is destructive. . . . That there's something destructive in the All strikes a curious chord with the famous, difficult, saying (no. 70) from the Coptic Gospel of Thomas: "That which you have will save you if you bring it forth from yourselves. That which you do not have within you will kill you if you do not have it within you."[9] Translator Thomas O. Lambdin has made a variant translation of the same text: "If you bring forth what is within you, what you bring forth will save you. If you do not bring forth what is within you, what you do not bring forth will destroy you." Stephen J. Patterson and James M. Robinson have undertaken another translation for The Gnostic Society Library: "If you bring it into being within you, (then) that which you have will save you. If you do not have it within you, (then) that which you do not have within you [will] kill you." In order to be "saved," or transformed, something has to be turned inside out, and outside in.

Arguably the most rounded statement of equating knowing oneself with knowing the All, and knowing Christ, occurs in the supposedly Syrian, largely encratite Book of Thomas the Contender, also in the Nag Hammadi library, and dated to the first half of the third century.

It purports to be a dialogue between Jesus and twin brother Thomas, who "stands in" for the would-be gnostic reader.

> Now, since it has been said that you are my twin and true companion, examine yourself, and learn who you are, in what way you exist, and how you will come to be. Since you will be called my brother, it is not fitting that you be ignorant of yourself. And I know that you have understood, because you had already understood that I am the knowledge of the truth. So while you accompany me, although you are uncomprehending, you have (in fact) already come to know, and you will be called "the one who knows himself." For he who has not known himself has known nothing, but he who has known himself has at the same time already achieved knowledge [gnosis] about the depth of the all. So then, you, my brother Thomas, have beheld what is obscure to men, that is, what they ignorantly stumble against.[10]

What men *stumble against* probably refers to Luke 20:18: "Whomsoever shall fall on that stone [the "stone the builders rejected"] shall be broken; but he on whom the stone falls shall be winnowed [from Greek verb *likmaō*]." To winnow is to separate the wheat from the chaff by means of air (wind = Hebrew *ruach* = mind, spirit), with the chaff consigned to fire. In Jesus's saying the stone (or head of the corner, "cornerstone") acts as spiritual agent, purifying and transforming the one on whom it descends is another intriguing alchemical analogy.*

---

*Such is the frequent ignorance of such recondite subjects among our clergy that readers may be amused, but perhaps not surprised, by the following anecdote. Some thirty years ago I introduced the then Dean of Lichfield (a respected Anglican theologian from Oxford) to this saying and its alchemical analogy. Quickly dismissing the idea, he told me there was no such thing as alchemy in the first century CE! He was clearly unfamiliar with either Mary the Prophetess or pseudo-Democritus but perhaps might have wondered what Jesus may have learned in Egypt and why he was removed there in the first place; but the knowledge of the ignorant is always well guarded.

244 ◓ A Strange Relation

◓

Such analogies as presented above suggest an apparent symbiosis, mysterious and intriguing, between the spheres of alchemy and gnostic thought, or spiritual illumination. Both are concerned with what is within and with hidden properties and potentials for transforming natural states, mineral, organic, spiritual. Observing such an apparent symbiosis has led me on numerous occasions to wonder if the central conceit of the Gnostic gospels and associated writings—the determination to pit pneuma (spirit in contact with higher being) against the world and set the bodies at nought—may have been stimulated by what alchemists were doing, or saying, or both. Could there have been deliberate reapplication of a symbolic language of *transformation, rising,* and *becoming* to the formidably analogous issue of human salvation from the Hades (or furnace?) or fiery hell of earth and its lower regions? Could the secret hidden in the earth be exposed and transfigured? Or is it that such symbolism, allegory, and metaphor were imported *into* chemical practice from adjacent founts of spiritual speculation? Or alternatively, can we discern a two-way dynamic of mutual communication?

Rarely shall we find such a straight crossover of metaphor as we find in the Nag Hammadi Gospel of Philip, possibly composed in Syria in the second half of the third century (roughly Zosimos's time). It advocates a Valentinian take on two becoming one, in that the fall of man is typified by an androgynous primal unity of heavenly Man sundered and divided into male and female in the lower world, with Christ descending to repair the deficiency through sacramental marriage—earthly prefiguration of a heavenly reunion of pneuma with angelic source and spouse: the soul's higher being beyond, not subjected to, the lower world of division and suffering.

In this free-associative, somewhat tendentious text, the author actually homes in on the practice of *tinctures* not only as salvific metaphor but also as indicating divine identity! Thus:

God is a dyer. As the good dyes, which are called "true," dissolve with the things dyed in them, so it is with those whom God has dyed. Since his dyes are immortal, they become immortal by means of his colors. Now God dips what he dips in water [dyeing is here metaphor for baptism, and vice versa].

It is not possible for anyone to see anything of the things that actually exist unless he becomes like them. This is not the way with man in the world: he sees the sun without being a sun; and he sees the heaven and the earth and all other things, but he is not these things. This is quite in keeping with the truth. But you saw something of that place, and you became those things. You saw the Spirit, you became spirit. You saw Christ, you became Christ. You saw the Father, you shall become Father. So in this place you see everything and do not see yourself, but in that place you do see yourself—and what you see you shall become.[11]

Later we learn that Levi (renamed by Jesus "Matthew," meaning "gift of God," in the canonical gospels) owned a *dye works,* whereas Levi-Matthew is known exclusively in orthodox tradition as a tax collector.

The Lord went into the dye works of Levi. He took seventy-two different colors and threw them into the vat. He took them out all white. And he said, "Even so has the Son of Man come as a dyer."[12]

It may be that "the dye works of Levi" is a symbolic name for Judaism (Levite ministry), with the idea that the Son of Man united, completed, simplified, and synthesized complex practices taught to the Jews before Christ, where the "tinctures" were deemed imperfect, or rather, incomplete, but this is speculation only. The seventy-two-color idea may well derive from seventy-two names of God, themselves derived from a kabbalistic reading of Exodus 14:19–21 (the pillar of cloud and the parting of the Red Sea), whose three verses, remarkably, are each of seventy-two letter length and from which verses letter-triplets can be formed with the seventy-two names being deduced by reversing the middle verse letters. The first work of Jewish speculative mysticism, the "Book of Formation" (*Sefer Yetzirah*), was probably in existence between the second and fourth centuries, and may have influenced the author of the Gospel of Philip or a source he used. Anyhow, the meaning seems straightforward. Through baptism, the Lord unites the dyer and the dyed, which encompasses all colors and divine possibilities and attributes as one pure tinctured substance (white): all variants returning to light-source. Isaac Newton would have been intrigued to find a variant spectrum combining in divine light.

Later in the text we find this unity theme recapitulated in another statement of the Hermetic and gnostic "things above like things below; things outside and inside" type.

[The Lord] said, "I came to make [the things below] like the things [above, and the things] outside like those [inside. I came to unite] them in that place.[13]

Yes, the dyer metaphor works well here. However, relating authentic dyeing texts to Gnostic material proves considerably more problematic as one goes along. There is something about trying to separate completely spiritual and physical processes in this context that bamboozles the mind. If we banish utterly the spiritual (as in modern materialist science), there is of course no problem; nor is there any question, for the question is disallowed automatically. How nice for the moderns! But it wasn't that way for our ancestors in late antiquity. Physical and spiritual processes were perceived in relation. If there was a "natural" order, it was because spiritual intelligence ordained it that way, and when you approached the edges of the natural, the pull of the spiritual orbit grew stronger. The most radical Gnostic thinkers wished to sunder the relation altogether: "I am spirit, therefore I am not body." The Hermetic strain, as we have seen, attempted to keep the glue in place. The spirit was in the body—not the *most* desirable place of all for sure—but, while here, the spirit, or *nous,* need not be dominated *by* an imperfect body and its celestial determinants. Whereas the radical Gnostic saw the body as the very clutches of the world, the Hermetist (if Zosimos be an exemplar of the type) saw it as a vehicle with hidden potential.

While gnostic influence was discernible in the second, third, and fourth centuries throughout the empire (if not earlier), there seems little doubt that its epicenter was Alexandria and the Thebaid, with a strong link to Syria. When back in 1959 one of the first works on the Nag Hammadi library discovery was published, it was called *The Secret Books of the Egyptian Gnostics,* and no one deferred from author Jean Doresse's designation: "Egyptian Gnostics." When Berthelot and Ruelle worked on the Graeco-Egyptian alchemical corpus in the 1880s, they, too, considered the "Gnostics" as chiefly an Egyptian phenomenon involved with esoteric and occult speculation (like the "occult revival" in Paris in their own day). They could feel the presence because they were aware of numerous Gnostic works with heavenly travel itineraries and secret sayings, with some attributed to Jesus in his risen state, that had emerged from Egypt since James Bruce returned from Ethiopia and Egypt with the Bruce Codex (containing the Gnostic *Books of Jeu* in 1773, the same year, curiously, in which the "Askew Codex" was also brought from Egypt, containing Gnostic text *Pistis Sophia.* Egyptians in late antiquity seemed to have developed a penchant for producing rather disturbing, heretically freeform speculative trance texts of a peculiarly otherworldly, hybrid, riddle-strewn bent, with cousinhood to the Egyptian magical corpus of the same period, so different in tone to the familiar gospels and Pauline letters.

As we've seen, Zosimos seems to have grown up and pursued his living in a cultural milieu permeated by gnostic and magical beliefs and groups. While it's going too far to speak of gnosis as popular culture in the second to fourth centuries CE, gnostic ideas were certainly prevalent enough among the minority of educated folk for revered Egyptian Platonist philosopher Plotinus (ca. 204–270) to write a tract against "gnostics" (in the *Enneads*) who, he believed, abused Plato's philosophy by being, according to him, too loose with it, while indulging excessive criticism of the world's imperfections. Zosimos had ample opportunity to soak in as much gnostic material as was then current—and that, even from what has survived, was a great deal. And who knows what else was available to him in the period around 300 CE?

Indeed, there are some instances in the Zosimian corpus where it's plain that he has imported gnostic motifs and myths into his diatribe against daimonic and unnatural tinctures for Theosebeia's benefit. The influence, though empathetic, is still coming from outside the chemical practice. The chief example of this is his distinguishing between the heavenly, or inner, man, called *phōs* (light, and "man") who was tricked into life below the *heimarmēnē* (zodiacal powers) to become "Adam" (of the earth), whereafter "Our intelligence says: The Son of God, who can do everything and becomes everything when he wants to, manifests himself as he wants to each one. Jesus Christ added himself to Adam and brought (him) back to Paradise, where mortals previously lived."[14]

Another quote from Zosimos's treatise *On the Apparatus and Furnaces; Authentic Commentaries on the Letter Omega* actually serves to clarify the meaning of a quite difficult passage in the Nag Hammadi *Second Treatise of the Great Seth,* the passage being: "For my [Jesus's] death, which they think happened, (happened) to them in their error and blindness, since they nailed their man unto their death."[15] Zosimos explains (unwittingly) for us what was meant by nailing "their man unto their death," writing about Jesus's instruction to followers to get beyond the powers by killing their own Adam:

"Thus stripped of appearances [writes Zosimos], he [Jesus] advised his followers also secretly to exchange their mind (or spirit) with that of the Adam which they had in them, to beat him and to put him to death, this blind man being led to compete with the spiritual and luminous man: it's thus that they kill their own Adam."[16] According to Zosimos, the hostile crucifiers were actually slaughtering themselves when they thought they were killing Jesus. "And I was laughing at their ignorance," adds the Sethian treatise as a postscript, or punchline.

If we attempt to answer the question of whether alchemy influenced, or even created, the gnostic conceit, or whether gnosis fed into alchemical practice, the simplest answer would be to proceed from dated texts. There are two main problems here. One is that nearly all dates are rough with middling degrees of certainty, and second, the surviving number of Graeco-Egyptian alchemical texts up to the time of Zosimos is very small and very far from what we may legitimately expect to have been the case in late antiquity. Still, we must base our conclusions on the evidence.

Pseudo-Democritus is usually dated to the first century CE; so are the sources for Mary in Zosimos's works. The "Dialogue of Cleopatra and the Philosophers" is thought to date from the first or second century CE, and of course the Leiden and Stockholm Papyri are thought to be third century, but with much in common with first-century pseudo-Democritus. The earliest surviving material is predominantly practical, with very little mythical or symbolic color. An exception is the rather beautiful speech given to Cleopatra in the aforementioned "Dialogue." Here the practical process is directly described in terms of a mystical epiphany, where one is not simply an analogy of the other but the same events seen simultaneously with corporeal and with non-corporeal vision. We cannot simply blow this away because it appears inconvenient to the weight of surviving evidence. The complete speech is on pages 66–68, but here is an extract as a reminder:

But when the dark and fetid spirit is rejected, to the point of leaving no smell or dark color, then the body becomes luminous and the soul rejoices, as well as the spirit. When the shadow has escaped from the body, the soul calls the body now luminous and said to him: Awaken from the depths of Hades and rise from the tomb; wake up from the darkness. Indeed, you have assumed the spiritual and divine character; the voice of the resurrection has spoken; the preparation of life has entered into you. For the spirit [above this word is the sign for cinnabar] rejoices in its turn in the body [in *Codex Marcianus* ("M") above this word is an abbreviation for lead], as well as the soul in the body where it resides. He runs with a joyful rush to embrace him; he embraces him and the shadow no longer dominates him, since he has reached the light [above "light" is the sign for native sulfur]; the body does not bear to be separated from the spirit forever, and he rejoices in the dwelling [in "M" above this word is the sign for gold] of the soul, because after the body has been hidden in the shadow he found it filled with light [the sign for native sulfur above the word]. And the soul has been united to her, since he became divine in relation to her, and dwells in her.[17]

The historical facts seem to be these: alchemy developed, as far as we can tell, in an era and place rife with spiritual and economic ferment. We take so much for granted when we consider the past that it's difficult to put one's feet in the shoes of an intelligent, spiritually attuned person who heard about Christianity for the first time, for example, within decades of the actual crucifixion, with a stream of new, related, never-before-seen material (gospels, etc.) becoming available over subsequent generations. The practice of alchemy undoubtedly will have raised questions about the nature of absolute reality in the minds of intelligent persons and stimulated the imaginations of all. The phenomenon of blown glass likewise affected thought about the cosmos. Those cosmic "spheres" around the earth, for example, were likened to glass; quite an innovation of vision! There was a new age of technical, industrial, and religious development; that is, a period of innovation, and inevitably, reaction.

Athanasios Rinotas has written an interesting paper titled "Spiritual and Material Conversion in the Alchemical Work of Zosimus of Panopolis."[18] The title suggests that Zosimos was pursuing both aims simultaneously and gives much consideration to his alchemy being an awakening of a divine spark, so that "pneumatic man" can be extracted from the Adamic body and released unto redemption. The only trouble with this view of Zosimos's intentions is that by all his own accounts, Zosimos was himself *already* released from dependence on his old Adam and had already hastened with his own "race" to the bliss of *Poimenandres,* as he called the sovereign Nous of Corpus Hermeticum I; that is, he carried on dyeing and advising Theosebeia on dyeing arts afterward, when he was in no need of salvation from the practice. Nor does he advocate, as far as I can tell, pursuing the art as a means of salvation, only that the enlightened, raised mind will judge right practice and avoid deleterious practice. When he advises Theosebeia about opening herself to God, he doesn't say, "Fire up your furnace and burn away the old Adam to reveal the tincture of divinity," he says she should quiet herself in a neutral space without apparatus or any physical hindrance and wait upon God, who will come. As St. Paul maintained, *spiritual things are spiritually discerned* ("But the natural man receiveth not the things of the Spirit of God: for they are foolishness unto him: neither can he know them, because they are spiritually discerned"; 1 Corinthians 2:14). He urges her to develop spiritual discernment as an achievement prior to practicing the art. He doesn't even suggest that it was the holy art that introduced him to noetic liberation. He found the activities mutually congenial, and as we have seen, that is hardly surprising, since the analogies of dyeing and purification and transformation and all the rest are many and profound and sometimes obvious, so much so that in his own practice he has internalized the processes in almost sacramental fashion. However, it will be noted that when he talks dyeing methods through his treatises, it's predominantly dyeing methods he is discussing, with practical aims.

The problem (of symbolical obscurity) has come *after* Zosimos, it seems. After Zosimos, in some cases, the analogy *becomes* the practice and leads to so many blind alleys—blind but compelling all the same, ever afterward. Modern writers then have often simply backdated what they learned about post-Zosimian alchemy and projected it onto Zosimos, and that mechanism can be seen as early as the formation of the Byzantine alchemical corpus. Later commentators simply could not tell what was the earliest stratum of Graeco-Egyptian alchemy. They inherited a variegated property, pullulating with any number of disparate ideas, foreshortened paths, and symbols. The garden needed weeding, for sure, but how and where could one begin? There was no original plan, or if there had been, it was lost.

Mercury and Christ

We referred earlier (pages 241–42) to the alchemical text, sometime attributed to Zosimos, titled *Authentic Memoirs on Divine Water,* which appears to describe mercury.

Fig. 12.1. Sign of Hermes, badly drawn from *Codex Marcianus* (*Codex Parisinus Graecus* 2327, fol. 297v)

This is the divine and great mystery; the object we seek. This is the All. From him (comes) the All, and through him (exists) the All. Two natures, one sole essence [Greek *duo phuseis, mia ousia*]; for one attracts one; and one dominates one.

There is another key word that also expresses the idea of two natures in one substance, one involving a conception familiar to Catholic and orthodox Christians. The word is *homoousios,* translated as "of like (or one, or same) substance." It became the key word of the Nicene Creed of 325 CE, a creed intended to standardize Christological doctrine officially throughout the Roman Empire. It was understood as meaning that the Son (Jesus) was "of one substance" with the Father. Athanasios of Alexandria had vociferously opposed the beliefs of Arius, who believed a substantial distinction between Father and Son a necessity on account of Jesus's humanity. Constantine insisted that the word *homoousios* was the solution. It was not a familiar word to the bishops assembled in terms of describing the nature of the Trinity.

I was most interested recently to read a paper by Pier Franco Beatrice putting the case forward that the word's special application derived not from orthodox Christian sources but from, among other sources, an anonymous alchemical text referring to "Orphic consubstantiality" and the "Hermaic chain."[19]

The phrase referred to a doctrine of Egyptian priests that a universal harmony existed based on kindred sympathy linking natures consubstantial with one another. We have seen a similar conception attributed to Ostanes in pseudo-Democritus. More than that, the word appears specifically dealing with *God's* nature in the first tract of the *Corpus Hermeticum,* where it is taught that Nous is supreme, with the Logos proceeding from "Mind" (*nous*) as Son. Nous and Logos are not divided in substance but in function. A second Nous is generated from Nous: the demiurge who crafted the seven rulers who ordain fate. In the *Poimandres,* Logos leaps up from the elements of nature to unite with Nous-Demiurge "because he was of the same substance" (*homoousios gar ēn*). According to Beatrice: "The concept, if not the term *homoousios* characterizes the overall Hermetic conception of the Godhead."[20] Beatrice justifiably asserts that Egyptian theology already was familiar with consubstantiality of *nous* and pneuma. In the *Poimandres, pneuma* is breath of *nous* hovering on the watery chaos; *nous* expands like the light of the sun throughout the universe.

Beatrice presents another source text for the term: four books called *Theosophia,* from numerous sources dating back to the early sixth century CE. According to the first book, in the fortress town Ombos in the Thebaid, five Egyptian oracles exalted a supreme God known as Nous, or Logos, and Son Logos, who share the nature of *pneuma.* The last of five oracles was allegedly drawn from a lost work by Antiochus, priest of Heliopolis, said to be taken from an inscription in a vault beneath the Valley of the Kings. The inscription declared a unique Nous, source of Logos, Son, universal creator "being from the Father, *homoousios* eternally incorruptible with the prime holy Pneuma and beginning of life."[21] Of course similarities with pre-sixth-century Nicene credal statements arouse suspicion that the oracles could be forgeries. On the other hand, they are consistent with the *Poimandres* and known Graeco-Egyptian Hermetic theologies.

"Homoousios" was not popular among bishops at Nicea but was included at the insistence of Emperor Constantine. In youth, Constantine had contact with pagan philosophers at Diocletian's Nicomedian court at the time of Porphyry's attack on Christianity before Diocletian's great persecution of Christians. Constantine saw the ruins of Memphis and refused to make bloody sacrifices, perhaps familiar with Hermetic disdain for such practices. Constantine made a special effort to justify the use of the word *homoousios.* Bishop Eusebius of Caesarea was very grateful for his ameliorative explanation, when the emperor said there was no consubstantiality of bodily affection twixt Father and Son, for such could not exist in incorporeal, intellectual, and immaterial nature. The relationship was unique, and proper to the Father who must be Father to his Logos, who must be called Son for he issued from the Father and as such was consubstantial with him and at one with the Father's will. Constantine's victory arch inscription for the battle of the Milvian Bridge against Maxentius was attributed to divine inspiration and the "greatness of the divine mind" (*instinctu divinitatis mentis magnitudine*).[22] Besides Lactantius (ca. 250–325), who had good things to say about Hermes as a prophet of Christianity (while deploring the idol-making passage in *Asclepius*), Constantine was also advised by Neoplatonist Soter of Apamea, successor to Iamblichus, who combined Platonist philosophy with Egyptian, Hermetic sources.

An idea of Christ having two natures in one substance seems to have eventually entered alchemical circles in another way. We started this section with an alchemical description of what appears to be mercury, which as a substance contains a dual nature of liquid and solid, and which was considered all penetrating, awe inspiring, and transformative. Again it is impossible now to disentangle whether the idea of Christ as mercurial stone comes from an alchemical reading of Christian homoousios creed or from a consideration of the nature of mercury. The analogy of giving up the old Adam, the earthy nature, for transformation by elemental piercing by active agents to reveal the formerly hidden new body seems to be an analogy inseparable from the chemistry of the era. It became particularly resonant with the strange, profoundly invocative phases of the Christ narrative: mixture of two natures without confusion in Mary's womb; transformative miracles (water to wine, to name but one); walking on water; thrashing of the body; division of the garments; raising to the cross (the elements); two thieves on either side caduceus-like (Mercury was god of thieves); piercing; dying of the "old" man (Adam); burial; the stone moved; rising in the body; ascension; and removal from sight by a cloud.

While the key events of the Christian story have often been

likened to a ritual process, they also resonate with alchemical processes in an enigmatic manner whose apparent mystery has exercised some of the finest minds of our earthbound species for the 1,700 years since Zosimos's day. The survivor has indeed survived, and how strangely.

THIRTEEN

Legacy

FROM THE BEGINNINGS traced as far and as accurately as possible in this book, alchemy proceeded to find a place in scientific history throughout the 1,700 years after Zosimos, and even to the present day, when the subject is being reexamined in a more generous light than has been the case in mainstream scholarship since the eighteenth century's somewhat partial "Enlightenment."

I made the point earlier in the book that to my observation, Zosimos could be said to represent the classical stage of alchemical development, where the most fruitful aspects have flourished to a completeness, with indications of grounds for a progressive future. Of course we're accustomed to think that after a classical period, one may expect a decline, and even a thorough decadence, especially if one accepts a rather cyclic or wave pattern in the development, or comings and goings, of civilized pursuits. Nowadays, though, we like to think of progress as being linear, with each generation building on what has preceded it. Tangible advances, though perhaps forestalled or delayed by obstructions, are considered fairly inevitable. This was not the view of our ancestors, for whom progress was anything but straightforward. For a start, the nature of learning in late antiquity was based on authority; the future required the sanction of the past. We see this in Zosimos's own work. While he was enthusiastic about improvements to the art, the keys to improvement were all based on practicing more closely what had been recommended in the past. He liked to refer to the elders or the ancients, from whom he expected and received clear guidance. It was simply a case of taking the trouble to understand what they were referring to. Mary and "Democritus" and Moses and Cleopatra and Pebichius and Hermes Trismegistos: these were the names to watch out for, as far as he was concerned. Nevertheless, Zosimos was also an innovator.

One gets a sense of this from his letter to Theosebeia about his having observed a cook "steaming" a chicken in her kitchen, and wondering whether a steaming technique might be applicable to the art. What is noteworthy, though, is that instead of going home and trying it out, he said he consulted a Jewish text in Theosebeia's house to see if there was any prior mention of this, for him untried, technique. Though he might indeed have experimented directly later, one senses a "push-me-pull-you" approach to innovation. He was intrigued to find improvements, but he wanted to find the improvement guaranteed by the respected practitioners of the past. Despite his scientific credentials in relying on proven success and repeatable demonstration as being guides, he did not *take possession* of the future in the way that we expect science to do today. We are familiar with obsolescence. For Zosimos, any notion of obsolescence indicated that someone had gone very wrong in the past, with subsequent decline being proof of original error. If one stuck to the original guidelines, preferably coming from God enlightening the *nous,* one could avoid pitfalls of folly and enjoy the fruits of well-earned wealth.

Where we can speak of innovation in Zosimos is the degree to which he placed his alchemical practice within the context of gnostic itineraries and a life of spiritual virtue and ascent. Success in practice required spiritual integrity and a proper understanding of what was "natural" as against what he considered illegitimate attempts to manipulate nature by calling on daimons or excessive dependence on astrological fate. It is arguable that it was precisely in this area of innovation that he inadvertently may have prevented progress in the art as a practical means to increasing scientific knowledge. That point of view, however, is a mark of how far our perspective differs from his. He was not conscious of attempting to increase knowledge but simply of putting into practice what *was* known more effectively and responsibly. Spiritual analogy of chemical processes was something that conditioned successful practice, and while it could be argued that the analogy was just a mite secondary to practical knowledge, he would have tolerated none of this. For Zosimos, there was no theoretical dividing line between cultivation of noetic consciousness and recipe practice. The whole creation of the universe was imbued with divinity at every level. The cosmos could be said to represent the success of the holy art writ large. He did not say so, but he seems to imply as much.

Nevertheless, it is arguable that after him the analogical potential of the art appears to have become the dominant emphasis to the detriment of the practical, and in the process, the practical became redirected toward the symbolic, analogical, and, some would say, the impossible.

One thing is for sure, whatever may have happened to the first-class Egyptian dyers employing the art, it now appears that the persons who found the written works associated with the art worthy of commentary were not themselves servants or masters of industry or commerce.

Now, it may have been the case that the trade continued using straightforward recipe texts of the kind discovered in the Thebaid, which are now lodged at Leiden and Stockholm; we may only presume such may have been the case for lack of evidence. What evidence we have from the tenth-century Byzantine corpus suggests strongly that the preservation, commentary, and copying of early alchemical writings was in the hands either of educated Christian clerics, especially monks alive to Christian symbolism and to mysticism, or simply people of imaginative intellects, or Neoplatonic philosophers such as Synesius, Olympiodorus, and Stephanus of Alexandria. None of these commentators, or any others, show any interest whatever in issues of manufacturing ornamental goods. The predominant interest is chrysopoeia and argyropoeia. The notion that fundamental transmutation was possible from base metals to gold and silver constituted the primary interest. This was encouraged by a philosophical rather than practical approach to minerology and chemistry. That the interest in transmutation was often set in pious-sounding and mystically symbolic texts only increased fascination in transmundane, rather than visceral, worldly achievements. The superstition arose that success in producing gold was an act of divine grace dependent on spiritual advancement and purity: something for the monk, solitary or in community. This was doubtless a misleading exaggeration of Zosimos's position, while it may be added that such beliefs did nothing, of course, for practicable science.

As far as we know, sciences in Egypt suffered long decline after the triumph of Christianity and the eventual closure of pagan philosophical schools in the fifth and sixth centuries. The Greek spirit of inquiry waned in the face of an educated and uneducated preoccupation with salvation, while a hatred of fleshly existence that went to extremes of curiously elaborate body-denying asceticism neither looked for, nor expected, anything from this world. The conquest of Egypt by Arab Muslims in the 640s did nothing, for the time being, to alleviate the loss of vigorous cultural competition in thought and knowledge that had characterized Alexandria in its long heyday. In Constantinople, meanwhile, there was an emphasis on systematizing—that is, collecting and ordering—classical works from the past. The encyclopaedia became the ideal text. All must be "safely gathered in" before the Second Coming would take the world by surprise. Knowledge was something chiefly to be possessed, and guarded, not something to be created. And knowledge had to be acceptable to the powerfully unified church and state, which meant it had to accord with what was known; that is, what had been collected and interpreted.

The chief intermediary between Greek-language and Arabic medicine and science was not Egypt, but the Syriac-speaking world, neo-Aramaic or Syriac idiom having dominated learned circles in western Asia. Chief bearers of Syro-Hellenistic civilization were the heretical Nestorians. Founded in 428 CE, they first moved to Edessa until expelled in 489 by Byzantine emperor Zeno. They were in due time received well by Persians under Sasanian rule and were enormously successful as a civilizing influence even farther to the east. From Nisibis, Nestorians moved to Jundeshapur in southwest Persia, where King Chosroes Nushirwan (531–579) made the city a great intellectual center, to which came Greek scholars who left Athens when Justinian closed the philosophical schools in 529. Translation of Greek works into Syriac became a key activity. Among these translation works we may suppose we owe at least some of our rare Syriac versions of Zosimos's works. The great towns in the northern and eastern Persian provinces became the main centers for alchemical and astrological study. The Arab conquest left much of the Persian administrative and scientific institutions to pursue familiar paths. Jundeshapur's academy continued as the new Islamic empire's science center.

Arabic Alchemy

In about 750, the rise of the Abbasids brought power and prosperity to the Muslim world. From that time to 900 was inaugurated an era of translations. Abbasid Caliph al-Manṣūr (754–775), encouraged translating from Greek into Arabic at Jundeshapur. In the ninth century, Nestorian Christians did much of the work with their knowledge of Greek, Syriac, Persian, and Arabic. Caliph al-Ma'mūn (813–833) established a translation school and library in Baghdad. Notable there was translator Ḥunayn ibn Isḥāk (809–877), who translated an immense corpus of Galen's writings on medicine. The first half of that century was dominated by Syriac translations, but in the second half, Arabic translations grew more numerous, by which time the old school at Jundeshapur had given way to new academies at Baghdad and Samarra. While a firm basis in Greek medicine, botany, minerology, mechanics, and physics came into Islamic possession, and while many Greek alchemical works were translated, though most under false ascriptions, there was no recorded progress in chemistry during the ninth century.

Ḥunayn and the great Arab natural philosopher al-Kindī (died ca. 873) both opposed alchemy, condemning its practice as fraudulent.

One outstanding figure, however, took an interest at that century's end: Persian Muslim al-Rāzī (ca. 865–925), known to the West as "Rhazes." Possessing encyclopaedic knowledge of theology, philosophy, mathematics, astronomy, and physics (including meteorology, optics, and growth), he also wrote on alchemy, penning a great *Book of the Art (of Alchemy)*. Al-Rāzī's precise classification of substances and clear exposure of chemical processes and apparatus is notably free of mystical or obscurantist elements. While works that circulated under the ubiquitous name of "Jābir" and other Arabic-writing alchemists divided minerals into the familiar bodies (gold, silver, copper, etc.), souls (sulfur, arsenic, and so on), and spirits (such as mercury and sal-ammoniac), al-Rāzī invented the classification of animal, vegetable, or mineral. Minerals were divided by him into spirits, bodies, stones, vitriols, boraxes, and salts. Distinguishing volatile bodies and non-volatile spirits, he placed with the latter sulfur, mercury, arsenic, and salmiac.[1]

When Arabic *al-kīmiyā* spread to Latin Europe, it was frequently to be found in texts attributed to Jābir. In the West, that name appeared as "Geber," and works attributed to "him" dominated alchemical collections during the Middle Ages, the Renaissance, and beyond. Otherwise known as an eighth-century mystic and scholar, works attributed to Jābir emerged in the early tenth century, contemporaneous with the gathering of the Byzantine corpus. According to great orientalist Max Meyerhof (1874–1945), "certain mystical tendencies derived from the Gnostics and the neo-Platonists had a very detrimental effect upon the experimental spirit. Alchemy, which in the hands of 'Jābir' was a matter for experimental research, tended to become the subject of ineffable speculation and superstitious practice, passing into fraudulent deception."[2]

While many of the hundred or so works that bear the name are confused and obscure, others raise the banner of experimentation in a manner unique to the period. Through experimentation, the practitioner was able to improve methods of evaporation, filtration, sublimation, melting, distillation, and crystallization. The Jābir corpus offers many clear preparations of chemical substances, with instructions to obtain pure vitriols, alums, alkalis, sal-ammoniac,* and saltpeter. The works demonstrate knowledge of preparing fairly pure mercury oxide and sublimate, as well as acetates of lead and other metals, often crystallized. Jābir could prepare crude sulfuric and nitric acids and their admixture (called *aqua regia,* or royal water), and he could dissolve gold and silver in this acid.

The Jābir texts have given us terms such as realgar (red sulfide of arsenic), tutia (zinc oxide), alkali and antimony (Arabic *ithmid*), as well as common apparatus names like alembic for the upper vessel and aludel for the lower part of the distillation vessel.

The most comprehensive collection of pseudo-Geber compositions on alchemy is the *Book of the Seventy* (*Kitāb al-Sab'īn*). It has seven parts, with ten treatises for each part. Three of the parts describe preparing an elixir from animal, vegetable, and mineral substances; two parts are concerned with reducing substances to the four elements, and those elements to hot, cold, moist, and dry; another part is devoted to animal substances; while the last part expatiates on minerals and metals.

It is clearly the case that when we consider the passage of alchemy to western Europe—that is, Latin Catholic Europe—we do not find the Greek-speaking Byzantine empire leading the path to their Christian brethren. In 1053 the Eastern Orthodox Church and the Western Catholic Church entered a long schism that permanently damaged the whole Christian world. Its effects continue, sometimes bitterly and

---

*"Sal-ammoniac" comes from the Jābir corpus and was apparently unknown to Greek writers. While Pliny (*Natural History* 31) knew of an "ammoniacon," a rock salt named after the temple of Jupiter Amun in Cyrenaica (from which the name derives), it seems from its qualities that this was not identical to the substance first referenced in the pseudo-Geber work *De inventione veritatis*, where a preparation of sal ammoniac (ammonium chloride) is given in the chapter *De Salis armoniaci præparatione*.

painfully, to this day. The Greek *Corpus Hermeticum,* for example, did not enter the West until 1460, after Constantinople fell to the Turks in 1453, four hundred years after the Great Schism began. The impetus in the West came through translations of Arabic works. Gérard of Cremona (ca. 1114–1187) translated the *Book of the Seventy* into Latin in Spain, while Englishman Robert of Chester translated Jābir into Latin in the work called the *Book of the Composition of Alchemy,* which appeared in 1144. Together with the *Book of the Seventy* these rare works launched the career of alchemy in medieval western Europe, more than eight hundred years after Zosimos. Who says progress is inevitable?

The Inheritance

Predominantly Arabic works translated into Latin introduced western Europe to a legacy of knowledge derived from the first Graeco-Egyptian alchemists. Ability to read Latin limited the transmission of these works primarily to the educated clergy, and this factor clearly conditioned reception of alchemical ideas. Analogies for chemical processes were early on bound up with Christian mythology and doctrine, though often in a way that rendered doctrine somewhat transmuted in import, sometimes, we might say, subliminally. This was partly because of the legacy of gnostic logic inherent to the received tradition, suffusing the texts, coloring them: the release of spirit from body; resurrection as a symbolic, chemical experience; crucifixion as a symbol and a process; baptism as tincture. The Christian mystery could be seen as ongoing, repeated at all levels of creation, from the above to the below.

The mystical transformation of the individual was not a doctrine normally stressed in Catholic teaching, whose approved path to salvation lay in divine grace, faith in Christ, obedience to the church, and a store of good works. Knowledge of science was not deemed of salvific value during the Middle Ages, though it was chiefly educated churchmen and monks and nuns who were custodians of such classical knowledge as was available. Alchemy did appeal to some senior churchmen for sure (many of whom were aristocrats with aristocratic priorities), and the lucrative promise of alchemy appealed to monarchs and barons in need of gold and silver and who were able to pay for self-appointed masters of the field. To pursue alchemy required time and money, for there was no obvious link with a trade to generate capital—with the exception of masons and decorative craftsmen who might have opportunity to experiment with stained glass and dyeing of stones—with information held in monastic and college libraries.

Precisely what, then, did the Western world inherit from late antique alchemy?

The first thing we might mention takes us all the way back to pseudo-Democritus and the phrase that author allegedly took from Ostanes: "Nature delights in nature, nature conquers nature, nature masters nature." Western sages acquired a different slant, a new perspective on Nature—that is to say, a *dynamic* insight into her, not a static, flat, once-and-for-all creation, but Nature as *process* within an optimistically unified system both symbolic and demonstrable, whose watchword was "Hen to pan": the *One is All*. Applied to the doctrine of the Catholic Trinity, for example (or rather, applied with the Holy Trinity in mind), it became possible to see the divine persons of the Trinity involved actively in the inner life of Nature. This invited *in* to Nature some brave experimental souls, among whom we may name the following medieval stars of alchemy, who wedded their interests and discoveries to the fruits of Arabic science: Albertus Magnus (died 1280); Roger Bacon (1220–1292); Ramon Llull (ca. 1232–1316); Arnaldus de Villa Nova (ca. 1240–1311); Nicholas Flamel (1330–1418); Sir George Ripley (ca. 1415–1490); and Thomas Norton (1433–1531).

Alchemists learned to prioritize certain materials. All of the following ingredients were mentioned in the Leiden Papyrus, and we see the same materials time and again in Western alchemical literature: arsenic; orpiment; sandarac (our realgar); misy (basic iron sulfate mixed with copper sulfate); cadmia (impure zinc oxide mixed with copper oxide, or even lead oxide, antimony oxide, or other substances); chrysocolla solder (alloy of gold and silver or lead, or malachite and various congeners); alum; antimony; cinnabar; and, of course, sulfur; tin; gold; silver; copper; and mercury. Interestingly, those substances all appeared in Dioscorides's ten recipes at the end of the Leiden Papyrus and show there was an early relation between alchemy and medicine, though our knowledge of it is limited by limited evidence. Certainly, this aspect of alchemy was of interest to Arabic-speaking practitioners. It was they who gave us the word *al-'iksīr,* from a Greek word for powder to dry wounds, the word we know as *elixir.* In receiving the word, the West received the idea at least that there *could* be manufactured a cure for all diseases—or at least some—cures that were not dependent on miracles or Galenic authority with its herbal-based medicines.

Unfortunately, this chemical knowledge was hardly applied, until the towering figure of Paracelsus (ca. 1493–1541) appeared to make the revolutionary step of introducing chemistry into medicine. It took great, almost foolhardy, courage to challenge openly the medical establishment, but Paracelsus had the tenacity and fire of the prophet, and he looked to a new age of practical hands-on, firsthand, experimental knowledge. When you see those lines of pills at the chemist's shop, or in your bathroom or handbag, they are there thanks to Paracelsus and his application of alchemical wisdom. Paracelsus, keen reformer of the church as well as the medical establishment, introduced his own system of theological alchemy, dominated not by the Aristotelian four elements but three principles he called mercury (spirit), sulfur (soul), and salt (body): a tripartite system familiar as a doctrine to late antique Egyptian Valentinian Gnostics, and one that got Paracelsus into much posthumous controversy when his theological works appeared after his death, and Catholic inquisitors tarnished readers of them with the capital charge of heresy.

As for the basic equipment of the art, it had hardly changed from Zosimos's time. Paracelsus would have known immediately what

Zosimos was talking about when he mentioned the ambix (alembic), the phial, the distillation tube, the tribikos, the Bath of Mary, the kērotakis, and, of course, the furnace. These were the first vessels to be associated with scientific laboratory experiment, and while late antique alchemy did not pass on a theory of experimentation in the sense of that associated with Sir Francis Bacon, the very nature of the recipes made experiment a necessity, and the keeping of notes essential to record degrees of heat or more accurate quantities, better conditioning, and so on. And all the time, the legacy offered textual encouragement for transmutation and other unseen wonders.

It was inevitable that transmutation would become the dominant interest, especially when the link between the recipes and the trade of dyeing was forgotten, or hardly glimpsed. As a result, alchemy would acquire a bad name among its critics, for gold-making looked for all intents and purposes like counterfeiting, which again is not surprising since the early recipes were not unknowing of the fact that people could be deceived, and deceived out of money, by effective dyes. Criticism further encouraged the view among practitioners that not only was secrecy and initiation highly significant, but that one's best defense was to assert by implication that this was a sacred pursuit in tune with God's holiest purposes: the restitution of Adam to his first estate and the reconciliation of Man, Nature, and God.

Conversely, this very emphasis further obscured any likelihood that alchemists would realize the once practical, artistic, and commercial nature of the art, while rendering the transmutational potential of the chemistry even more mysterious and compelling. The element of trade having been practically extinguished, the question "Why do these things?" would be answered by the promise of transmutation, coupled with initiation into a divine secret. That attitude itself further alienated alchemists from seeing the practical and applicable aspects of chemistry, and doubtless limited the possibility for scientific advances.

However, with the period of Renaissance or rebirth of classical learning, beginning in the fifteenth century, and building on a twelfth-century Renaissance stimulated by Arabic translations and revolutions in masonry and education, the mentality moved away from mere repetition and preservation of past wisdom into a more positive view of exploring the unknown, based on a reassessment of the nature of Man. Here, the Hermetic tradition enjoyed its own revival. As Hermes taught: "Man is a great miracle, O Asclepius. Honor and reverence to such a being!" That first statement from the Latin *Asclepius* (*magnum miraculum homo est*) became the guiding text for Pico della Mirandola's epoch-marking text, the *Oration on the Dignity of Man* (1486). Intelligent men and women sympathetic to alchemy, convinced it had an experimental and theological role in natural philosophy, became contemptuous of what were called the "puffers"—that is, would-be gold-makers going up in smoke in their desperation for gold—and non-puffing alchemists began to see something in alchemy of a transcendent science of the spirit.

The following nineteen names from the sixteenth century all shared serious interest in alchemical priorities: Gerolamo Cardano (1501–1576); Gerhard Dorn (ca. 1530–1584); Martin Ruland the Elder (1532–1602); Tycho Brahe (1546–1601); Andreas Libavius (1550–1616); Edward Kelley (1555–1597); Raphael Eglin (1559–1622); Heinrich Khunrath (1560–1605); Adam Haslmayr (1562–1630); Oswald Croll (ca. 1563–1609); Michael Sendivogius (1566–1636); Benedictus Figulus (born 1567); Michael Maier (1568–1622); Martin Ruland the Younger (1569–1611); Robert Fludd (1574–1637); Jacob Böhme (1575–1624); Jan Baptist van Helmont (1580–1644); Carl Widemann (fl. 1588–1612); and Daniel Mögling (1596–1635).

One thing that is striking from these lists of luminaries of the tradition is that we can glean from them, at a glance, when the subject was most able to be pursued openly. We saw four names from the thirteenth century; one born in the fourteenth; three born in the fifteenth; but lo and behold! *nineteen* born in the sixteenth (and this list is by no means exhaustive). Well, we must consider that this was also the golden age of widespread access to printing presses, and that fact distorts the picture somewhat, for everyone who published invited others to comment in print, so inevitably, it looks like more people were hot about the subject than in times when copying manuscripts and distributing was a considerably smaller affair. Nevertheless, in the sixteenth and seventeenth centuries we do see in the West a tolerance to pursue the subject seriously by educated men (and it is predominantly men in this period) who enjoyed the leisure to investigate.

The absence of serious thought about dyeing, or industry, among alchemists definitely had an effect on the legacy inherited about coloring. Whereas Zosimos was adamant that it was not just whitening and yellowing that was important to the art but the generation of all colors, we find that by medieval times processes of making the "stone" vital for transmutation had been repeatedly written up as being marked by a color-changing process as mere means to transmutational end, not in the dyeing sense but as regulatory markers that one was pursuing the right path to the magnum opus. A key stage was whitening, yet it is apparent from the earliest known texts that whitening was concerned with making dyes for silver, where *white* meant silver, as *yellowing* meant the dye to render metals golden. However, the colors that mattered to those living with the legacy were those appearing in the crucible to be seen as vital stages to completion (often regularized as black > green > red > white), so the experimentation was too often guided by false, and often imaginary, values, since there was only a limited number of conceived outcomes.

One might argue that when the science aspect improved in the seventeenth and eighteenth centuries, it was largely a result of *accidents* in normal processes that engaged logical thought, curiosity, and practical inquiry as to what had gone "wrong." Progress is very much an issue of asking the right questions at the right moment. If we are wise, we really do learn from our mistakes, if we are to learn at all. Most book learning is learning from others' mistakes, and those lessons are not always so well learned.

One aesthetically delightful, and spiritually suggestive, aspect of the late antique alchemical legacy was of course the range of imagery stimulated in the imagination from the original recipes and commentaries. We have very little pictorial material from late antiquity, unfortunately, but a considerable amount from Arabic and Western sources throughout the Middle Ages; then in the sixteenth and seventeenth centuries we get a flood of remarkable printed works with extraordinary emblems of almost cinematic scope engraved to the highest standards depicting quite dramatically the extravagant language of alchemical relationships. It may be for us that this treasury of curious images is the greatest legacy for our own times; they definitely get under the skin. I recommend anyone interested in the field look into the Michael Maier book *Atalanta Fugiens* (1617) for a visual feast of almost surreal otherworldliness.

Readers may recall the "Dialogue of Cleopatra and the Philosophers" (page 65) from the *Book of Komarios*. It's instructive to see how much visual material lies within it, waiting for an artist.

Ostanes could be advising such an artist when he says to Cleopatra: "In thee is concealed a strange and terrible mystery. Enlighten us, casting your light upon the elements." Cleopatra verbally creates visual analogues between plants and distillation. She speaks of the union of bride and bridegroom as nature rejoices in nature. She imagines the nourishing of ingredients in the fire as being like the action of the mother's womb for the child-to-be (the *Work*). When the time comes, she will give birth. Cleopatra speaks of the path ingredients must take to the tomb (Hades), but after a time, are enabled to mount from the flames as a child might leap from its mother. And all this could be seen in a glass! The eye was the camera, the vial the lens, the cosmos the movie. In such eyes, religious ideas were not just ideas or things hoped for, but experiential realities, seen and imagined. Look at illustrations from alchemy-inspired texts and you will eventually see something like that which Cleopatra urges the philosophers to see when she says to them: "Go up to the highest peak, to the bushy mountain, in the middle of the trees, and see: (there is) a stone at the top." At the height is the prize of the stone. We shall find this mountain and stone in the writings of enthusiasts for the fraternity Rose Cross in the seventeenth century and long afterward, where it is called Mount Abiegnus, a mount that adepts must ascend for initiation. In the words of alchemist Thomas Vaughan in his *Lumen de Lumine, or a New Magical Light* (1651): "There is a Mountain situated in the midst of the earth or center of the world, which is both small and great. It is soft, also above measure hard and stony. It is far off and near at hand, but by the providence of God invisible. In it are hidden the most ample treasures, which the world is not able to value." The mountain is one of spiritual ascent, an ascent in virtue and knowledge disclosed simultaneously; it is the symbol of the effort of refinement. It is a mountain because the path is hard, but the prize unimaginable to those who dare not make the ascent.

The influence of Mary the Prophetess on alchemical typology is incalculable. Not only did she prioritize the fundamental practice of distillation, but she also gave us the notion of what would later be called the *mysterium coniunctionis,* a union of "male" and "female" that produces a new thing and reconciles opposites: water and fire, if you like, an unimaginable thing. Mary it was who is most identified as having named "fixed and not fleeting things" *bodies.* The bodies are copper, iron, tin, and lead; bodies because they don't evaporate in the fire. She writes of a union of body and an incorporeal, where the bodies become incorporeal and the incorporeals body, declaring: "If two don't become one; that is to say, if the volatile (materials) don't combine with the fixed materials, nothing will happen of what is expected." Only then can they rise as sublimated vapor and become bodies again. Born-again ingredients! Bodies, souls, males, females, conjoining, rising. Here are the beginnings of what might be called sexual alchemy, something intuited from the alchemical legacy that will outlive alchemy as laboratory practice in the classic sense. "Join the male with the female and you will find what is sought," says Mary.

Effected by fire, the union suggests passion, nay, requires it ("the healing of the passions of matter"): "Do not touch with your hands, for it
is an igneous preparation."

The seventeenth century sees the Renaissance alchemical revival
reach its near-apocalyptic apogee as the arguably gnostic works of
Jacob Böhme blend with those of Rosicrucian supporters and generate
an expectation of a new spiritual age as the cosmos goes through an
alchemical turning inside-out and the true heart of Christianity is
expected to be revealed with the dissolution of all false religion and
all that hinders the spiritual reformation and knowledge reformation of the world. As German alchemy suffers in the Thirty Years
War, it is in England that a late flowering of Rosicrucian-inspired
alchemy has its day in a period of republican violence and political
revolution. The following names stand out in the annals of the art:
Elias Ashmole (1617–1692); Thomas Vaughan (1621–1666); George
Starkey (1627–1665); Robert Boyle (1627–1691); Lady Anne Conway
(1631–1679); and Isaac Newton (1643–1727).

A figure of six notable alchemists from the seventeenth century
seems a significant drop from the previous century, which is partially
surprising because the seventeenth was the century in which the mystery of the Rose Cross movement was first thrust across the continent, producing hundreds of responses to a series of tracts that bound
alchemy to a vision of the end of an old world and the inauguration of
a new age of enlightened knowledge and Christian tolerance.

Admirer of the idea of the Rose Cross fraternity, Elias Ashmole
had as his personal motto: *Ex Uno Omnia* (From the One, All).
Profoundly concerned with alchemy (preserving the words of English
alchemists in his publication *Theatrum Chemicum Britannicum* in
1653), this great antiquarian and founder of the first public museum
in the world (the Ashmolean), was made "son" to alchemist recluse
William Backhouse (1593–1662) and henceforth considered himself of "Hermes's tribe," working to transform England and the

globe of knowledge according to an ideal of spiritual unity. An astrologer, he believed 1663 would see the appearance in the world of a great change, when the "more enlightened philosophers" would make their appearance. He might have had to be content, if not satisfied, with the foundation at that time of the Royal Society, of which he was founder-member, the first royally patronized scientific, experimental-based organization of the new scientific age, of which Isaac Newton would become famous president and emblem.

Science had arrived, and it was promoted by students of alchemy: Elias Ashmole, Robert Boyle, Isaac Newton.

One legacy of late antiquity they all adhered to: that alchemical secrets are sacred, and communication of them should be made only to those whose virtue and receptivity is fully attested. Nevertheless, the work was to be for the good of all, albeit pursued discreetly and with spiritual advancement as the highest goal. We can hear Hermes's son, Zosimos, speaking here, for Zosimos knew that the sky was no limit to the successful practitioner.

It is perhaps ironic that both Isaac Newton and Robert Boyle have been called fathers of modern science, for Newton has also been called "the last sorcerer" on account of his alchemical pursuits, which began in late 1669 with the purchase of alchemical books and laboratory equipment. Like Zosimos, Newton believed that the ancients had the secrets, and those secrets went back to the earliest times, and humankind had deviated from them; yet they could be recovered. Alchemy for Newton was part of his quest for the ancient science, into which quest he integrated all his work. Newton's serious efforts to get to the experimental basis of what was known of alchemy seem to have confirmed his belief that the ultimate upholder of universal order was the spiritual Logos. In this, he was no different to the essential Mind that produced many statements in the *Corpus Hermeticum* in this regard, and Newton would, I think, have found himself in fraternal accord with the outlook of Zosimos of Panopolis.

The next century would see a pinion of that ancient science fall into disrepute. The discovery of oxygen and the recognition of what we now consider true elements left alchemy with nothing new to say. Adherents who valued the legacy tended to associate in societies like Freemasonry, which still respected the link with ancient knowledge, and were mindful of a spiritual imperative and a world beyond physical appearances. In Germany, the alchemist who called himself "Hermann Fictuld" (ca. 1700–1777) founded the extra-Masonic Order, the Gold und-Rosenkreuz, which practiced alchemy, chiefly for medicinal purposes, with alchemical laboratories well organized and established throughout the German states. Christopher McIntosh has recorded numerous successes of the organization with healing elixirs produced by members using ancient alchemical techniques, but with additional experimentally based knowledge.

Looked at as a whole, we can see the curious relationship between alchemy and gnosis continuing in the ongoing life of late antique alchemy's legacy, such that it would not be going too far to call the alchemical tradition a vehicle through time for condemned beliefs about man, the world, and the spirit, and most particularly, those beliefs we call gnostic, concerned with spiritual knowledge beyond appearances, and the transformation of the human being through freed Mind. One joins the fraternity through sympathetic understanding and intuitive loyalty to it.

One of the more influential of neo-gnostic, post-scientific-revolution figures must be Rudolf Steiner (1861–1925). His influence in forming out of theosophy and Rosicrucian sources, and his own scientific and spiritual discoveries, the umbrella field of Anthroposophy, or "spiritual science," as he called it, has been very great. A keen reader of alchemical texts, his biodynamic farming methods are filled with a Paracelsian sense of the wisdom of Ostanes and pseudo-Democritus: that nature and the cosmos are a single, unified, interacting system, spiritually and materially bound by a discernible, if invisible, network of correspondences, sympathies, and antipathies, which when applied intuitively and practically produce real, observable results in the fields. I do not think he would object to being described as an alchemist for today and the future.

The world sadly never got to witness the full flowering of French genius Albert Poisson (1868–1893), friend of Paris's Ordre Kabbalistique Rose-Croix, a chemist who published important works on alchemy but who died tragically young. Such minds are rare and give witness to the legacy of the first alchemists.

"Good Health!"

Carl Jung (1875–1961) is of course a neo-gnostic who has redrawn alchemy as a form of depth psychology for healing the mind, valuing above all the idea of the stone as symbol of individuation, which Zosimos would call salvation.

In the twentieth century, alchemy becomes the inspiration and type for new arts of visual and aural language, truly adorning our world once more. Despite Western alchemy having long lost sight of the practical and commercial nature of the art, Zosimos's efforts have held fast in one respect. The value of the art as an abstract of man's spiritual engagement with the cosmos, that it could be a means to stimulate spiritual progress and vision, this surely is Zosimos's legacy to us now. Alchemy has become an internationally recognized spectrum for perceiving artistic and spiritual life and progress. Its metaphors and allegories have found universal application not only in religion and the myths of creation but also in the arts of painting, sculpture, cinema, music-making, acting, and many more fields of educative value at all levels, including agriculture, design, and computer modeling.

And contrary to the body-denying puritan, there's nothing wrong with decorative arts, for the greatest form of decoration is the revelation, not the obscuring, of the essence of substance.

The curious legacy of the first alchemists is that they have left us an open-ended prism for viewing all fields of creative endeavor and a means of grasping imaginatively the profound links that we still believe exist among mind, spirit, soul, and matter—or as the vapor said to the flask: "The only way is Up!"

Alchemy will be what we make of it, and we shall be what it makes of us.

Notes

One.
Ancient Recipes for Gold—and Other Things

1. Dawson, "Anastasi, Sallier, and Harris and Their Papyri," 158.
2. Chrysikopoulos, "À l'aube de l'égyptologie hellénique et de la constitution des collections égyptiennes," 2.
3. Dawson, "Anastasi, Sallier, and Harris and Their Papyri," 158.
4. Chrysikopoulos, "À l'aube de l'égyptologie hellénique et de la consitution des collections égyptiennes," 3.
5. Chrysikopoulos, "À l'aube de l'égyptologie hellénique et de la consitution des collections égyptiennes," 5.
6. Halbertsma, *Scholars, Travellers and Trade,* 99–107.
7. Lagercrantz, *Papyrus Graecus Holmiensis (P.Holm). Recepte für Silber, Steiner und Purpur,* 45.
8. Betz, *The "Mithras Liturgy,"* 8.
9. Dosoo, "A History of the Theban Magical Library," 251–74.
10. Dosoo, "A History of the Theban Magical Library," 260.
11. D'Athanasi, *A Brief Account of the Researches and Discoveries in Upper Egypt,* 10.
12. Dosoo, "A History of the Theban Magical Library," 269.
13. Berthelot and Ruelle, *Collection des Anciens Alchmisites Grecs,* vol. 1, 5.
14. Berthelot and Ruelle, *Collection des Anciens Alchmisites Grecs,* vol. 1, 8.
15. Berthelot and Ruelle, *Collection des Anciens Alchmisites Grecs,* vol. 1, 6–7.
16. Berthelot and Ruelle, *Collection des Anciens Alchmisites Grecs,* vol. 1, 12.

17. Berthelot and Ruelle, *Collection des Anciens Alchmisites Grecs,* vol. 1, 14.

18. Berthelot and Ruelle, *Collection des Anciens Alchmisites Grecs,* vol. 1, 19.

19. Caley, *The Leyden and Stockholm Papyri,* 42.

20. Caley, *The Leyden and Stockholm Papyri,* 19.

21. Caley, *The Leyden and Stockholm Papyri,* 37.

22. Caley, *The Leyden and Stockholm Papyri,* 37.

23. Caley, *The Leyden and Stockholm Papyri,* 43.

24. Caley, *The Leyden and Stockholm Papyri,* 42.

25. Berthelot and Ruelle, *Collection des Anciens Alchmisites Grecs,* 20.

26. Berthelot and Ruelle, *Collection des Anciens Alchmisites Grecs,* 26–27.

27. Caley, *The Leyden and Stockholm Papyri,* 85.

28. Jackson, "The Origin in Ancient Incantatory *Voces Magicae* of Some of the Names in the Sethian Gnostic System," 74.

29. Van den Broek, "Religious Practices in the Hermetic 'Lodge,'" 77–95.

30. Martelli, *The Four Books of Pseudo-Democritus,* 29–31.

31. Martelli, "Pseudo-Democritus' Alchemical Works."

32. Mosshammer, *Georgii Syncelli Ecloga chronographica,* 297, lines 24–28.

33. Martelli, "Pseudo-Democritus' Alchemical Works," 6.

34. Martelli, "Pseudo-Democritus' Alchemical Works," 8.

35. Berthelot and Ruelle, *Collection des Anciens Alchmisites Grecs,* vol. 1, 71.

36. Berthelot and Ruelle, *Collection des Anciens Alchmisites Grecs,* vol. 1, 72.

37. Berthelot and Ruelle, *Collection des Anciens Alchmisites Grecs,* vol. 1, 72.

38. Berthelot and Ruelle, *Collection des Anciens Alchmisites Grecs,* vol. 1, 73.

Two.
The Origins of Alchemy in Roman Egypt

1. Synkellos, *The Chronography of George Synkellos,* 18–19.

2. Cambridge manuscript Mm. 629 (folio 49r ff.).

3. Martelli and Rumor, "Near Eastern Origins of Graeco-Egyptian Alchemy."

4. Martelli and Rumor, "Near Eastern Origins," 40–41; Berthelot and Ruelle, *Collection des Anciens Alchmisites Grecs,* vol. 1, 61–62.

5. Mosshammer, *Georgii Syncelli Ecloga chronographica,* 23–25, 297.

6. Berthelot and Ruelle, *Collection des Anciens Alchmisites Grecs,* vol. 3, 4.2, 250–52.

7. Berthelot and Ruelle, *Collection des Anciens Alchmisites Grecs,* vol. 2, 3.28, 193.

8. Berthelot and Ruelle, *Collection des Anciens Alchmisites Grecs,* vol. 2, 3.6, 129–30.

9. Bidez and Cumont, *Les mages hellénisés Zoroastre Ostanèe et Hystaspe d'après la tradition grecque,* 329–31; Berthelot and Ruelle, *Collection des Anciens Alchmisites Grecs,* vol. 3, 4.3, 254.

10. Berthelot and Ruelle, *Collection des Anciens Alchmisites Grecs,* vol. 3, 5.8, 336–37.

11. Cambridge Ms. Mm. 629, folios 130r, 131r–131v4; Berthelot and Duval, *La Chimie au Moyen Age,* vol. 2, *L'Alchimie Syriaque,* 309–12; Bidez and Cumont, *Les mages hellénisés,* A16; cited in Martelli and Rumor, "Near Eastern Origins," 44.

12. Martelli and Rumor, "Near Eastern Origins," 45.

13. Martelli and Rumor, "Near Eastern Origins," 46.

14. Martelli and Rumor, "Near Eastern Origins," 46.

15. Martelli and Rumor, "Near Eastern Origins," 48.

16. Martelli and Rumor, "Near Eastern Origins," 49.

17. Martelli and Rumor, "Near Eastern Origins," 50; Leichty, "A Collection of Recipes for Dyeing," 15–20.

18. Martelli and Rumor, "Near Eastern Origins," 56.

19. Beretta, *The Alchemy of Glass,* ix.

20. Oppenheim, Brill, Barag, and Von Saldern, *Glass and Glassmaking in Ancient Mesopotamia,* 52.

21. Beretta, *The Alchemy of Glass,* 4.

22. Stern and Schlick-Nolte, *Early Glass of the Ancient World,* 19.

23. Beretta, *The Alchemy of Glass,* 21.

24. Beretta, *The Alchemy of Glass,* 22, adding the following citations: "On the theoretical importance of colors in ancient alchemical thought, see Arthur John Hopkins, 'Transmutation by Color' in *Studien zur Geschichte der Chemie,* Festgabe Edmund O. von Lippmann zum siebzigsten Geburtstag dangebracht (Berlin: Springer, 1927), pp. 9–14; Robert Halleux, 'Pigments et colorants dans la Mappae Clavicula' in *Pigments et colorants de l'Antiquité et du Moyen Age. Teinture, peinture,enluminure-études historiques et physico-chimiques* (Paris: CNRS Editions, 2002), pp. 173–180."

25. Oldfather, *Diodorus Siculus: The Library of History,* 2:55–57.

26. Grimes, "Secrets of the God Makers," 69.

27. Grimes, "Secrets of the God Makers," 68.

Three.
The Pioneers of Graeco-Egyptian-Jewish Alchemy

1. Berthelot and Ruelle, *Collection des Anciens Alchimistes Grecs*, vol. 1, 3.9: "Names of the Goldmakers," 26.

2. Berthelot and Ruelle, *Collection des Anciens Alchimistes Grecs*, vol. 2, 3.15 "On this question must one undertake the work at any time," 158.

3. Berthelot and Ruelle, *Collection des Anciens Alchimistes Grecs*, vol. 2, 3.18, 168.

4. Berthelot and Ruelle, *Collection des Anciens Alchimistes Grecs*, vol. 2, 3.28, 192.

5. Berthelot and Ruelle, *Collection des Anciens Alchimistes Grecs*, vol. 2, 3.28, 191.

6. Linden, "ANONYMOUS (first or second century AD): Dialogue of Cleopatra and the Philosophers," 44–45.

7. Luck, *Arcana Mundi*, 452.

8. Berthelot and Ruelle, *Collection des Anciens Alchimistes Grecs*, vol. 3, "Book of Komarios," 283–84.

9. Berthelot and Ruelle, *Collection des Anciens Alchimistes Grecs*, vol. 3, "Book of Komarios," 286.

10. Berthelot and Ruelle, *Collection des Anciens Alchimistes Grecs*, vol. 1, 1.10, 29.

11. Berthelot and Ruelle, *Collection des Anciens Alchimistes Grecs*, vol. 1, 1.16, 38.

12. Berthelot and Ruelle, *Collection des Anciens Alchimistes Grecs*, vol. 3, 4.23, 302–3.

13. Berthelot and Ruelle, *Collection des Anciens Alchimistes Grecs*, vol. 1, 2.4, 103.

14. Berthelot and Ruelle, *Collection des Anciens Alchimistes Grecs*, vol. 1, 128, 132 (figure 11).

15. Berthelot and Ruelle, *Collection des Anciens Alchimistes Grecs*, vol. 2, 3.41, 205.

16. Berthelot and Ruelle, *Collection des Anciens Alchimistes Grecs*, vol. 2, 3.42, 206–7.

17. Multhauf, *The Origins of Chemistry*, 104.

18. Grimes, "Zosimus of Panopolis," 94.

19. Berthelot and Ruelle, *Collection des Anciens Alchimistes Grecs,* vol. 2, 3.43, 208.

20. Berthelot and Ruelle, *Collection des Anciens Alchimistes Grecs,* vol. 3, 4.22, 287

21. Berthelot and Ruelle, *Collection des Anciens Alchimistes Grecs,* vol. 3, 4.22, 287.

22. Berthelot and Ruelle, *Collection des Anciens Alchimistes Grecs,* vol. 3, 4.22, 291.

23. Patai, *The Jewish Alchemists,* 30–34.

24. Berthelot and Ruelle, *Collection des Anciens Alchimistes Grecs,* vol. 3, 287–88.

25. Berthelot and Ruelle, *Collection des Anciens Alchimistes Grecs,* vol. 2, 3.24, 180.

26. Berthelot and Ruelle, *Collection des Anciens Alchimistes Grecs,* vol. 2, 3.50, 228–29.

27. Berthelot and Ruelle, *Collection des Anciens Alchimistes Grecs,* vol. 2, 216.

28. Berthelot and Ruelle, *Collection des Anciens Alchimistes Grecs,* vol. 2, 3.28, 188.

29. Berthelot and Ruelle, *Collection des Anciens Alchimistes Grecs,* vol. 2, 3.28, sect 5, 190, 192.

30. Berthelot and Ruelle, *Collection des Anciens Alchimistes Grecs,* vol. 2, 3.28, sect 9, 192.

31. Here Mary is quoted again on the subject of lead and the necessary depriving of metallic bodies of that state, in Berthelot and Ruelle, *Collection des Anciens Alchimistes Grecs,* vol. 2, 3.29 *On the Philosophers' Stone* (an expression that does not appear until the seventh century), 194.

32. Berthelot and Ruelle, *Collection des Anciens Alchimistes Grecs,* vol. 2, 3.29, sect. 13, 196.

Four.
Zosimos I: Clearing the Decks

1. Festugière, *La Révélation D'Hermès Trismégiste,* 260–62.

2. Grimes, "Zosimus of Panopolis," 119–20; Stolzenberg, "Unpropitious Tinctures," 4, 29–31; Fowden, *The Egyptian Hermes,* 153n43.

3. Berthelot and Ruelle, *Collection des Anciens Alchimistes Grecs,* vol. 2, 3.49.6, 223–24; for use of the word *lodge,* see van den Broek and van Heertum, *From Poimandres to Jacob Boehme,* 199.

4. Grimes, "Zosimus of Panopolis," 35.

5. Reymond, *From the Records of a Priestly Family of Memphis,* 133 (on Stele 82, Vienna).

6. Grimes, "Zosimus of Panopolis," 35; regarding Theosebeia's followers, Grimes cites Berthelot and Duval, *La Chimie au Moyen Age,* vol. 2, *L'Alchimie Syriaque,* 2.8.1, 239.

7. Berthelot and Duval, *La Chimie au Moyen Age,* vol. 2, *L'Alchimie Syriaque,* II. 6.4, 224.

8. Berthelot and Ruelle, *Collection des Anciens Alchimistes Grecs,* vol. 2, 3.51, sect. 5, 233.

9. Grimes, "Secrets of the God Makers," 75.

10. Berthelot and Duval, *La Chimie au Moyen Age,* vol. 2, 6.4, 223–24.

11. Berthelot and Ruelle, *Collection des Anciens Alchimistes Grecs,* vol. 2, 3.51, sects. 5–6, 233–34.

12. Dufault, "Zosimus, Client and Scholar," in *Early Greek Alchemy,* 128–29.

13. Berthelot and Duval, *La Chimie au Moyen Age,* vol. 2, 8.1, 238–39.

14. Berthelot and Ruelle, *Collection des Anciens Alchimistes Grecs,* vol. 2, 3.51, sect. 7, 234–35.

Five.
Zosimos II: Alchemical Yoga

1. Jung, *Psychology and Alchemy,* 299–300.

2. Berthelot and Ruelle, *Collection des Anciens Alchimistes Grecs,* vol. 2, 3.1, 117.

3. Berthelot and Ruelle, *Collection des Anciens Alchimistes Grecs,* vol. 2, 3.1, 117–18.

4. Copenhaver, *Hermetica,* 1.

5. Berthelot and Ruelle, *Collection des Anciens Alchimistes Grecs,* vol. 2, 3.51, 235–36; see also Fowden, *The Egyptian Hermes,* 122–23.

6. Fowden, *The Egyptian Hermes,* 118–19.

7. Grimes, "Zosimus of Panopolis," 74.

8. Berthelot and Ruelle, *Collection des Anciens Alchimistes Grecs,* vol. 2, 3.1, sects. 4–5, 119–20.

9. Hopkins, "A Study of the Kerotakis Process," 329–36.

10. Berthelot and Ruelle, *Collection des Anciens Alchimistes Grecs,* vol. 2, 3.5, sects. 1–3, 125–26.

11. Berthelot and Ruelle, *Collection des Anciens Alchimistes Grecs,* vol. 2, 3.5b, "Work of the same Zosimos," 126–27.

Six.
Zosimos III: From *Omega* to the *Final Quittance*

1. Berthelot and Ruelle, *Collection des Anciens Alchimistes Grecs,* vol. 2, 3.24, 180–81.
2. Berthelot and Ruelle, *Collection des Anciens Alchimistes Grecs,* vol. 2, 3.9, 146.
3. Berthelot and Ruelle, *Collection des Anciens Alchimistes Grecs,* vol. 2, 3.26, 183–84.
4. Berthelot and Ruelle, *Collection des Anciens Alchimistes Grecs,* vol. 2, 3.27, 184–88.
5. Berthelot and Ruelle, *Collection des Anciens Alchimistes Grecs,* vol. 2, 3.49, 221.
6. Berthelot and Ruelle, *Collection des Anciens Alchimistes Grecs,* vol. 2, 3.49, 221.
7. Fowden, *The Egyptian Hermes,* 120n17, 202.
8. Berthelot and Ruelle, *Collection des Anciens Alchimistes Grecs,* vol. 2, 3.49, 221–22.
9. Copenhaver, *Hermetica,* 16.
10. Berthelot and Ruelle, *Collection des Anciens Alchimistes Grecs,* vol. 2, 3.49, 222.
11. Berthelot and Ruelle, *Collection des Anciens Alchimistes Grecs,* vol. 2, 3.49, 223–24.
12. Berthelot and Ruelle, *Collection des Anciens Alchimistes Grecs,* vol. 2, 3.49, 223–24.
13. Berthelot and Ruelle, *Collection des Anciens Alchimistes Grecs,* vol. 2, 3.49, 224–25.
14. Bullard and Gibbons, "Second Treatise of the Great Seth," Codex 7, para. 9.
15. Brashler and Bullard, "Apocalypse of Peter."
16. Berthelot and Ruelle, *Collection des Anciens Alchimistes Grecs,* vol. 2, 3.49, 225.
17. Berthelot and Ruelle, *Collection des Anciens Alchimistes Grecs,* vol. 2, 3.49, 225–26.
18. Berthelot and Ruelle, *Collection des Anciens Alchimistes Grecs,* vol. 2, 3.49, 227.

19. Berthelot and Ruelle, *Collection des Anciens Alchimistes Grecs,* vol. 2, 3.51, 231.
20. Berthelot and Ruelle, *Collection des Anciens Alchimistes Grecs,* vol. 2, 3.51, 235.
21. Berthelot and Ruelle, *Collection des Anciens Alchimistes Grecs,* vol. 2, 3.51, 235–36; see also Fowden, *The Egyptian Hermes,* 122–23.
22. Copenhaver, *Hermetica,* 5–6.
23. Berthelot and Ruelle, *Collection des Anciens Alchimistes Grecs,* vol. 2.

Seven.
What Did the First Alchemists Do?

1. Grimes, "Zosimus of Panopolis," 36–39.
2. Berthelot and Duval, *La Chimie au Moyen Age,* vol. 2, 6.1, 222–23.
3. Berthelot and Duval, *La Chimie au Moyen Age,* vol. 2, 6.1, 223.
4. Berthelot and Duval, *La Chimie au Moyen Age,* vol. 2, 6.1, 224.
5. Berthelot and Duval, *La Chimie au Moyen Age,* vol. 2, 6.1, 224–25.
6. Berthelot and Duval, *La Chimie au Moyen Age,* vol. 2, 6.1, 226–27.
7. Berthelot and Duval, *La Chimie au Moyen Age,* vol. 2, 6.1, 228.
8. Berthelot and Duval, *La Chimie au Moyen Age,* vol. 2, 6.1, 228.
9. Berthelot and Duval, *La Chimie au Moyen Age,* vol. 2, 6.1, 228–29.
10. Berthelot and Duval, *La Chimie au Moyen Age,* vol. 2, 12.1, 260.
11. Berthelot and Duval, *La Chimie au Moyen Age,* vol. 2, 12.1, 260–63.
12. Berthelot and Duval, *La Chimie au Moyen Age,* vol. 2, 12.1, 263.
13. Berthelot and Duval, *La Chimie au Moyen Age,* vol. 2, 12.1, 264–66.
14. Berthelot and Duval, *La Chimie au Moyen Age,* vol. 2, 12.1, 264–66.

Eight.
How Did They Do It?

1. Halleux, *Les alchimistes Grecs,* 116.
2. Berthelot and Ruelle, *Collection des Anciens Alchimistes Grecs,* vol. 1, 2.3, 165.
3. Martelli, "'Divine Water,'" 8.
4. Martelli, "'Divine Water,'" 13.
5. Berthelot and Ruelle, *Collection des Anciens Alchimistes Grecs,* vol. 1, "Democrite: Questions Naturelles," 23, 55.

6. Martelli, "'Divine Water'" 21.

7. Flinders Petrie, *Athribis,* 11, and plate XXXIV.

8. Martelli, "Greek Alchemists at Work," 286–87.

9. Martelli, "Greek Alchemists at Work," 291.

10. Martelli, "Greek Alchemists at Work," 296.

11. Martelli, "Greek Alchemists at Work," 296.

12. Berthelot and Ruelle, *Collection des Anciens Alchimistes Grecs,* vol. 2, 3.15.2, 157; cited by Martelli, "Greek Alchemists at Work," 298.

13. Berthelot and Ruelle, *Collection des Anciens Alchimistes Grecs,* vol. 1, 1.13, 36.

14. Martelli, "Greek Alchemists at Work," 309.

15. Marchini et al., "Quicksilver and Quick-Thinking," 1.

16. Marchini et al., "Quicksilver and Quick-Thinking," 2.

17. Marchini et al., "Quicksilver and Quick-Thinking," 5.

18. Marchini et al., "Quicksilver and Quick-Thinking," 6.

19. Marchini et al., "Quicksilver and Quick-Thinking," 6.

20. Conniff, "Alchemy May Not Have Been the Pseudoscience We All Thought It Was."

Nine.
Where Did They Do It?

1. See Haas, *Alexandria in Late Antiquity,* 59, 236, cited in Grimes, "Zosimus of Panopolis," 39n76.

2. Grimes, "Zosimus of Panopolis," 39.

3. Grimes, "Zosimus of Panopolis," 40.

4. Wischnitzer, "Notes to a History of the Jewish Guilds," 252–53.

5. Grimes and College, "Divine Images," 69–70, further details of the integration of metallurgy in Egyptian temples, as regards Zosimos, may be found in Grimes, "Secrets of the God Makers," 67–89.

6. Grimes, "Secrets of the God Makers," 84.

7. Van den Broek, "Religious Practices in the Hermetic 'Lodge,'" 80.

8. Van den Broek, "Religious Practices in the Hermetic 'Lodge,'" 85.

9. Van den Broek, "Religious Practices in the Hermetic 'Lodge,'" 95.

10. Bull, "Part III: Religious Diversity in Egypt," 215; for papyrus of Theophanes, see Rees, *Papyri from Hermopolis,* and Moscadi, "Le lettere dell 'archivio di Teofane,'" 88–154.

11. Bull, "Part III: Religious Diversity in Egypt," 219.
12. Bull, "Part III: Religious Diversity in Egypt," 223–24.
13. Bull, "Part III: Religious Diversity in Egypt," 227–29.
14. Dufault, *Early Greek Alchemy,* 121. See translation by Matteo Martelli in "The Alchemical Art of Dyeing," 1–22. See also the translation of Rubens Duval in Berthelot and Duval, *La Chimie au Moyen Age,* vol. 2, 238–39.
15. Dufault, *Early Greek Alchemy,* viii.
16. Dufault, *Early Greek Alchemy,* 118, 122.
17. Martelli, "Greek Alchemists at Work," 275.
18. Martelli, "Greek Alchemists at Work," 278.
19. PGM XII, 96–106, 100; Betz, *Greek Magical Papyri,* 156–57.

Ten.
The Myth of Transmutation

1. Grimes, "Secrets of the God Makers," 68.
2. Berthelot and Ruelle, *Collection des Anciens Alchimistes Grecs,* vol. 1, 2.3, 64–65.
3. Berthelot and Ruelle, *Collection des Anciens Alchimistes Grecs,* vol. 2, 3.28, 191.
4. Berthelot and Ruelle, *Collection des Anciens Alchimistes Grecs,* vol. 2, 3.28, 191.
5. Berthelot and Ruelle, *Collection des Anciens Alchimistes Grecs,* vol. 2, 3.29, 194.
6. Berthelot and Ruelle, *Collection des Anciens Alchimistes Grecs,* vol. 2, 3.29, 380.
7. Berthelot and Ruelle, *Collection des Anciens Alchimistes Grecs,* vol. 2, 3.29, 194–99.
8. Berthelot and Ruelle, *Collection des Anciens Alchimistes Grecs,* vol. 1, 1.3, 18–21.
9. Berthelot and Ruelle, *Collection des Anciens Alchimistes Grecs,* vol. 1, 1.4, 21.
10. Berthelot and Ruelle, *Collection des Anciens Alchimistes Grecs,* vol. 3, 6.17, 419–20.
11. Berthelot and Ruelle, *Collection des Anciens Alchimistes Grecs,* vol. 2, 3.2, 122.
12. Burnham, "Nature Rejoicing in Nature."
13. Burnham, "Nature Rejoicing in Nature," 2.

14. Hallum, "The Tome of Images," 82.

15. Hallum, "The Tome of Images," 83.

16. Hallum, "The Tome of Images," 82.

17. Hallum, "The Tome of Images," 78–79.

18. Hallum, "The Tome of Images," 81.

19. Burnham, "Nature Rejoicing in Nature," 3.

20. Hallum, "The Tome of Images," 84.

21. Hallum, "The Tome of Images," 85.

22. Burnham, "Nature Rejoicing in Nature," 4.

23. Berthelot and Ruelle, *Collection des Anciens Alchimistes Grecs,* vol. 2, 3.2, 121.

24. Berthelot and Ruelle, *Collection des Anciens Alchimistes Grecs,* vol. 2, 3.2, 124.

25. Berthelot and Ruelle, *Collection des Anciens Alchimistes Grecs,* vol. 2, 3.2, 121–22.

26. Berthelot and Ruelle, *Collection des Anciens Alchimistes Grecs,* vol. 2, 3.2, 122.

27. Burnham, "Nature Rejoicing in Nature," 5.

28. Burnham, "Nature Rejoicing in Nature," 8.

29. Berthelot and Ruelle, *Collection des Anciens Alchimistes Grecs,* vol. 2, 4.1, 247.

30. Burnham, "Nature Rejoicing in Nature," 9.

31. Burnham, "Nature Rejoicing in Nature," 10.

32. Burnham, "Nature Rejoicing in Nature," 11.

33. Dufault, "Transmutation Theory in the Greek Alchemical Corpus," 1.

34. Dufault, "Transmutation Theory in the Greek Alchemical Corpus," 3.

35. Dufault, "Transmutation Theory in the Greek Alchemical Corpus," 5.

36. Dufault, "Transmutation Theory in the Greek Alchemical Corpus," 13.

Eleven.
Forbidden Knowledge

1. Berthelot and Duval, *La Chimie au Moyen Age,* vol. 2, 8.1, 238.

2. Larson, "On the Identification of Two Greek Texts of I Enoch," 157–58.

3. Torijiano, *Solomon the Esoteric King,* 181–82.

4. Fraser, "Zosimos of Panopolis and the Book of Enoch," 125–47.

5. Fraser, "Zosimos of Panopolis and the Book of Enoch," 131.

6. Fraser, "Zosimos of Panopolis and the Book of Enoch," 131.

7. Fraser, "Zosimos of Panopolis and the Book of Enoch," 131–32.

8. Fraser, "Zosimos of Panopolis and the Book of Enoch," 132.

Twelve.
A Strange Relation: Alchemy and Gnosis

1. Lambdin, "Gospel of Thomas," 121.

2. Berthelot and Ruelle, *Collection des Anciens Alchimistes Grecs,* vol. 2, 3.24, sect 9, 192.

3. Berthelot and Ruelle, *Collection des Anciens Alchimistes Grecs,* vol. 2, 3.29, *On the Philosophers' Stone* [an expression that does not appear until the seventh century], 194.

4. Berthelot and Ruelle, *Collection des Anciens Alchimistes Grecs,* vol. 2, 3.29, sect. 13, 196.

5. Robinson, *The Nag Hammadi Library in English,* 119.

6. Berthelot and Ruelle, *Collection des Anciens Alchimistes Grecs,* vol. 1, 2.3, 64–65.

7. Robinson, *The Nag Hammadi Library in English,* 126.

8. Berthelot and Ruelle, *Collection des Anciens Alchimistes Grecs,* vol. 2, 3.9, 146.

9. Robinson, *The Nag Hammadi Library in English,* 126.

10. Robinson, *The Nag Hammadi Library in English,* Codex III.7 (translation by John D. Turner), 189.

11. Robinson, *The Nag Hammadi Library in English,* Codex II.3 (translation by Wesley W. Isenberg), 137.

12. Robinson, *The Nag Hammadi Library in English,* Codex II.3 (translation by Wesley W. Isenberg), 138.

13. Robinson, *The Nag Hammadi Library in English,* Codex II.3 (translation by Wesley W. Isenberg), 141.

14. Berthelot and Ruelle, *Collection des Anciens Alchimistes Grecs,* vol. 2, 3.49, 224.

15. Robinson, *The Nag Hammadi Library in English,* Codex VII.2, 332.

16. Berthelot and Ruelle, *Collection des Anciens Alchimistes Grecs,* vol. 2, 3.49, 224–25.

17. Berthelot and Ruelle, *Collection des Anciens Alchimistes Grecs,* vol. 2, 3.49; vol. 3, "Book of Komarios," 283–84.

18. Rinotas, "Spiritual and Material Conversion in the Alchemical Work of Zosimus of Panopolis," 1008.

19. Beatrice, "The Word 'Homoousios' from Hellenism to Christianity," 243–72.

20. Beatrice, "The Word 'Homoousios' from Hellenism to Christianity," 244.

21. *Theosophia* I, 45 (Greek text in Beatrice, *Anonymi Monophysitae Theosophia,* 23); in Beatrice, "The Word 'Homoousios' from Hellenism to Christianity," 262.

22. Beatrice, "The Word 'Homoousios' from Hellenism to Christianity," 268.

Thirteen.
Legacy

1. Meyerhof, "Science and Medicine," 325.

2. Meyerhof, "Science and Medicine," 327.

Bibliography

Beatrice, Pier Franco. "The Word 'Homoousios' from Hellenism to Christianity." *Church History* 71, no. 2 (2002): 243–72.

Beretta, Marco. *The Alchemy of Glass: Counterfeit, Imitation, and Transmutation in Ancient Glassmaking.* Sagamore Beach, Mass.: Science History Publications, 2009.

Berthelot, Marcellin, and Rubens Duval. *La Chimie au Moyen Age.* 2 vols. 1893. Reprint. Osnabruck: Otto Zeller, 1967.

Berthelot, Marcellin, and C. E. Ruelle. *Collection des Anciens Alchimistes Grecs.* 3 vols. bound in 2. Paris: Georges Steinheil, 1888.

Betz, Hans Dieter, trans. *The Greek Magical Papyri in Translation.* Chicago: University of Chicago Press, 1986.

———. *The "Mithras Liturgy": Text, Translation, and Commentary.* Tübingen, Germany: Mohr Siebeck, 2003.

Bidez, Joseph, and Franz Cumont. *Les mages hellénisés Zoroastre Ostanèe et Hystaspe d'après la tradition grecque.* Vol. 2, *Les textes.* Paris: Les Belles Lettres, 1938.

Brashler, James, and Roger A. Bullard, trans. "Apocalypse of Peter." In *The Nag Hammadi Library in English,* edited by James M. Robinson. Leiden: Brill, 1996.

Bull, Christian H. "Part III: Religious Diversity in Egypt." In *The Nag Hammadi Codices and Late Antique Egypt,* edited by Hugo Lundhaug and Lance Jenott. Studies and Texts in Antiquity and Christianity. Tübingen, Germany: Mohr Siebeck, 2018.

Bullard, Roger A., and Joseph A. Gibbons, trans. "Second Treatise of the

Great Seth." In *The Nag Hammadi Library in English,* edited by James M. Robinson. Leiden: Brill, 1996.

Burnham, Daniel. "Nature Rejoicing in Nature: On the Origin of the Philosophical Stone." Available online at Academia.edu, 2014.

Caley, Earle Radcliffe, ed., trans. *The Leyden and Stockholm Papyri: Greco-Egyptian Chemical Documents from the Early 4th Century AD.* Oesper Collections in the History of Chemistry. Cincinnati: University of Cincinnati, 2008.

Chrysikopoulos, Vassilis I. "À l'aube de l'égyptologie hellénique et de la consitution des collections égyptiennes: Des nouvelles découvertes sur Giovanni d'Anastasi et Tassos Néroutsos." In *Proceedings of the Tenth International Congress of Egyptologists,* edited by P. Kousoulis and N. Lazaridis, 2. Leuven: Peeters, 2013.

Churton, Tobias. *Aleister Crowley in India.* Rochester, Vt.: Inner Traditions, 2019.

Conniff, Richard. "Alchemy May Not Have Been the Pseudoscience We All Thought It Was." *Smithsonian Magazine,* February 2014.

Copenhaver, Brian P., trans. *Hermetica.* Cambridge: Cambridge University Press, 1992.

D'Athanasi, Giovanni. *A Brief Account of the Researches and Discoveries in Upper Egypt, made under the direction of Henry Salt, Esq.* London: John Hearne, 1836.

Dawson, Warren R. "Anastasi, Sallier, and Harris and Their Papyri." *Journal of Egyptian Archaeology* 35 (Dec. 1949): 158.

Dosoo, Korshi. "A History of the Theban Magical Library." *Bulletin of the American Society of Papyrologists* 53 (2016): 251–74.

Dufault, Olivier. *Early Greek Alchemy, Patronage and Innovation in Late Antiquity.* Berkeley, Calif.: California Classical Studies, 2019.

———. "Transmutation Theory in the Greek Alchemical Corpus." *Ambix* 62, no. 3 (August 2015): 215–44.

Festugière, A. J. *La Révélation D'Hermès Trismégiste.* Vol. 1, 2nd ed. Paris: Gabalda, 1950.

Flinders Petrie, William M. *Athribis.* London: B. Quaritch, 1908.

Fowden, Garth. *The Egyptian Hermes: A Historical Approach to the Late Pagan Mind.* Cambridge: Cambridge University Press, 1986.

Fraser, Kyle A. "Zosimos of Panopolis and the Book of Enoch: Alchemy as Forbidden Knowledge." *Aries* 4, no. 2 (2004): 125–47.

Fuad, Salwa, and Theodor Abt, trans. *Zosimos of Panopolis, The Book of Pictures: Muṣḥ af aṣ -ṣ uwar.* Zurich: Living Human Heritage, 2011.

Grimes, Shannon L. "Secrets of the God Makers: Re-thinking the Origins of Greco-Egyptian Alchemy." *Syllecta Classica* 29 (2018): 67–89.

———. "Zosimus of Panopolis; Alchemy, Nature and Religion in Late Antiquity." Doctoral Thesis, Graduate School of Syracuse University, 2006.

Grimes, Shannon, and Meredith College. "Divine Images: Zosimos of Panopolis's Spiritual Approach to Alchemy." *La Rosa di Paracelso: Non Omnis Moriar: Alchemical, Hermetic and Mystical Models in Western Esotericism* 2, no. 2 (2019): 69–70.

Haas, Christopher. *Alexandria in Late Antiquity: Topography and Social Conflict.* Baltimore: John Hopkins University Press, 1997.

Halbertsma, R. B. *Scholars, Travellers and Trade: The Pioneer Years of the National Museum of Antiquities in Leiden, 1818–1840.* London: Routledge, 2003.

Halleux, Robert, ed. *Les alchimistes Grecs.* Paris: Les Belles Lettres, 1981.

Hallum, B. C. "The Tome of Images: An Arabic Compilation of Texts by Zosimos of Panopolis and a Source of the Turba Philosophorum." *Ambix* 56, no. 1 (2009): 76–88.

———. "Zosimus Arabus: The Reception of Zosimos of Panopolis in the Arabic/Islamic World." Thesis: University of London, 2008.

Hopkins, A. J. "A Study of the Kerotakis Process as Given by Zosimus and Later Alchemical Writers." *Isis* 29, no. 2 (1938): 329–36.

Jackson, H. M. "The Origin in Ancient Incantatory *Voces Magicae* of Some of the Names in the Sethian Gnostic System." *Vigiliae Christianae* 43 (1989): 74.

Jung, Carl. *Psychology and Alchemy.* Vol. 12 of *Collected Works of C. G. Jung.* London: Routledge & Kegan Paul, 1981.

Lagercrantz, Otto. *Papyrus Graecus Holmiensis (P.Holm). Recepte für Silber, Steiner und Purpur.* Uppsala: Akademiska bokhandeln, 1913.

Lambdin, Thomas O., trans. "Gospel of Thomas." In *The Nag Hammadi Library in English,* edited by James M. Robinson. Leiden: Brill, 1984.

Larson, Erik W. "On the Identification of Two Greek Texts of I Enoch." In *The Dead Sea Scrolls,* edited by Lawrence H. Schiffman and Shani Tzoref, 60. Leiden: Brill, 2010.

Leichty, Erle. "A Collection of Recipes for Dyeing." In *Studies in Honor of Tom B. Jones,* edited by M. A. Powell and R. H. Sack, 15–20. *Alter Orient und Altes Testament* 203. Neukirchen-Vluyn: Neukirchner Verlag, 1979.

Linden, Stanton J., ed. "ANONYMOUS (first or second century AD): Dialogue of Cleopatra and the Philosophers." Chap. 5 in *The Alchemy Reader. From Hermes Trismegistus to Isaac Newton.* Cambridge: Cambridge University Press, 2003.

Luck, Georg. *Arcana Mundi: Magic and the Occult in the Greek and Roman Worlds; A Collection of Ancient Texts.* Baltimore: Johns Hopkins University Press, 2006.

Marchini, Marianna, Massimo Gandolfi, Lucia Maini, Matteo Martelli, and Lucia Raggetti. "Quicksilver and Quick-Thinking: Insight into the Alchemy of Mercury. A New Interdisciplinary Research to Discover the Chemical Reality of Ancient Alchemical Recipes." Department of Chemistry and Department of Philosophy and Communication Studies, University of Bologna, June 2021. Available online at ReasearchGate.net.

Martelli, Matteo. "The Alchemical Art of Dyeing: The Fourfold Division of Alchemy and the Enochic Tradition." In *Laboratories of Art,* edited by S. Dupré, 1–22. Cham: Springer, 2014.

———. "'Divine Water' in the Alchemical Writings of Pseudo-Democritus." *Ambix* 56, no. 1 (March 2009): 5–22.

———. *The Four Books of Pseudo-Democritus: Sources of Alchemy.* Sources of Alchemy and Chemistry: Sir Robert Mond Studies in the History of Early Chemistry, Supplement 1. Leeds: Maney, for the Society for the History of Alchemy and Chemistry, 2014.

———. "Greek Alchemists at Work: 'Alchemical Laboratory' in the Greco-Roman Egypt." *Nuncius* 26, no. 2 (2011): 271–311.

———. "Pseudo-Democritus' Alchemical Works: Tradition, Contents and Afterlife." Lecture Paper for Humboldt-Universität zu Berlin, undated. Available on Dacalbo Project website.

Martelli, Matteo, and Maddelena Rumor. "Near Eastern Origins of Graeco-Egyptian Alchemy." Chap. 4 in *Esoteric Knowledge in Antiquity,* edited by Klaus Geus and Mark Geller. TOPOI–Dahlem Seminar for the History of Ancient Sciences Vol. 2. Berlin: Max Planck Institute for the History of Science. 2014.

Meyerhof, Max. "Science and Medicine." In *The Legacy of Islam,* edited by Thomas Arnold and Alfred Guillaume, 311–55. Oxford: Oxford University Press, 1931.

Moscadi, Alessandro. "Le lettere dell 'archivio di Teofane.'" *Aeg* 50 (1970): 88–154.

Mosshammer, Alden A., ed. *Georgii Syncelli Ecloga chronographica*. Leipzig: Teubner, 1984.

Multhauf, R. *The Origins of Chemistry*. London: Bourne Press, 1966.

Oldfather, C. H., trans. *Diodorus Siculus: The Library of History*. Vol. 2. Loeb Classical Library. Cambridge, Mass.: Harvard University Press, 1933.

Oppenheim, Leo A., Robert H. Brill, Dan Barag, and Axel Von Saldern. *Glass and Glassmaking in Ancient Mesopotamia*. Vol. 3. New York: Corning Museum of Glass, 1970.

Patai, Raphael. *The Jewish Alchemists: A History and Source Book*. Princeton, N.J.: Princeton University Press, 2014.

Rees, Brinley R. *Papyri from Hermopolis: And Other Documents of the Byzantine Period*. London: Egypt Exploration Society, 1964.

Reymond, Eve A. E. *From the Records of a Priestly Family of Memphis*. Wiesbadan: Otto Harrassowitz Verlag, 1981.

Rinotas, Athanasios. "Spiritual and Material Conversion in the Alchemical Work of Zosimus of Panopolis." *Religions* 12, no. 11 (2021): 1008.

Robinson, James M. *The Nag Hammadi Library in English*. Leiden: Brill, 1984.

Stapleton, Henry Ernest, and R. F. Azo. "An Alchemical Compilation of the Thirteenth Century A.D." *Memoirs of the Asiatic Society of Bengal* 3, no. 2 (1910): 57–94.

Stern, Marianne, and Birgit Schlick-Nolte. *Early Glass of the Ancient World*. Ostfildern: Verlag Gerd Hatje, 1994.

Stolzenberg, Daniel. "Unpropitious Tinctures: Alchemy, Astrology and Gnosis According to Zosimos of Panopolis." *Archives internationales d'histoire des sciences* 49 (1999): 3–31.

Synkellos, George. *The Chronography of George Synkellos. A Byzantine Chronicle of Universal History from the Creation,* translated by William Adler and Paul Tuffin. Oxford: Oxford University Press, 2002.

Torijiano, Pablo A. *Solomon the Esoteric King.* Leiden: Brill, 2002.

Van den Broek, Roelof. "Religious Practices in the Hermetic 'Lodge': New Light from Nag Hammadi." In van den Broek and van Heertum, *From Poimandres to Jacob Böhme: Gnosis, Hermetism and the Christian Tradition,* 77–95.

Van den Broek, Roelof, and Cis van Heertum, eds. *From Poimandres to Jacob Böhme: Gnosis, Hermetism and the Christian Tradition.* Amsterdam: In de Pelikaan, 2000.

Wischnitzer, Mark. "Notes to a History of the Jewish Guilds." *Hebrew Union College Annual* 23, no. 2 (1950–1951): 245–63.

Index

Abt, Theodore, 214, 215, 217
　on *Book of Keys,* 214
　on *The Sulfurs,* 214, 216
Agathocles, 22
Agathodaimon, 115, 151
Albertus Magnus, 265
Alchemical Lexicon, 210
Alexander the Great, 46, 154–55
al-Kindī, 262
Allogenes, 126
al-Ma'mūn, Caliph, 261
al-Manṣūr, Caliph, 261
al-Rāzī (Rhazes), 262
Anastasiou, Ioannis (Giovanni),
　9–11, 13, 17
Anaxilaus, 35
Antimimos, 134–35
Apion, 47
Apocalypse of Peter, 134, 231
Apocryphon of John, 69, 132
Archimedes, 228
Aristotle, 12, 156–57
　Metaphysics, 12
　Meteorologica, 201, 204

　on substance, 198, 201–2, 204,
　　224–25
　Zosimos on, 136, 156–57, 200,
　　205
Arnaldus de Villa Nova, 265
Ashmole, Elias, 272, 273
　*Theatrum Chemicum
　　Britannicum,* 272
Athanasi, Giovanni ("Yanni"),
　13
Athanasios (or Athanasius), 187
Avigad, Nahman, 84

Backhouse, William, 272
Bacon, Roger, 265
Bacon, Sir Francis, 267
Barbelo, 38
Beatrice, Pier Franco, 253
　on *Theosophia,* 254
Belzoni, Giovanni Battista, 10
Benedetti, Vincent, 10
Berbeloch, 34
Beretta, Marco (*The Alchemy of
　　Glass*), 56, 59

297

Berthelot, Marcellin, 18, 23
  La Chimie au Moyen Age, 40, 145
  on *Chrysopeia of Cleopatra,* 72
  on Gnostics and alchemy, 20, 22
  on Papyrus V, 21
  and pseudo-Democritus, 41
  on transmutation, 28
  on "unqualified substrate," 42–43
Betz, Hans Dieter, 13
Bidez, Joseph, *Catalogue des manuscrits alchimiques grecs* (CMAG), 36
Böhme, Jacob, 3, 268
Bolos of Mendes,
  and Ostanes, 47
  and pseudo-Democritus, 6, 38, 78
Book of Komarios, 65, 71, 270
Book of the Watchers (I Enoch), 45, 46, 230–31
Books of Jeu, 247
Bouriant, Urbain, 231
Boyle, Robert, 272, 273
Brahe, Tycho, 268
Bull, Christian H., 186,
  on Zosimos and Hermes, 187, 188
Burnham, Daniel, 212
  on *Tome of Images,* 212–23

Caley, E. R., 19, 25, 28, 35
  on alchemical symbols, 27
Cambyses II, 46
Cardano, Gerolamo Cardano, 268
Cebes of Thebes (*Pinax*), 129
Champollion, Jean-François, 10

Chosroes Nushirwan, King, 261
Chrysikopoulos, Vassilis, 9, 10, 11
Chthotho, 34
Chymes, 63, 81, 118–19, 172
Cleopatra (or Kleopatra, alchemist), 46, 64, 66, 67, 70, 75
  "Dialogue of Cleopatra and the Philosophers," 65, 249–50, 270
  "The Eight Tombs," 70–71
Cleopatra VII, 60
Codex Marcianus, 39, 49, 51, 70, 76, 104, 111, 120, 145, 169, 170, 191, 195, 198
  Chrysopeia of Cleopatra, 72, 112, 120, 229
Codex Panopolitanus, 231
Codex Parisinus Graecus, 73, 83, 143, 164, 206, 252
Conniff, Richard, 176
Conway, Lady Anne, 272
Corpus Hermeticum 1, 106, 131, 253, 254
Corpus Hermeticum 4, 127–28, 184
Corpus Hermeticum 13, 184
Croll, Oswald, 268
Crowley, Aleister, 139–40

Dawson, Warren R., 9
Democritus, 35, 36, 47
Diocletian, 29, 39, 160, 254
Dioscorides, Pedanius, 20, 174
  de materia medica, 20, 32

Doresse, Jean, 23
  Secret Books of the Egyptian Gnostics, 247
Dorn, Gerhard, 268
Dosoo, Korshi, 15, 17
Drovetti, Bernardino, 10
Dufault, Olivier, 189–90
  "Transmutation Theory," 223–26
Dugan, Elena (*Codex Panopolitanus*), 231–32
Duval, Rubens (*La Chimie au Moyen Age*), 40, 145–46, 152

Echnin, 34
Eglin, Raphael, 268
Epimetheus, 129, 131
Epiphanius, 34
  Panarion, 186
  and Sethian Gnostics, 34
Erotylos, 121, 242
Eusebius of Caesarea, 254

Festugière, A. J., 91
Fictuld, Hermann, 274
Figulus, Benedictus, 268
Flamel, Nicholas, 265
Fludd, Robert, 268
Fowden, Garth (*The Egyptian Hermes*), 53, 91, 135

Gallus, Gaius Cornelius, 61
Gérard of Cremona
  and *Book of the Seventy,* 264

Godwin, Charles Wycliffe, 12
  and Aleister Crowley, 12
  and Papyri Grecae Magicae, 12
Gospel of Peter, 231
Gospel of Thomas, 120–21, 202, 239–40, 242
Grimes, Shannon L., 60, 199
  alchemy and temple system, 62, 92, 178, 180
  on distillation, 77–78
  on guilds, 178–79
  on Theosebeia and Neilos, 92, 94
  on Zosimos, 91, 92, 95, 108, 180–81

Hallum, Bink C., 213, 214, 215, 217
Haslmayr, Adam, 268
Hemerius, 22
Heraclius (emperor), 69, 206
Hermes, 23, 24
Hermes Trismegistos (or Trismegistus), 129, 130
  Asclepius, 240, 255, 268
  On the Eighth and the Ninth, 182–83, 185, 188–89
  Poimandres (also Poimenandres), 107, 139, 140–41, 251, 253
  Prayer of Thanksgiving, 182–83
Hermetic lodges, 34, 182–89
Herodotus (on glass), 57
Hesiod, 129
Hopkins, A. J. (kerotakis), 110
Ḥunayn ibn Isḥāk, 261

Iamblichus, 91, 255
Iao, 12

Jābir ("Geber"), 262, 263
  Book of the Seventy, 263
Jackson, H. M. (Greek Magical
  Papyri), 34
Jesus Christ, 130–31, 134, 255–56
  and Mercury, 252
John of Antioch, 29, 39, 160
Josephus, 47
Julius Africanus (Chronographiai), 35
Jung, Carl, 4, 234, 241, 275
  Psychology and Alchemy, 4
  on Zosimos's "dreams," 101–3

Kelley, Edward, 268
Khunrath, Heinrich, 192–93, 268
Kopp, Hermann, xi
Kungliga Bibliotek, Stockholm, 12

Lactantius, 255
Larson, Erik W., 231
Leemans, Conrad, 17
  Papyri graeci musei antiquarii, 18
Leichty, Erle, 54
Lepsius, Karl Richard, 10
Levi (dyer in Gospel of Philip), 245
Libavius, Andreas, 194, 268
Llull, Ramon, 265

Macquer, Dictionary of Chemistry, 21
Maier, Michael, 268
  Atalanta Fugiens, 270

Marcus (Gnostic), 20, 23
  in Irenaeus's Against the Heretics,
    20
Martelli, Matteo, 36, 169
  cold extraction of mercury from
    cinnabar at Bologna University,
    171–75
  on "divine water," 164–66
  Four Books of Pseudo-
    Democritus, 36, 38, 39
  on laboratories, 196–97
  and Maddalena Rumor on Near
    Eastern origins of alchemy, 47,
    52, 53–56
Mary the Prophetess ("Mariam"),
    38, 46, 81
  apparatus, 84–87
  on bodies and incorporeals,
    87–88
  on distillation 82–83, 168
  influence, 271–72
  on the "stone," 207
  symbolism in distillation, 240
  on yellowing, 81, 119
McIntosh, Christopher, 274
Mertens, Michèle, 120
  on alabastron, 219
  cataloging Zosimos, 104,
    191
Meyerhof, Max, 262
Miach, 34
Mithra, 218
Mithras Liturgy, 14
Mögling, Daniel, 196, 268

Moses (alchemist), 22, 28, 79–81,
    118–19
  Chymia of Moses, 81
Muhammad Ali Pasha al-Mas'ud
    ibn Agha, 10

Nag Hammadi Library, 240
  Book of Thomas the Contender,
    242–43
  Gospel of Philip (God as "dyer"),
    245, 246
  Gospel of Truth, 241
  Patterson, Stephen J., 242
  Robinson, James M., 242
  Second Treatise of the Great
    Seth, 133, 248–49
Neilos (or Nilus), 94, 97, 118, 124, 152
Nestorians, 260–61
Newton, Isaac, 272, 273
Nicene Creed (homoousios), 252
Nocotheus, 125–26
Norton, Thomas, 265

Octavian, 61
Olympiodorus, 28, 71, 205, 259
Oppenheim, Adolf Leo, 54, 57
Osiris, 12
Osron, 62
Ostanes, 22, 37, 38, 46, 47, 51, 53,
    60, 62
  in "Anepigraphos Philosopher," 50
  *Ostanes the philosopher to
    Petasius,* 47–48
  and Rudolf Steiner, 274

Pammenes, 38
Pandora ("Eve"), 131
Paphnutia (alchemist), 96–97,
    118, 124
Paracelsus, 266
Pebechius (or Pebichius), 22, 46,
    62–63, 81, 118
  Pebichius to Osron, 51–52
Pelagius the Philosopher, 221
Pelekanos, Theodoros, 36, 66
Petrie, Flinders, 166
Pico della Mirandola, 268
Pistis Sophia, 247
Plato
  Critias, 41
Pliny (*Natural History*), 22, 27, 35,
    79, 147, 159, 167, 168, 263
Plotinus (*Enneads*), 248
Poisson, Albert, 275
  Ordre Kabbalistique
    Rose-Croix, 275
Porphyry (*Life of Plotinus*), 125,
    254
Principe, Lawrence, 176
pseudo-Democritus, 28, 36, 37,
    40, 175
  Physika kai mystika, 37, 38,
    165–66, 202
  and Rudolf Steiner, 274
Psherenamun I, 93
Pythian (serpent), 24

Quispel, Gilles (in *Gnostics*),
    241

Rijksmuseum van Oudheden,
  Leiden, 12
Rinotas, Athanasios, 251
Ripley, Sir George, 265
Robert of Chester,
  *Book of the Composition of
  Alchemy,* 264
Roberts, Alexandre M., 191
Rowling, J. K., 3
Ruelle, C. E., 18, 21
Ruland, Martin, the Elder,
  268
Ruland, Martin, the Younger,
  268

Sabaoth, 12, 75
Salmasius, Claudius (*Plinian
  Exercises*), 79
Salt, Henry, 10, 13, 16
Sandum, 34
Sefer Yetzirah, 246
Sendivogius, Michael, 268
Set, 13
Siculus, Diodorus (*Bibliotheca
  historica*), 59
Solomon, King, 139
  in Zosimos, 157–59, 232
Soter of Apamea, 255
Starkey, George, 272
Steiner, Rudolf, 274
Stephanus of Alexandria, 66, 167,
  169, 205, 211, 217, 259
  on the "stone," 210

Stolzenberg, Daniel (on theurgy), 91
Stournari, 11
St. Paul, 251
Suda, 29, 39, 104, 125, 194
  Svidae Lexicon (ed. Ada Adler),
  30
Synesius, 47, 205, 259
  "Synesius and Dioscorus,"
  163–64, 201–2, 241
  on transmutation, 202, 241
Synkellos (or Syncellus), George,
  45, 47
  Chronographica, 38

Tarpoktsis, Argyrios D., 11
Theophrastus of Lesbos
  (*On stones*), 172
Theosebeia,
  advice from Zosimos, 106,
  118, 123–24, 127, 138–39,
  233–38
  and guilds, 179–80, 189–92
  her name, 94
Thoth, 23
Tossiza Bros & Co., 11
Toth, 92

Urbicus, 22

Valentinus, 23, 185
van Helmont, Jan Baptist, 268
Vaughan, Thomas, 272
  Lumen de Lumine, 271

Widemann, Carl, 268

Zaguel, 34
Zeno (emperor), 261
Zizinia, Etienne, 11
Zminis the Tentyrite,
    22
Zoroaster, 129
Zosimos of Panopolis
    allegedly on the "stone,"
        210–11
    "Chapters of Zosimos to
        Theodore," 78–79
    condemns priestcraft, 98–100,
        123–24, 144
    "dreams," 104–17

and Enoch, 230, 233–34
The Final Account (or Quittance),
    97–98, 137–42, 231–33
"Imouth," 45, 46, 230–31, 232
inspects a furnace, 62
on Gnostic Passion, 133–34
on Lime (or Quicklime), 214, 215,
    216, 217
making a talisman (On electrum),
    153–56
on making images, 149–52
on Ocher, 122–23
on Ostanes, 48–49
and Theosebeia's chicken, 258
on transmutation, 64, 203
Zostrianos, 126

Books of Related Interest

The Lost Pillars of Enoch
When Science and Religion Were One
by Tobias Churton

Gnostic Philosophy
From Ancient Persia to Modern Times
by Tobias Churton

Aleister Crowley in Paris
Sex, Art, and Magick in the City of Light
by Tobias Churton

Occult Paris
The Lost Magic of the Belle Époque
by Tobias Churton

The Invisible History of the Rosicrucians
The World's Most Mysterious Secret Society
by Tobias Churton

The Mysteries of John the Baptist
His Legacy in Gnosticism, Paganism, and Freemasonry
by Tobias Churton

Aleister Crowley in India
The Secret Influence of Eastern Mysticism on Magic and the Occult
by Tobias Churton

Deconstructing Gurdjieff
Biography of a Spiritual Magician
by Tobias Churton

INNER TRADITIONS • BEAR & COMPANY
P.O. Box 388
Rochester, VT 05767
1-800-246-8648
www.InnerTraditions.com
Or contact your local bookseller